WHY ISRAEL MATTERS

Past • Present • Forever

Mathew D. Staver, Esq.
with John P. Aman

Morning breaks over the Sea of Galilee
with Golan Heights in the distance.

ISBN: 978-0-9831767-3-2

Printed in the United States of America

First Printing, 2017

Design by: Tad Crisp, crispgraphics.com

Published by:

New Revolution Publishers

Contents

Panoramic vista of Jerusalem, Israel's capital, as seen from the Mount of Olives.

The Russian Orthodox Church of Mary Magdalene, with its gilded onion domes, on the Mount of Olives.

CHAPTER 1

WHAT IS IT ABOUT ISRAEL?

After 1,900 years, it took just 30 minutes. A crowd of 250 Jewish officials and dignitaries, along with a handful of journalists, gathered in the Tel Aviv Museum at 4 pm sharp on May 14, 1948. Fearful of Arab bombs, organizers kept the ceremony's time and place secret. But that didn't stop a huge throng from congregating outside on Rothschild Street, awaiting news under the watch of Haganah soldiers brandishing Sten guns on the rooftop above.

Inside, attendees packed into the museum's cramped hall listened as the future prime minister of Israel, David

Israeli Government Press Office

Shershel Frank/Israeli Government Press Office

Top: *David Ben-Gurion reads Israel's Statehood Declaration on May 14, 1948 in Tel Aviv.*

Bottom: *Crowd awaits announcement of Israel's Statehood outside Tel Aviv Museum.*

Beautiful ancient mosaic pavements, as shown, beautified floors in synagogues, churches, and other buildings.

Pinn Hanns/Israeli Government Press Office

Top Left: *Citizens outside the Tel Aviv Museum cheer Israel's Statehood Declaration on May 14, 1948.*

Bottom Left: *Though much more colorful and ornate than the American Declaration of Independence, the Israeli Declaration of Statehood was likewise forged in the crucible of war.*

Ben-Gurion, read Israel's statehood declaration in Hebrew. His voice lifting, he pronounced, "We hereby proclaim the establishment of a Jewish State in Palestine, to be called the State of Israel." The audience stood and broke into heartfelt applause.

A rabbi, his voice quavering with emotion, offered a benediction, declaring: "Blessed art Thou, O Lord our God, King of the Universe, who hath kept us and sustained us and has brought us unto this time."[1]

Then, in reliance on the "Rock of Israel," the 37 members of the Provisional State Council signed modern Israel's founding document.

Cheers erupted outside the museum and across Tel Aviv. Israelis young and old danced in the streets. After centuries of exile and agony, pogroms and persecutions, and, finally, the killing of six million Jews in the Holocaust, the Jewish people had their own independent homeland.

They were also at war.

Israel extended an olive branch to its Arab neighbors in its statehood declaration, proposing "an offer of peace and good

Beautiful burnt orange rock in Judean Desert as seen from Masada.

neighbourliness," and seeking to "establish bonds of cooperation and mutual help." The new Jewish state urged Arabs living inside her boundaries "to preserve peace and participate in the upbuilding of the State on the basis of full and equal citizenship."[2]

But the Arab world answered with bullets and bombs. Israel declared statehood about 4:30 pm on May 14. Five Arab nations were on the attack that night. "It does not matter how many [Jews] there are," the Arab League's secretary-general promised. "We will sweep them into the sea."[3]

And that is what much of the Muslim world still seeks today.

In the nearly 70 years since statehood, modern Israel has been attacked eight times by enemies pledged "to uproot it just like a cancer," as Saudi Arabia's King Saud said in 1954.[4]

Israel today lives in what is easily the most toxic neighborhood on earth. Her next-door neighbors in the Gaza Strip and West Bank are ruled by Hamas and the Palestinian Authoritiy, both committed to Israel's destruction. Unwilling to make peace with Israel,

Top: *Saudi Arabia's King Saud called in 1954 for Israel to be removed "just like a cancer."*

Bottom: *Map shows Arab nations' invasion routes during their 1948 war to eliminate Israel.*

Majestic view across the Negev in southern Israel.

Top Left: *Iran's supreme Ayatollah Ali Khamenei*

Bottom Left: *Hezbollah leader Sheikh Hassan Nasrallah*

these Palestinian militants use suicide bombs, rocket attacks, and knifings, along with intifadas (uprisings) and international pressure to wage war against Israel.

In Lebanon, the ruling party, Hezbollah, has 45,000 fighters and an estimated stockpile of 120,000 rockets.[5] "Israel is a cancer" charges Hezbollah leader Sheikh Hassan Nasrallah, who says the "ultimate goal should be to remove it."[6]

On its southern border, Israel faces growing danger from ISIS in Sinai. A menacing recorded message said to be from ISIS leader Abu Bakr al-Baghdadi proclaimed: "We are getting closer to you day by day. Do not think that we have forgotten about you."[7]

And to the northeast, Iran is on its way to building a nuclear arsenal and achieving its aim, as the rogue nation's supreme leader Ali Khamenei put it, "to erase Israel from the map."[8]

Clearly, Israel "matters" to the Muslim world.

But Israel matters not just because its mere presence provokes Muslim outrage and anger. Israel also matters to the Jewish people. It is a source of pride and security for a nation which spent centuries wandering the world in exile and oppression. And it consolidates Jewish brilliance, which is why Israel, after

seven short decades, is already a source of stunning innovations like incision-free surgery.

A global leader in high-tech, pharmaceuticals, agriculture and military equipment, Israel is improving the lives of millions and is a vital part of the global economy. It is a channel of blessing to the world, just as God promised Abraham nearly 4,000 years ago when He said, "in you all the families of the earth shall be blessed" (Genesis 12:3 NKJV).

And yet Israel remains fixed in the cross-hairs of global controversy. Why? What is it about Israel? Why does this one nation on the eastern edge of the Mediterranean matter so much? What makes it the improbable focus of so much anger and interest?

With a population of just eight million, Israel attracts the attention of the world's sole superpower, the U.S., like a magnet, and roils our domestic politics. Israel is under near-constant critique and condemnation at the U.N. and is on sometimes stormy terms with the European Union. And almost seven decades after Israel became a nation, its Muslim-majority Arab and Persian neighbors still dream and work for its annihilation.

But why? What generates so much fascination, frustration, and fury over one small and densely populated state?

Why does Israel matter? To the Jewish people, to Muslims, to the world, and to you.

Let's take a look.

Desert rocks near Eilat, Israel's southernmost city.

Nazi Germany killed six million Jews, and almost one million died at the grim Auschwitz death camp in Poland. Nearly 2,000 years of Jewish anguish climaxed in the Holocaust, Adolf Hitler's (above) diabolical plan to eliminate God's chosen people.

CHAPTER 2

FROM DESOLATION TO DELIGHT

Jewish suffering over the last 2,000 years is beyond comprehension. The litany of terror and grief includes pogroms, persecutions, expulsions, forced conversion, enslavement, massacres, confiscations, mob attacks, mass arrests, public torture, burning at the stake, and genocide. All this has come at the hands of a variety of adversaries, some of whom professed a distorted view of Christianity or who abused it for political purposes. Others were Muslims advancing the cause of jihad, and social Darwinists who wanted to eliminate "undesirable" people in order to evolve a superior human race.

Anti-Semitism has forced the Jewish people

> to wander over the face of the earth, without rights, except by gracious concession, without a home, and without security; treated at all times,

The ruins of Masada, a cliff-top fortress in the Judean Desert where Jewish rebels made their last stand against Rome in 73 A.D.

lev radin / Shutterstock, Inc.

Left: *Elie Wiesel gave the world an unforgettable account of the Holocaust in his Nazi death camp memoir,* Night.

> in years of peace and in years of persecution, as if they were beings of an inferior species.[9]

Much of the world—including Christians—is barely aware of the pain, agony, and death visited upon the Jewish people. Too many pay too little heed to Jewish suffering and the plague of anti-Semitism—an ancient animus whose flames never dies. Not so with Jews.

THE ZIONIST SOLUTION

Theodor Herzl, the founder of Zionism, came face to face with anti-Semitism as a student in Austria. Later, he had a ring-side seat to Jew hatred in 1894 while a journalist in Paris covering the trial of French Captain Alfred Dreyfus, a Jewish military officer falsely accused of treason. Herzl concluded the only solution to seething anti-Semitism was a national homeland for the Jewish people, an idea he championed in *The Jewish State*, his 1896 Zionist manifesto setting forth the dilemma faced by Jews everywhere:

> No one can deny the gravity of the situation of the Jews. Wherever they live in perceptible

numbers, they are more or less persecuted. Their equality before the law, granted by statute, has become practically a dead letter.[10]

Writing some 40 years before Hitler introduced his "Final Solution," Herzl saw disaster ahead. "Anti-Semitism increases day by day and hour by hour among the nations," he announced in *The Jewish State*.[11] He said more to his diary:

> I cannot imagine what appearance and form this will take. Will it be expropriation by some revolutionary force from below? Will it be proscription by some reactionary force from above? Will they banish us? Will they kill us? I expect all these forms and others.[12]

The only avenue to safety, Herzl insisted, was the wholesale exodus of European Jewry to their ancient homeland—a region the Romans renamed "Palestine" around 135 A.D. to signal the end of Jewish sovereignty. But too few heeded the warnings Herzl and other Zionists issued. As late as spring 1944, it was still possible for Jews in Romania to purchase "emigration certificates to Palestine," Elie Wiesel recalls in *Night*, his searing Holocaust memoir. He urged his father to leave but the patriarch refused.

Right: *Journalist Theodor Herzl called for Jewish return to Palestine in* The Jewish State, *his 1896 Zionist manifesto. Herzl organized the first Zionist Congress in 1897.*

Israeli Government Press Office

HaMakhtesh HaGadol (the big crater) in the Negev Desert.

"I am too old, my son," he replied. "Too old to start a new life. Too old to start from scratch in some distant land. . . ."[13]

Supremely prescient about the dire threat and the Zionist solution, Herzl didn't get all the details right. He proposed a Jewish state run on socialist principles, with German as the vernacular, located in either Argentina or Palestine. And he did say the Jews, "once settled in their own State, would probably have no more enemies."[14]

But along with other Zionists, Herzl hoisted the banner of Jewish nationalism. "We shall live at last as free men on our own soil, and die peacefully in our own homes," wrote Herzl. And the new Jewish state, he predicted, would be a great boon to all nations, who "will be freed by our liberty, enriched by our wealth, magnified by our greatness"[15]— a strikingly accurate prophecy.

Herzl convened the first Zionist Congress in Basel, Switzerland in 1897, but Jewish pilgrims and pioneers were already returning to their ancient homeland by the mid-nine-

Above: *Theodor Herzl, center, at the first Zionist Congress in Basel, Switzerland, in 1897.*

teenth century. Those who came found a bleak and impoverished backwater. "For many centuries Jerusalem has lain in ruins," asserted David Baron (1855-1926), a Jewish believer in Jesus who visited Palestine seven times. While "naturally a fruitful land," Palestine, he wrote, "has been known preeminently 'as the land that is desolate.'"[16]

A Land in "Sackcloth and Ashes"

When Mark Twain toured Palestine in 1867, the American author called it a "hopeless, dreary, heartbroken, land." Palestine, he wrote, "sits in sackcloth and ashes.... [It] is desolate and unlovely."[17] Herman Melville walked the streets of Jerusalem ten years earlier and conjured a vision of Captain Ahab in stone: "The color of the whole city is grey & looks at you like a cold grey eye in a cold old man."[18]

Nineteen centuries after Rome sacked Jerusalem and leveled the Temple in 70 A.D., Palestine was just as God promised it would be. In a prophecy fulfilled during the first exile to Babylon—and since in the people of God's long diaspora from their homeland—Yahweh said of His beloved people:

***Right:** American authors Herman Melville (above) and Mark Twain labeled Palestine "gray" and "dreary" after visits there in 1857 and 1867, respectively.*

Parched and sun-baked landscape near the Dead Sea.

The "neglect of centuries" and the "blight of Ottoman rule" left Palestine desolate, dreary, and depopulated. The Kidron Valley outside Jerusalem in the early 20th century reveals a landscape notable for small trees, rocks, and sand.

Top Left: *Mounted Bedouin fighters near Jerusalem in Ottoman era, 1909.*

Left: *Ottoman soldiers.*

Right: *Jews pray at the Western Wall in photo taken between 1900 and 1920.*

American Colony/Israeli Government Press Office

Left: *Gamal Pasha, Ottoman ruler in Palestine who was notorious for cruelty and called "the Blood-Shedder." Shown in 1916.*

Salt deposits on the shoreline of the Dead Sea which has a salinity of about 30 percent and is the lowest spot on earth.

> But I scattered them with a whirlwind among all the nations which they had not known. Thus the land became desolate after them, so that no one passed through or returned; for they made the pleasant land desolate. (Zechariah 7:14 NKJV)

Instead of a land flowing with milk and honey, the land shared in God's punishment on His people, declining into a barren expanse distinguished for sand, rocks, malaria and nomadic Bedouin. It was anything but pleasant. Under Muslim Ottoman rule, Jerusalem in the mid-nineteenth century was a place of "little infrastructure, terrible corruption, a lack of hospitals, and an absence of social amenities and order. Assault and theft were daily occurrences...."[19]

Estimates vary greatly, but first century Jerusalem may have had 80,000 residents.[20] By 1845, the 3,000-year-old city had just 15,510 residents, claimed one count supplied by the Prussian consul to Jerusalem.[21] "The country is in a considerable degree empty of inhabitants and therefore its greatest need is that of a body of population," a British consul reported in 1857.[22]

Other reports cited by Harvard law professor Alan Dershowitz described Palestine's Arab population as "decreasing,"[23] and labeled the region "thinly populated,"[24] "unoccupied,"[25] "uninhabited,"[26] and "almost abandoned now." Surprisingly, more Jews than Muslims lived in Jerusalem by the mid-1850s.[27]

"MUSSULMAN OPPRESSION"

Living under the boot of Ottoman rule, the Jews were "the constant objects of Mussulman oppression and intolerance," Karl Marx stated in the *New York Daily Tribune*. An occasional journalist when not fomenting the overthrow of capitalism, Marx claimed the Jews in Palestine hailed from "different and distant countries," having arrived in the holy city to be "where the redemptor is to be expected."[28]

Jews in Jerusalem may have been the majority by mid-nineteenth century, but they lived in squalor and "walked with a shuffling, cringing step that told of blows received and blows expected," as one scholar put it.[29] Under Ottoman rule, the Jews were third-class citizens who had to pay exorbitant taxes and avoid Muslims on the street—stepping aside or walking past Muslims on their left side (the side of Satan). And any physical contact could quickly lead to a rain of fists, for which no justice could be had.[30]

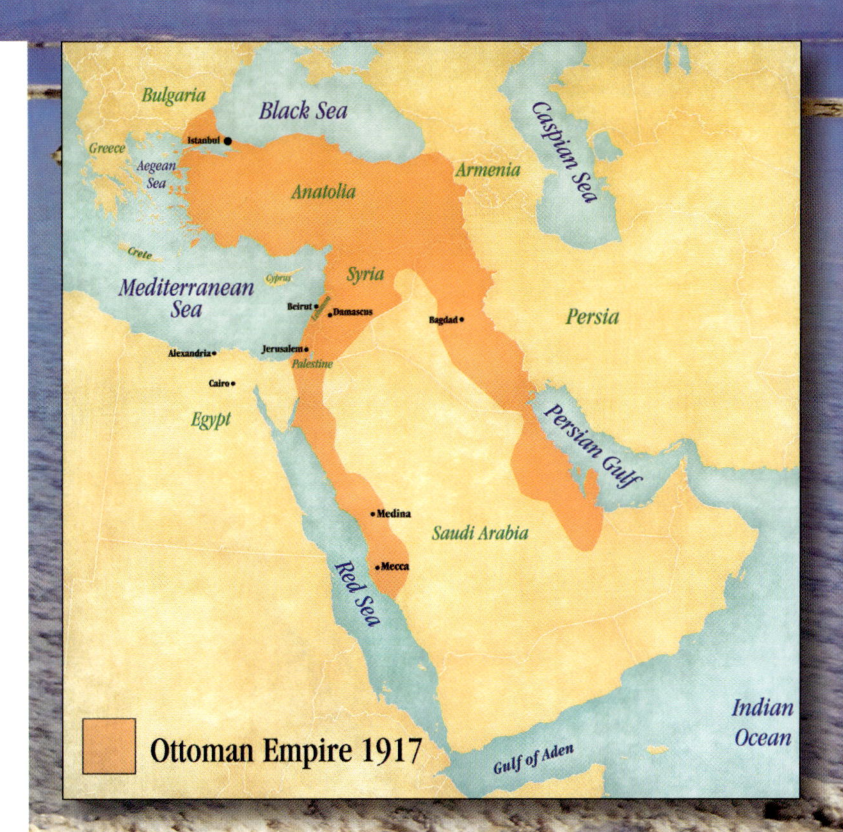

Right: *Map shows lands controlled by Ottoman Empire in 1917.*

Top: *British Foreign Secretary Lord Palmerston.*
Bottom: *Sir Moses Montefiore.*

The vicious persecution Jews endured at the hands of their Muslim masters is gruesomely revealed in a May 1839 British consul report to the British Foreign Office:

> In the early part of this week, a House was entered in the Jewish Quarter, and a robbery was committed—the House was in quarantine—and the guardian was a Jew—he was taken before the Governor—he denied having any knowledge of the thief or the circumstances. In order to compel him to confess, he was laid down and beaten, and afterwards imprisoned. The following day he was again brought before the Governor, when he still declared his innocence. He was then burned with a hot iron over his face, and various parts of the body—and beaten on the lower parts of his body to the extent that the flesh hung in pieces from him. The following day the poor creature died. He was a young Jew of Salonica about 28 years of age—who had been here but a very short time, he had only the week before been applying to enter my service.
>
> A young man—a Jew—having a French passport was also suspected—he fled—his character was known to be an indifferent one—his mother, an aged woman, was taken under the suspicion of concealing her son—She was tied up and beaten in the most brutal way....

Right: Elderly Jewish men in Jerusalem during Ottoman rule in Palestine. Circa 1910.

> I must say I am sorry and am surprised that the Governor could have acted so savage a part—for certainly what I have seen of him, I should have thought him superior to such wanton inhumanity—but it was a Jew—without friends or protection—it serves well to show, that it is not without reason that the poor Jew, even in the nineteenth century, lives from day to day in terror of his life.[31]

Over time, the great powers in Europe, especially the British, provided a measure of protection to Jews in Palestine. British Foreign Secretary Lord Palmerston instructed the consul in Jerusalem "to afford protection to Jews generally" and supply reports on their status in Palestine.[32] Somewhat improved conditions in Palestine led to a doubling of Jewish immigration between 1856 and 1880 and brought the Jewish population in Palestine to 25,000, with 14,000 living in Jerusalem.[33]

Pioneer Dreams

These Jewish immigrants, many from Eastern Europe, also had a champion in Moses Montefiore (1784-1885), perhaps the most

Israel Government Press Office

Verdant agricultural landscape shows how Jewish enterprise has transformed Israel.

David B. Keidan Collection, Central Zionist Archives

well-known Jewish philanthropist of his time and a forerunner of Zionism. A British citizen, Montefiore made seven visits to the Holy Land where he intervened to lighten the burden of the Jews' austere life, establishing a medical clinic and printing press, building synagogues, distributing funds for relief, building the first Jewish settlement outside the walls of Jerusalem, and an orchard in Jaffa to launch Israel's citrus industry.[34]

An observant Jew, Montefiore took up the task of serving the Jewish community in Palestine after a dream came to him three times in one night, prompting his initial 1827 visit to Palestine and the humanitarian largesse he lavished on Jews living there.[35]

Like Montefiore, another pivotal figure in the Jewish return was propelled into the Zionist cause by a life-transforming "revelation." Born in Lithuania, Eliezer Ben-Yehuda (1858-1922) pioneered the revival of the Hebrew language, arriving in Palestine in 1881 to launch his life's work of making Hebrew the modern tongue of the Jewish people. He did so in the wake of a blinding inspiration. "It was as if the heavens had suddenly opened, and a clear incandescent light flashed before my eyes, and a mighty inner voice sounded in my ears: the renascence of Israel on its ancestral soil." The more his dream of a national

***Left:** Eliezer Ben-Yehuda came to Palestine in 1881 and spearheaded the restoration of Hebrew as a spoken language.*

David Waterfall at Ein Gedi Nature reserve in the Judean Desert just west of the Dead Sea.

homeland for his people grew, Ben-Yehuda wrote, "the more I realized what a common language is to a nation...."[36]

Ben-Yehuda's arrival in Palestine could not have been better timed to obtain his goal: the rebirth of the Jewish nation in its own land, speaking its own language. He set foot in Palestine just as the first large-scale Jewish immigration, or aliyah (Hebrew for "going up"), began. This influx of almost 35,000 Jewish settlers from 1882-1903[37] was the first of five waves of pre-World War II Jewish immigrants. It brought young, idealistic, and educated Jews, mostly from Eastern Europe, who were willing to learn the language of Zion in their new land.

A fervent champion of "Hebrew only," Ben-Yehuda made his people's ancient tongue his exclusive vernacular when speaking with other Jews. He forbade any other language from being spoken in his own house. That rule, violated only with his wrath, made his son the first modern Jewish child to grow up speaking only Hebrew.

Because teaching the rising generation to speak Hebrew was indispensable to the success of his project, Ben-Yehuda promoted the use of Hebrew for classroom instruction. He published a Hebrew-language newspaper, creating new words for items unknown in biblical times, and devoted himself to the creation of a Hebrew dictionary. Working sometimes 18 hours a day, he produced the first six volumes of his *Complete Dictionary*

A fruitful vineyard in Kfar Tavor, a village near Mount Tabor in northern Israel.

A riot of colorful wildflowers bloom in a Golan Heights meadow.

Left: *Israeli settlers plow a field in central Israel in the 1940s.*

Bottom Left: *A worker waters a young tree in 1947 at Kibbutz Urim in the Negev desert in southern Israel.*

of Ancient and Modern Hebrew before his death in 1922. By then, his four decades of labor had made Hebrew—largely unused in daily communication for two millennia—the common language of the Jews in Palestine, a fact British mandate authorities acknowledged in 1922, just one month before his death.

RECLAIMING THE DESERT

Along with learning a new language, early Jewish settlers faced the almost impossible task of reclaiming the desert when they arrived in 1882. Joshua took the Israelites into a Promised Land of bucolic abundance, a place of "hills and valleys, which drinks water from the rain of heaven, a land for which the Lord your God cares" (Deuteronomy 11:11-12 NKJV). But by the late nineteenth century, the land was reduced to ruin. Walter Clay Lowdermilk, a U.S. soil specialist who visited the region in 1939, gave this assessment of what Jewish colonists encountered in 1882:

> the soils were eroded off the uplands to bedrock over fully one half the hills; streams across the

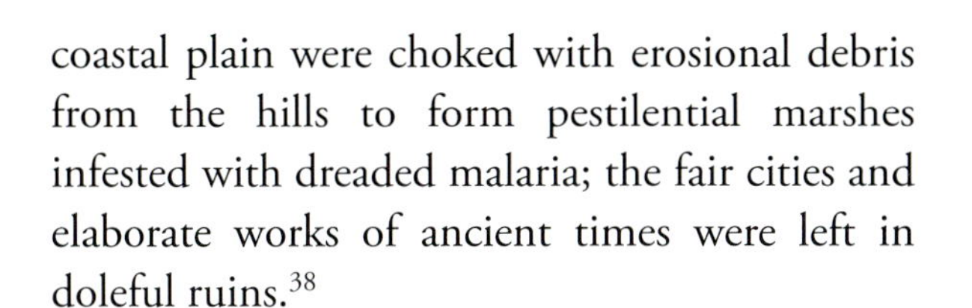

> coastal plain were choked with erosional debris from the hills to form pestilential marshes infested with dreaded malaria; the fair cities and elaborate works of ancient times were left in doleful ruins.[38]

Long years of backbreaking labor on lands purchased from absentee Arab landowners followed. Willing to pay sometimes huge sums for sand dunes and swampland, Jewish immigrants pushed back the desert, clearing land, planting citrus orchards and reforesting bare hills. Founded in 1901, the Jewish National Fund purchased land and planted more than 1.7 million trees by 1935.[39] All told, JNF has now planted almost 250 million trees in a century-long afforestation project to transform bald slopes into green forests.

One early Zionist testified in 1885 to the daunting task of reclaiming the land:

> Nobody knows of all the hardships, sickness and wretchedness they [the early Zionists] underwent. No observer from afar can feel what it is like to be without a drop of water for days, to lie for months

***Right:** Walter Clay Lowdermilk, a U.S. soil conservationist and Rhodes Scholar, supported Zionism and praised Jewish land reclamation efforts in Palestine.*

Israeli Government Press Office

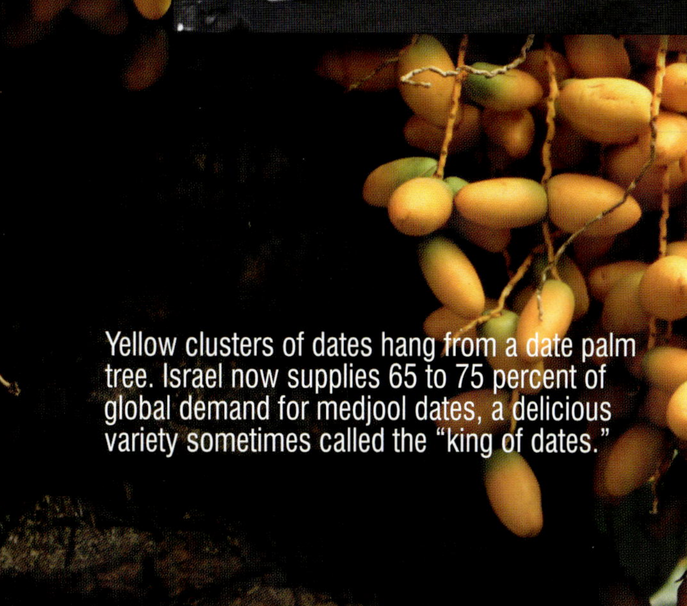

Yellow clusters of dates hang from a date palm tree. Israel now supplies 65 to 75 percent of global demand for medjool dates, a delicious variety sometimes called the "king of dates."

Teddy Brauner, Israeli Government Press Office

Amos Ben Gershom/Israeli Government Press Office

Top Left: *Israeli children in a 1952 Tel Aviv tree planting ceremony.*

Left: *Stand of trees in northern Israel. The Jewish National Fund has planted nearly 250 million trees in Israel since 1901.*

> in cramped tents visited by all sorts of reptiles, or understand what our wives, children, and mothers go through.... No one looking at a completed building realizes the sacrifice put into it.[40]

With fierce commitment and modern, scientific methods, striking improvements appeared in the land. Writing in 1925, David Baron remarked at the "wonderful changes" he witnessed in Palestine over the course of 34 years and seven visits. The "neglect of centuries" and the "blight of Turkish misrule," Baron declared, "are transformed by the labours of enthusiastic colonists into fruitful fields and vineyards and orchards."[41]

Just 24,000 Jews, or eight percent of the total population, lived in Palestine in 1882, but the Jewish population swelled to 60,000 by 1918 as modern Zionism gained strength and Jews fled persecution in Europe and Russia. Relaxed immigration allowances under the British mandate opened the door for greater Jewish immigration, lifting the number of Jews in Palestine to 384,000 by 1936.[42]

Detail from HaMakhtesh HaGadol (large crater), in the Negev desert in southern Israel.

JEWISH SETTLERS BLESS ARABS

With their arrival came socio-economic improvements that benefited Jew and Arab alike. A 1937 British commission of inquiry stated that the "general beneficent effect of Jewish immigration on Arab welfare is illustrated by the fact that the increase in the Arab population is most marked in urban areas affected by Jewish development."[43]

Aided by Jewish expertise and capital, Arab agriculture, especially citrus-growing, expanded rapidly between the two world wars. Israeli historian Efraim Karsh reports that Arab mortality rates declined dramatically, increasing life expectancy from 37.5 years in 1926-27 to 50 in 1942-44. Meanwhile, life expectancy in Egypt was just 33 years.

"That nothing remotely akin to this was taking place in the neighboring British-ruled Arab countries, not to mention India," Karsh writes, "can be explained only by the decisive Jewish contribution to mandatory Palestine's socio-economic wellbeing."[44] Today, some 5.5 million Arabs live in the region of the former British mandate and have a life expectancy of 70 years, a fact attributable, George Gilder writes, to the work of Jewish settlers.[45]

***Right:** Founding members of Moshav Batzra building the first solid house there in 1946. Tents can be seen in the background.*

Zoltan Kluger/Israeli Government Press Office

The Sorek Valley, west of Jerusalem, shows evidence of reforestation, turning brown slopes to green.

Solomon's Pillars, striking sandstone columns near Eilat in southern Israel.

An exquisite natural stone arch in Timna Valley, just north of Eilat on the Gulf of Aqaba.

***Left:** Workmen drill a well in 1946 to found Kfar Monash, a moshav (farming cooperative) in central Israel.*

The impact of Jewish know-how in Palestine was such that between 1921 and 1942 jobs increased by a factor of ten and total capital investment soared to $70 million from just several hundred thousand dollars.[46] "If we are interested in the regeneration of man," asserted Lowdermilk, a Rhodes Scholar married to a Christian missionary, "let all the righteous forces on earth support these settlements in Palestine as a wholesome example for the backward Near East, and indeed, for all who seek to work out a permanent adjustment of people to their lands."[47]

But despite the benefits gained, Muslim hostility prevailed. Arab mob violence took lives and destroyed property in the decades preceding Jewish independence. And they did so thinking they were doing the will of Allah.

CHAPTER 3

ISRAEL AND ISLAM

Allah wills it. Simple as it is, that is the best three-word explanation for the Arab-Israeli conflict.

The hostility between Arabs and Jews is not, first and foremost, a nationalistic struggle between two peoples seeking to live on the same land. Nor does the conflict primarily stem from the ancient rift between Isaac and Ishmael. Jews and Arabs lived together on the Arabian Peninsula for centuries[48] until Mohammad announced he was Allah's prophet in 622 A.D., and almost eliminated Jewish presence on the Peninsula.

Instead, the engine driving the bitter dispute between Jew and Arab is the religion of Islam. Extreme prejudice against Jews radiates from Islam's holy book, the Qur'an. It is a catechism for hating Jews. "The Qur'an portrays the Jews as the craftiest, most persistent, and most implacable enemies of the Muslims," asserts Islam scholar Robert Spencer.[49]

The Eilat Mountans in Southern Israel.

Indeed, the Qur'an showers Jews with contempt. In it, Allah denounces Jews, making them apes, pigs, and slaves for violating the Sabbath and distorting the Torah:

- And you had already known about those who transgressed among you concerning the sabbath, and We said to them, "Be apes, despised." (Sura 2:65)[50]
- So when they were insolent about that which they had been forbidden, We said to them, "Be apes, despised." (Sura 7:166)[51]
- Say, "Shall I inform you of [what is] worse than that as penalty from Allah? [It is that of] those (the Jews) whom Allah has cursed and with whom He became angry and made of them apes and pigs and slaves of Taghut. Those are worse in position and further astray from the sound way." (Sura 5:60)[52]

"Fight with the Jews"

One especially vicious hadith (revered report of what Mohammad allegedly said or did) instructs believers the end times will be marked by the killing of Jews at the hands of Muslims: "The Hour will not be established until you fight with the Jews, and the stone behind which a Jew will be hiding will

The striking expanse of the Ramon Crater in Israel's Negev desert.

Right: *Bangladeshi passport declares prohibition on travel to Israel.*

say, 'O Muslim! There is a Jew hiding behind me, so kill him'" (Sahih Bukhari, 4:52:177).[53]

Mohammad, who Muslims celebrate as their "excellent example,"[54] spent one day watching, along with his 12-year-old wife, as his soldiers beheaded some 800 Jewish men and boys in Medina in 627 A.D. After the atrocity, the Jewish women and girls became Muslim war booty—slaves and concubines.[55]

Islam infuses the entire Muslim world, not just the Arab states, with a malign ill-will toward Israel. Almost every non-Arab Muslim state—including Iran, Pakistan, Afghanistan, Indonesia and Malaysia—rejects normal diplomatic relations with Israel. Passports for Pakistan and Bangladesh read: "valid for all countries of the world, except Israel."

Muslims view the land of Israel itself as their proper possession. Under Islam, any land once subjugated by Islam must remain so—even if the occupants are predominantly non-Muslims. That is why Muslim countries, with the notable exception of Egypt and Jordan, refuse to make peace with Israel. Despite painful concessions on the part of Israel, Muslim rulers reject the Jewish state's existence and refuse to live in peace. That's what Islam requires.

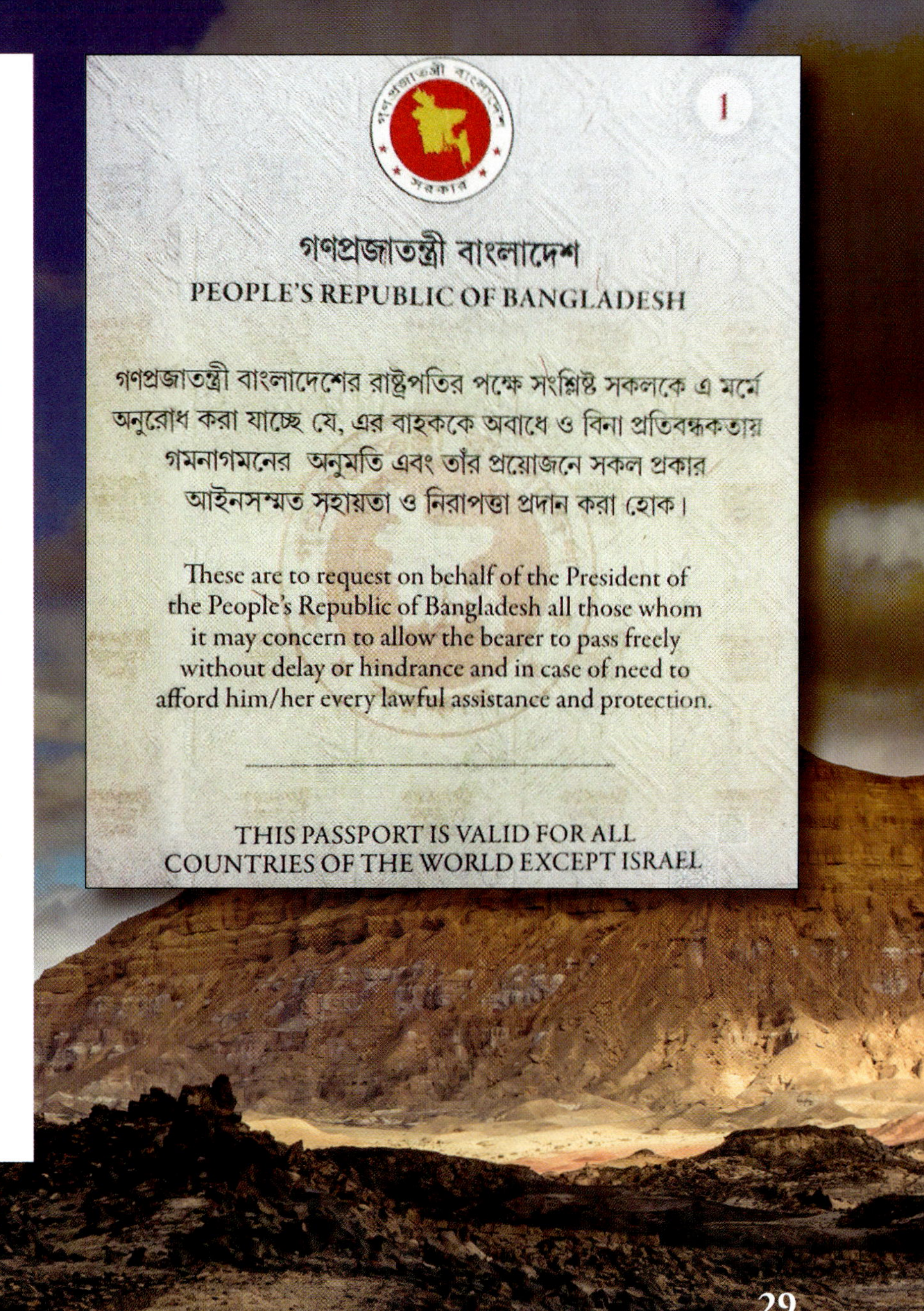

1

গণপ্রজাতন্ত্রী বাংলাদেশ

PEOPLE'S REPUBLIC OF BANGLADESH

গণপ্রজাতন্ত্রী বাংলাদেশের রাষ্ট্রপতির পক্ষে সংশ্লিষ্ট সকলকে এ মর্মে অনুরোধ করা যাচ্ছে যে, এর বাহককে অবাধে ও বিনা প্রতিবন্ধকতায় গমনাগমনের অনুমতি এবং তাঁর প্রয়োজনে সকল প্রকার আইনসম্মত সহায়তা ও নিরাপত্তা প্রদান করা হোক।

These are to request on behalf of the President of the People's Republic of Bangladesh all those whom it may concern to allow the bearer to pass freely without delay or hindrance and in case of need to afford him/her every lawful assistance and protection.

THIS PASSPORT IS VALID FOR ALL COUNTRIES OF THE WORLD EXCEPT ISRAEL

1948 JIHAD ON ISRAEL

Israeli historian Benny Morris spent three years poring over dusty archives in the U.S., Britain and Israel, and concluded "the central element in the [1948] war was an imperative to launch jihad." He calls Israel's war for independence "an Islamic holy war" and says the religious character of the conflict makes compromise then or since all but impossible.[56]

En route to Palestine in 1882, a group of Russian Jews issued a manifesto declaring their desire for "a home in our country" and pledged their willingness "to help our brother Ishmael in the time of his need."[57] Likewise, some Arab leaders adopted a welcoming posture, viewing arriving Jews as a source of Arab jobs.[58]

But peace and harmony between the two people was always in doubt. Attempts were made to stop European Jews from taking refuge in Palestine and "organized gangs of Arabs attacked unprotected and unarmed Jewish settlements" in the 1880s, asserts Alan Dershowitz.[59]

The King-Crane Commission, a U.S. government panel which sampled Arab opinion in the dissolving Ottoman

***Top Left:** Haganah soldiers patrol outside Nazareth in early 1948.*

***Bottom Left:** Israeli soldiers in combat in 1948 during Israel's War of Independence.*

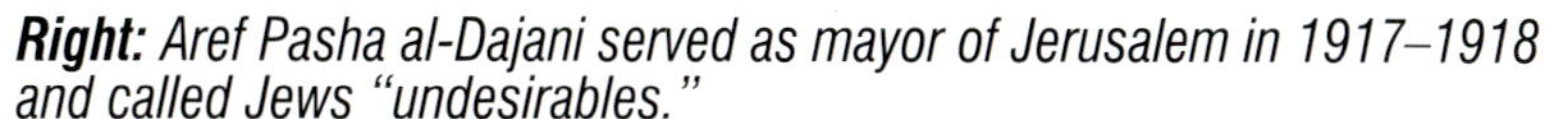

Right: *Aref Pasha al-Dajani served as mayor of Jerusalem in 1917–1918 and called Jews "undesirables."*

Empire in 1919, warned that a wholesale repatriation of Jews to their homeland would only worsen resentment toward Jews. "[T]he complete Jewish occupation of Palestine," the Commission reported, "... would intensify, with a certainty like fate, the anti-Jewish feeling both in Palestine and in all other portions of the world which look to Palestine as 'the Holy Land.'"[60]

Aref Pasha al-Dajani, a former mayor of Jerusalem, expressed the raw version of that resentment, telling the King-Crane Commission:

> It is impossible for us to make an understanding with them [Jews] or even to live [with] them together.... Their history and all their past proves that it is impossible to live with them. In all the countries where they are at present they are not wanted and undesirables, because they always arrive to suck the blood of everybody, and to become economically and financially victorious. If the League of Nations will not listen to the appeal of the Arabs this country will become a river of blood.[61]

Reproduced from http://www.passia.org with permission

Canyon in En Gedi Nature Reserve overlooking the Dead Sea.

MIRAGE OF HOPE

At least one Arab leader stirred hope for a future of Arab-Jew good-will. Emir Feisal, who led the Arab delegation to the Versailles Peace Conference in 1919, struck an agreement there with Chaim Weizmann, president of the Zionist Organization. In it, Feisal accepted the terms of the historic Balfour Declaration, which announced the British government's support for a Jewish homeland in Palestine.

A stunning triumph for Zionism, the Balfour Declaration was a one-paragraph note British Foreign Secretary Arthur Balfour sent to Lord Rothschild, head of the British Zionist Federation, on Nov. 2, 1917. In it, Balfour announced

> His Majesty's Government view with favour the establishment in Palestine of a national home for the Jewish people, and will use their best endeavors to facilitate the achievement of this object, it being clearly understood that nothing shall he done which may prejudice the civil and religious rights of existing non-Jewish communities in Palestine, or the rights and political status enjoyed by Jews in any other country.

Left: *Emir Feisal, center, during the Paris Peace Conference of 1919.*

Right: *Chaim Weizmann, President of the World Zionist Organization, and later the first President of Israel.*

Lower Right: *Chaim Weizmann and Emir Feisal.*

In concert with the Balfour Declaration, the Feisal-Weizmann agreement notably encouraged Jewish immigration and settlement "on a large scale, and as quickly as possible."[62] Feisal offered more felicities in a letter to Felix Frankfurter, the legal adviser to the Zionist delegation. "We Arabs…look with deepest sympathy on the Zionist movement," he wrote. "We will wish the Jews a hearty welcome home…our two movements complete one another…. I think that neither can be a real success without the other."[63]

But the Feisal-Weizmann agreement was never implemented.[64] Feisal, who became king of Iraq in 1921, disowned the pact, announcing ten years later through his royal staff, "His Majesty does not remember having written anything of that kind with his knowledge."[65]

Despite Feisal's forgetfulness, an enduring legal basis for the Jewish claim to their ancient homeland was established in April 1920 when Great Britain, France, Italy, and Japan, with the U.S. as a neutral observer, met at a villa in San Remo, Italy. The postwar gathering to parcel out the former Ottoman empire made Britain responsible, in what became known as the San

The Judean Desert is east of Jerusalem and stretches south to the Dead Sea.

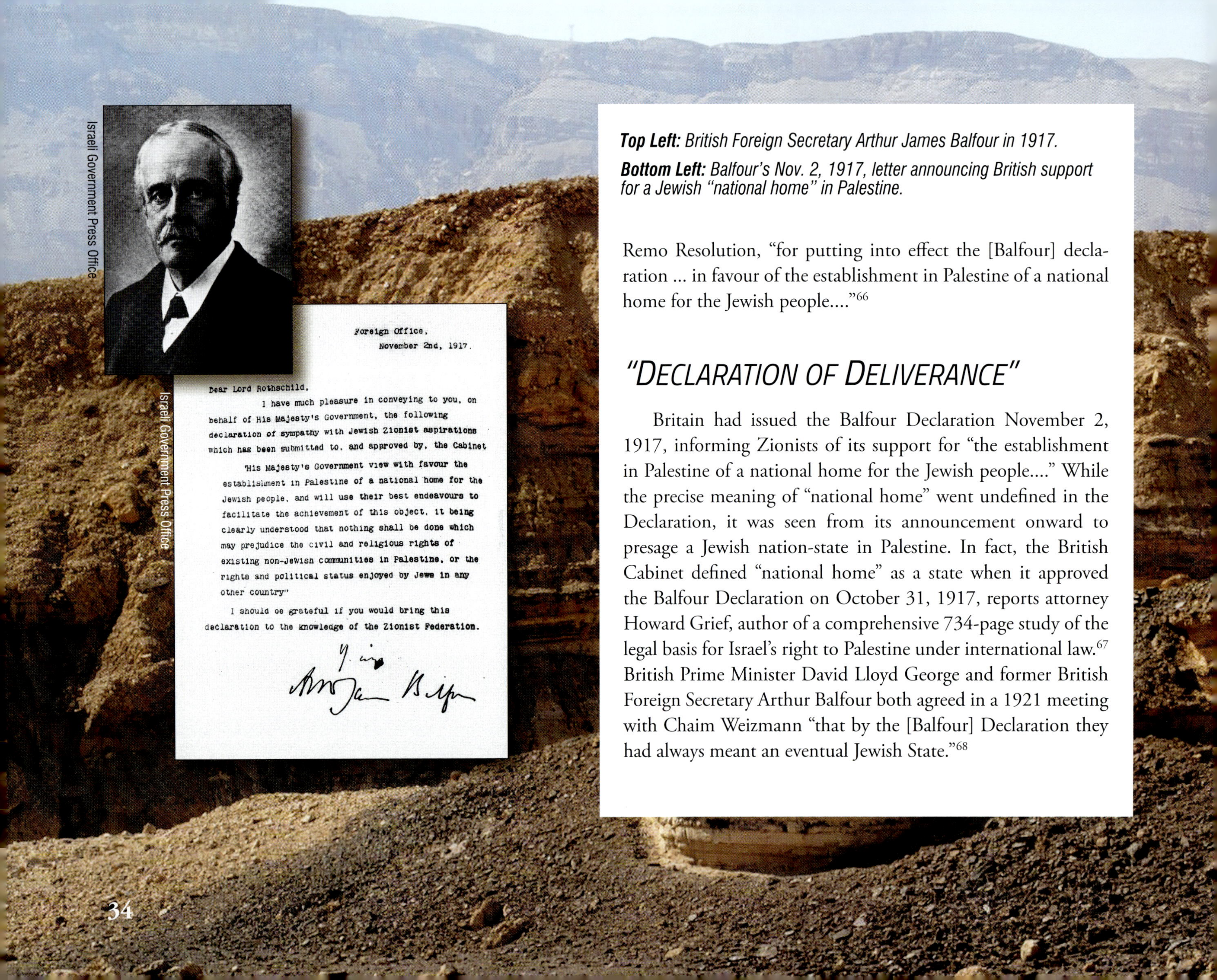

Foreign Office,
November 2nd, 1917.

Dear Lord Rothschild,

I have much pleasure in conveying to you, on behalf of His Majesty's Government, the following declaration of sympathy with Jewish Zionist aspirations which has been submitted to, and approved by, the Cabinet

"His Majesty's Government view with favour the establishment in Palestine of a national home for the Jewish people, and will use their best endeavours to facilitate the achievement of this object, it being clearly understood that nothing shall be done which may prejudice the civil and religious rights of existing non-Jewish communities in Palestine, or the rights and political status enjoyed by Jews in any other country"

I should be grateful if you would bring this declaration to the knowledge of the Zionist Federation.

Yours
Arthur James Balfour

Israeli Government Press Office

Israeli Government Press Office

Top Left: *British Foreign Secretary Arthur James Balfour in 1917.*

Bottom Left: *Balfour's Nov. 2, 1917, letter announcing British support for a Jewish "national home" in Palestine.*

Remo Resolution, "for putting into effect the [Balfour] declaration ... in favour of the establishment in Palestine of a national home for the Jewish people...."[66]

"DECLARATION OF DELIVERANCE"

Britain had issued the Balfour Declaration November 2, 1917, informing Zionists of its support for "the establishment in Palestine of a national home for the Jewish people...." While the precise meaning of "national home" went undefined in the Declaration, it was seen from its announcement onward to presage a Jewish nation-state in Palestine. In fact, the British Cabinet defined "national home" as a state when it approved the Balfour Declaration on October 31, 1917, reports attorney Howard Grief, author of a comprehensive 734-page study of the legal basis for Israel's right to Palestine under international law.[67] British Prime Minister David Lloyd George and former British Foreign Secretary Arthur Balfour both agreed in a 1921 meeting with Chaim Weizmann "that by the [Balfour] Declaration they had always meant an eventual Jewish State."[68]

Top Right: *Lord Rothschild, a British banker and active Zionist.*
Bottom Right: *David Lloyd George, British Prime Minister,1916-1922.*

Because it created a legal framework to establish a Jewish national home and, ultimately, a Jewish state, the San Remo Resolution sparked Jewish celebrations around the world. Chaim Weizmann called it "the most momentous political event in the whole history of our [Zionist] movement" and a "great declaration of deliverance."[69]

The San Remo Resolution, agreed to on April 24-25, 1920, is one of three "founding documents of mandated Palestine and the modern Jewish state of Israel that arose from it."[70] The two others are the Mandate for Palestine, which was confirmed by the League of Nations on July 24, 1922, and the Franco-British Boundary Convention established on December 23, 1920.

Under the Franco-British Boundary Convention, the lines drawn for Palestine encompassed the modern state of Israel—including Jerusalem, Judea and Samaria (West Bank), and Gaza—and the modern state of Jordan, as the nearby map shows (top left, page 36). Britain soon acted to limit the territory granted for Jewish settlement to only land west of the Jordan River. The territory to the east, some 77 percent of the land originally designated for Jewish settlement, was transferred to the Arab population and became Transjordan, what is now the

Wikipedia, public domain

Wikipedia, public domain

Ha-Makhtesh Ha-Katan (The Small Crater), a vast depression encompassed by limestone cliffs in the Negev.

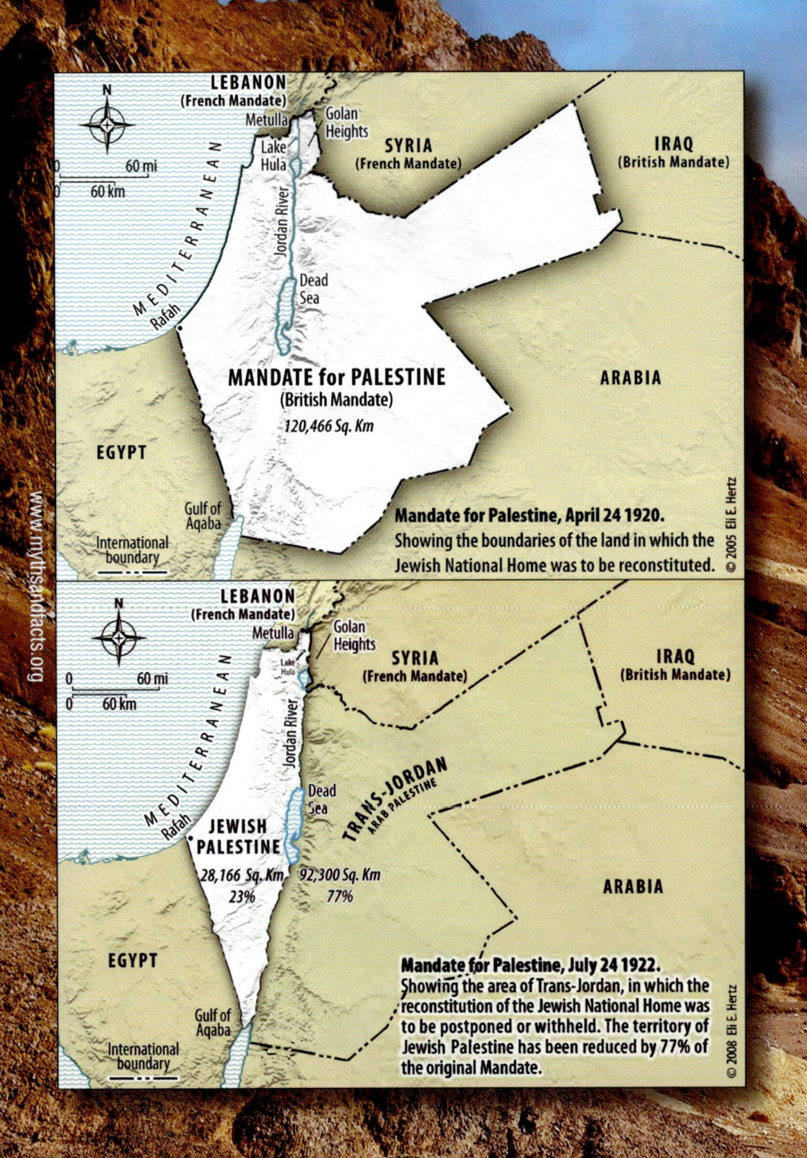

Richly colored Eilat Mountains in Israel's southern Negev.

modern nation state of Jordan. Transjordan became a "judenrein" (cleansed of Jews) territory where Jews were forbidden to live. The same is true today in Jordan where Jews—including Israeli Jews—are allowed to visit but forbidden to become citizens or own property.[71]

The Mandate did not, however, limit Jewish settlement inside Palestine west of the Jordan. It authorized the British, as the Mandate authority, to "encourage, in co-operation with the Jewish agency ... close settlement by Jews on the land, including State lands and waste lands not required for public purposes."[72]

And while Emir Feisal raised hopes for the happy coexistence of Jew and Arab in Palestine, other Arabs sharply protested Jewish presence in Palestine. The Haifa Congress of Palestinian Arabs rejected Jewish immigration in a petition delivered on March 14, 1921 to Winston Churchill, then British Secretary of State for the Colonies. "We energetically protest," the Arab delegation told Churchill, "against the Balfour Declaration to the effect that our Country should be made the Jewish National Home."[73] Churchill dismissed the Arab petition, arguing it was "manifestly right that the Jews, who are scattered all over the world, should have a national centre and a National Home where some of them may be reunited."[74]

Churchill, however, fundamentally reshaped the Mandate for Palestine by inserting Article 25, which allowed the British to prohibit Jews from Palestine east of the Jordan. And the 1922

Top Right: *British Colonial Secretary Winston Churchill (left), T. E. Lawrence ("Lawrence of Arabia"), and Emir Abdullah (later King Abdullah of Transjordan) in the gardens of the Government House, Jerusalem in 1921.*

Bottom Right: *Churchill (center right) escorted by British high commissioner for Palestine Herbert Samuel in Jerusalem in 1921.*

Churchill White Paper redefined "Jewish national home" "to mean not an eventual independent Jewish state but ... a cultural or spiritual center for the Jewish people," Grief contends.[75]

GRAND MUFTI: "KILL THE JEWS"

The British also fueled Arab grievance toward Jews in 1921 when British high commissioner for Palestine Herbert Samuel appointed anti-Semitic extremist Haj Amin Husseini Grand Mufti of Jerusalem. As the supreme Muslim leader in Palestine, Husseini soon silenced voices of compromise. Instead, as Dershowitz observes, he imposed the non-negotiable rule that "it would violate Islamic law for even one inch of Palestine to be controlled by Jews."[76] By 1937, if not earlier, Husseini's "hatred" for a Jewish homeland in Palestine had "permeated the Arab population as a whole," as a Royal British Commission determined.[77]

The Grand Mufti supported Muslim terrorists, or *fedayeen* ("one who sacrifices himself"), who attacked Jewish civilians.[78] He instigated violent anti-Jewish riots in 1929 and 1936, and made

Library of Congress

Israeli Government Press Office

Stony heights of Masada in the Negev.

Bundesarchiv, Bild 146-1987-004-09A/ Heinrich Hoffmann / CC-BY-SA 3.0

Left: *Grand Mufti Haj Amin Husseini with Adolf Hitler in November 1941. Husseini issued a call to "kill the Jews" on Radio Berlin.*

common cause with Hitler during World War II by broadcasting bitter attacks on Jews in Palestine. In 1944, Husseini called on his fellow Arabs to "rise as one man and fight for your sacred rights. Kill the Jews wherever you find them. This pleases God, history, and religion. This saves your honor. God is with you."[79]

"STEALING" ARAB LAND?

Husseini was also a surprise witness on behalf of the Jews, undermining the persistent Arab charge that Jewish settlers stole their land. That claim is a centerpiece of the Arab case against Israel—an easy-to-understand accusation that plays to anti-Semitic stereotypes and remains widely believed today. But the evidence is not there.

Theodor Herzl, Zionism's leading progenitor, proposed the creation of a "Jewish Company" in *The Jewish State* to, among other things, gain title to land which "must, of course, be privately acquired."[80] Herzl's proposal came to fruition, in modified form, when the fifth Zionist Congress founded the Jewish National Fund in 1901. The JNF purchased its first tract of land in 1904 and has bought 2.6 million dunams (quarter acre) since.[81]

Right: *An aging Lord Balfour with Herbert Samuel, British high commissioner for Palestine in 1925. Samuel was the first Jew to govern the historic land of Israel in 2,000 years.*

A British investigation in 1929 found that, far from "stealing" land, Jews in Palestine "paid high prices for the land, and in addition they paid to certain of the occupants of those lands a considerable amount of money which they were not legally bound to pay."[82]

The much more frequent complaint within the Arab community was that land sales to Jews *were* taking place. An article in the Arab press in 1911 decried the transfer of property into Jewish hands:

> You are selling the property of your fathers and grandfathers for a pittance to people who will have no pity on you.... This is a crime that will be recorded in your names in history, a black stain and disgrace that your descendants will bear, which will not be expunged even after years and eras have gone by.[83]

Israel critics also allege land sales to Jews led to the eviction of poor Arab tenants—robbing them and their families of their livelihoods, and sending them deeper into poverty. But liberal Israeli historian Benny Morris suggests such transactions were relatively rare: "Historians have concluded that only 'several

Israeli Government Press Office

Evrona Nature Reserve, with majestic sunlight-splashed mountains beyond.

thousand' families were displaced following land sales to Jews between the 1880s and the late 1930s."[84]

And possibly less. The British looked into the extent of Arab landlessness in 1931, and offered land to Arabs who had been dispossessed, as Mitchell Bard notes in *Myths & Facts*. While over 3,000 applications for land grants came in, the vast majority were judged unfounded since those applying were not, in fact, landless Arabs. Ultimately, just 600 Arabs were determined to be landless and only 100 accepted land offers.[85]

Moreover, David Ben-Gurion called on Jews in 1920 not to buy land from *fellahin* (native peasants). The Labor Zionist leader insisted that "under no circumstances must we touch land belonging to *fellahs* or worked by them."[86] Nor did the Jews "cherry-pick" the best land. The Palestine Royal Commission, a British investigation also known as the Peel Commission, reported the opposite in 1937: "Much of the land now carrying orange groves was sand dunes or swamps and uncultivated when it was bought."[87] Jews founded Tel Aviv in 1909 on sand hills purchased "piecemeal, from European, Turkish and (principally) Arab landlords, mostly at extremely high prices."[88]

Top Left: *Jewish pioneers carting soil in 1910 over the sands of what is now Tel Aviv.*

Bottom Left: *Aerial view of Tel Aviv in the 1920s shows dramatic development.*

BEN-GURION: "BIBLE IS OUR MANDATE"

In his testimony to the Peel Commission, Ben-Gurion was asked to define the basis of the Jewish claim to Palestine. "The Bible is our mandate,"[89] he answered. He later told French President Charles de Gaulle, "It was from the Bible that we drew the strength to withstand a hostile world and to perpetuate our faith that we would one day return to our land and that peace would reign in the world."[90]

The Peel Commission also took testimony in early 1937 from Haj Amin Husseini, the British-appointed political and religious chief in Palestine. Husseini called for an end to Jewish immigration into Palestine and alleged widespread Arab evictions from their lands due to Jewish land purchases. But under close questioning by a Royal Commissioner, Husseini said most land was obtained through commercial transactions and acknowledged land sales were voluntary, not forced:

> **SIR L. HAMMOND:** His Eminence gave us a picture of the Arabs being evicted from their land and villages being wiped out. What I want to know is, did the Government of Palestine, the

Fritz Cohen/Israeli Government Press Office

Right: *Israeli Prime Minister David Ben-Gurion meeting with French president Charles de Gaulle in Paris in 1961.*

The ancient rocks of Masada bear witness to Jewish courage, endurance and strength of will.

Left: *Peel Commission vice chairman Sir Horrace Rumbold, left, and chairman Lord Peel at Jerusalem War Graves Cemetery in 1936.*

Administration, acquire the land and then hand it over to the Jews?

MUFTI: In most cases the lands were acquired.

SIR L. HAMMOND: I mean forcibly acquired-compulsory acquisition as land would be acquired for public purposes?

MUFTI: No, it wasn't.

SIR L. HAMMOND: Not taken by compulsory acquisition?

MUFTI: No.[91]

After fleeing Palestine in July 1937 when the British sought to arrest him for his part in a violent Arab uprising, Husseini arrived in Germany in 1941 where he met with Nazi dictator Adolf Hitler. Husseini urged both Germany and Italy to give Palestinian Arabs "the right to solve the problem of the Jewish elements in Palestine ... by the same method that the question is now being settled in the Axis countries."[92]

The Long History of "No"

Whether instigating violence against Jews in Palestine or broadcasting a call to "kill the Jews" on Radio Berlin, Husseini models the consistent approach adopted by almost every Arab leader since. Their strategy, "from the very beginning," says Harvard law professor Alan Dershowitz, "has been to eliminate the existence of any Jewish state, and indeed any substantial Jewish population, in what is now Israel."[93] It's a strong statement, but one with ample support in the long history of modern Arab-Israeli relations.

"No" to Partition in 1937

Some 400,000 Jews, along with about one million Arabs, lived in Palestine by 1937 when the British Peel Commission, unable to identify any other plan with "a chance of ultimate peace,"[94] recommended dividing Palestine into Jewish and Arab states. Even though Jews were nearly half the total population, the Peel proposal allotted the Jews just 18 percent of the land left in Palestine (5,000 of the 26,700 square kilometers).[95] While unhappy with their tiny

Top Right: *Arab protest delegation against British policy in Palestine, circa 1929. Haj Amin Husseini, the Grand Mufti of Jerusalem, is in front row (white fez).*

Right: *Haj Amin Husseini, a fiery anti-Semite and supreme Muslim leader in Palestine.*

Library of Congress

Israeli Government Press Office

Cattle graze in the Judean Desert near the Dead Sea.

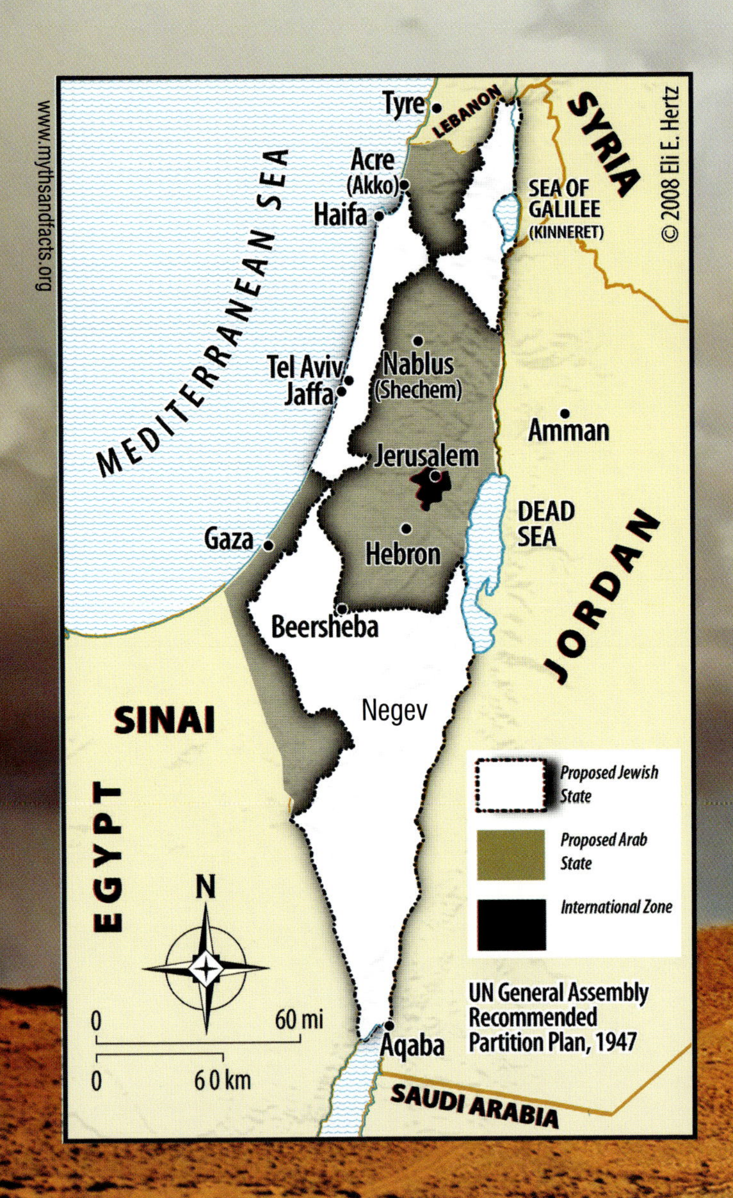

Mustard-hued desert under cloudy sky.

***Left:** UN-approved partition proposal gave Jews 55 percent of Palestine and sparked Jewish celebrations. Arabs flatly rejected it.*

slice of Palestine, the Jews accepted the British solution. Not so the Arabs who rejected the proposal unanimously, including the "whole principle of awarding territory to the Jews."[96]

"NO" TO PARTITION IN 1947

Ten years later, Jews danced in the streets of Tel Aviv after the UN approved a partition plan giving Jews 55 percent of Palestine (although more than 60 percent was in the Negev desert), as the map at left reveals. "We are happy and ready for what lies ahead," Zionist leader Golda Meir said after the UN vote. "Our hands are extended in peace to our neighbors," declared the future Israeli prime minister. "Both States can live in peace with one another and cooperate for the welfare of their inhabitants."[97]

But two months before the UN approved the partition plan, Arab League Secretary-General Abdul al-Rahman Azzam flatly rejected all talk of dividing the land between Jews and Arabs. "The Arab world is not at all in a compromising mood," Azzam told Jewish Agency representatives:

> You will achieve nothing with talk of compromise or peace. You may perhaps achieve something by

Right: *Tel Aviv residents celebrate the United Nations decision on the partition of Palestine, November 29, 1947.*

Pinn Hans/Israeli Government Press Office

> force of your arms. We will try to rout you. I am not sure we will succeed, but we will try. We succeeded in expelling the Crusaders, but lost Spain and Persia, and may lose Palestine. But it is too late for a peaceable solution.[98]

Three weeks later Azzam predicted "a war of extermination and momentous massacre which will be spoken of like the Tartar massacre or the Crusader wars."[99]

Likewise, an Arab Higher Committee spokesman told the UN Arabs would drench "the soil of our beloved country with the last drop of our blood."[100] As promised, hostilities erupted almost immediately after the UN partition vote on November 29, 1947, killing 427 Arabs and 381 Jews from November 30 to February 1, with more bloodshed after that.[101]

"No" to Peace in 1948

When Israel declared statehood on May 14, 1948, Arab irregular forces had already been assaulting Jews in Palestine for five-and-a-half months. Despite that, Israel's Declaration of Statehood appealed

A gorgeous sunrise seen from Masada with the Dead Sea in the distance.

Israeli Government Press Office

Left: *Israeli soldier takes aim from behind boulders at Castel, a rock-hewn stronghold east of Jerusalem, during Israel's War of Independence.*

> to the Arab inhabitants of the State of Israel to preserve peace and participate in the upbuilding of the State on the basis of full and equal citizenship and due representation in all its provisional and permanent institutions.[102]

Instead, five Arab nations invaded Israel in a failed attempt to drive the infant nation into the sea. And when a UN envoy proposed a revised partition plan, giving Israel Western Galilee while handing the entire Negev to the Arabs in exchange for recognizing Israel, the answer came back "No."[103]

"No" to Peace in 1956

Egypt closed the Suez Canal to Israeli shipping in 1949 and in 1955 it sponsored terrorists who infiltrated Israel and staged murderous assaults and sabotage. Egypt also blocked Israeli shipping in the Straits of Tiran, at the southern tip of Sinai. Egyptian president Gamal Abdel Nasser explained why:

> I am not solely fighting against Israel itself. My task is to deliver the Arab world from destruction

The sharp peaks of Sinai with sunlight

Wikepedia, public domain

Israeli Government Press Office

Right: *Egyptian strongman Gamal Abdel Nasser, right, declared, "Our hatred [against Israel] is very strong."*

Bottom Right: *IDF soldiers surround Army Chief Chaplain, Rabbi Shlomo Goren, on June 6, 1967, as he blows the shofar in front of the Western Wall, celebrating Israeli control of the Old City of Jerusalem.*

> through Israel's intrigue, which has its roots abroad. Our hatred is very strong. There is no sense in talking about peace with Israel. There is not even the smallest place for negotiations.[104]

With no room for talks and in a de facto state of war with Egypt, Israel attacked Egypt on October 29, 1956, seizing the Gaza Strip and much of the Sinai Desert—territory it soon returned under pressure from the U.S., which, in turn, guaranteed open shipping channels for Israel.[105]

"No, No, No" in 1967

Some 250,000 Arab troops, along with 2,000 tanks and 700 aircraft were staged and ready to strike Israel on June 4, 1967. The armies of Egypt, Jordan, Syria, and Iraq were gathered with one purpose. "The existence of Israel is an error which must be rectified," Iraq's president announced on May 31. "This is our opportunity to wipe out the ignominy which has been with us since 1948. Our goal is clear—to wipe Israel off the map."[106]

The harsh and forbidding Sinai Desert.

Left: *Israeli Defense Minister Moshe Dayan.*

Lower Left: *IDF soldiers march Egyptian prisoners of war captured on the west bank of the Suez Canal during the 1973 Yom Kippur War.*

But things didn't go quite as planned. Recognizing its existence was at stake, Israel seized the initiative on June 5, destroying the Egyptian Air Force on the ground and executing a stunning defeat of the nations gathered against her. Within six days, Israel had taken Jerusalem, the West Bank, and the Golan Heights.

And then Israeli Defense Minister Moshe Dayan announced he was "waiting for a telephone call from King Hussein" to discuss a land for peace swap.[107] The call never came. Instead, the heads of 13 Arab states retired to Khartoum, Sudan, for a summit conference where they issued their famous "Three Nos" declaration: "no peace with Israel, no negotiations with Israel, no recognition of Israel."[108]

Six years after the Arab world suffered humiliating defeat in the Six-Day War, Egypt and Syria—aided by nine Muslim nations—attacked Israel again on October 6, 1973. The surprise assault came on Yom Kippur, the holiest day in the Jewish calendar, and caught Israel by surprise. Israeli forces suffered initial losses but turned the battle around, aided by a massive infusion of tanks, munitions, spare parts, and helicopters from the U.S. By the time the U.N. imposed a truce on October 22, Israeli forces were threatening Cairo and Damascus.

"YES" TO SINAI AND PEACE IN 1978

In the one land-for-peace swap which has endured, Israel gave Sinai, which it acquired in the 1967 Six-Day War, back to Egypt in 1978. In return, Egypt, under Anwar Sadat, signed a peace treaty recognizing Israel and establishing a "cold peace" with the Jewish state. For that, the other members of the Arab League banished Egypt from the Pan-Arab body in 1980. Two years later, Muslim Brotherhood forces assassinated Sadat in Cairo.

"YES" AND "NO" IN OSLO IN 1993

An apparent breakthrough came in 1993 when the Palestinian Liberation Organization, under Yasser Arafat, said it would, like Egypt, recognize the right of Israel to exist in both peace and security. While the PLO's 1964 founding charter called for the destruction of Israel, Arafat promised to end terrorism against Israel and erase the anti-Israel charter provision.

In reward, Arafat, along with Israel's Shimon Peres and Yitzhak

Top Right: *President Anwar Sadat and Prime Minister Menachem Begin during joint session of Congress, September 18, 1978.*

Bottom Right: *Nobel Peace prize laureates for 1994, from left, PLO Chairman Yasser Arafat, Foreign Minister Shimon Peres, and Prime Minister Yitzhak Rabin.*

Ya'acov Sa'ar/Israel Government Press Office

Judean Desert near Beit El (House of God), suggested as place where Jacob slept, dreaming of angels ascending and descending from heaven.

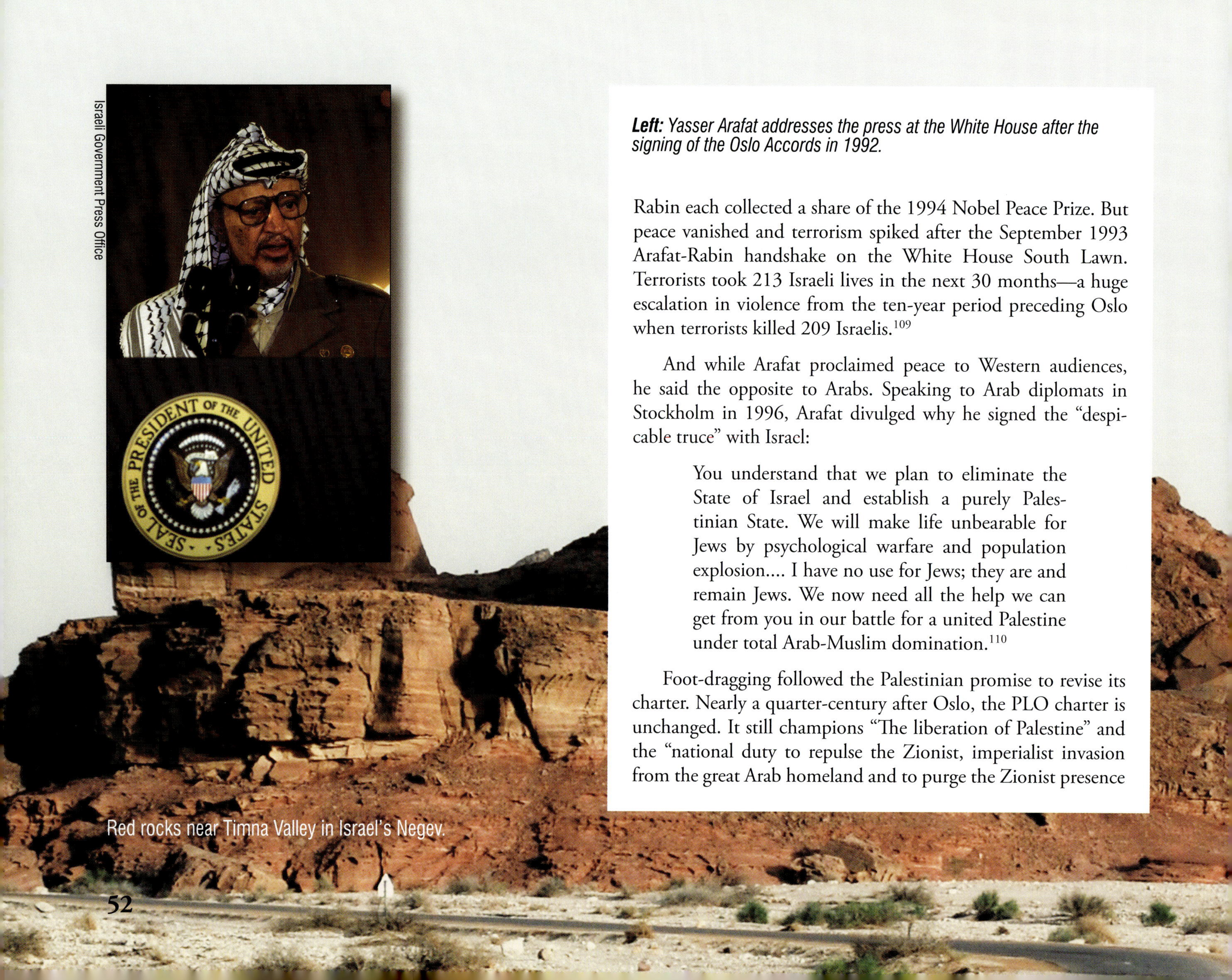

Israeli Government Press Office

***Left:** Yasser Arafat addresses the press at the White House after the signing of the Oslo Accords in 1992.*

Red rocks near Timna Valley in Israel's Negev.

Rabin each collected a share of the 1994 Nobel Peace Prize. But peace vanished and terrorism spiked after the September 1993 Arafat-Rabin handshake on the White House South Lawn. Terrorists took 213 Israeli lives in the next 30 months—a huge escalation in violence from the ten-year period preceding Oslo when terrorists killed 209 Israelis.[109]

And while Arafat proclaimed peace to Western audiences, he said the opposite to Arabs. Speaking to Arab diplomats in Stockholm in 1996, Arafat divulged why he signed the "despicable truce" with Israel:

> You understand that we plan to eliminate the State of Israel and establish a purely Palestinian State. We will make life unbearable for Jews by psychological warfare and population explosion.... I have no use for Jews; they are and remain Jews. We now need all the help we can get from you in our battle for a united Palestine under total Arab-Muslim domination.[110]

Foot-dragging followed the Palestinian promise to revise its charter. Nearly a quarter-century after Oslo, the PLO charter is unchanged. It still champions "The liberation of Palestine" and the "national duty to repulse the Zionist, imperialist invasion from the great Arab homeland and to purge the Zionist presence

Top Right: *Prime Minister Yitzhak Rabin and King Hussein of Jordan confer at the Sea of Galilee after signing Israel Jordan Peace Treaty.*

Bottom Right: *Prime Minister Yitzhak Rabin (left) shaking hands with PLO Chairman Yasser Arafat (right) on White House lawn as President Bill Clinton looks on.*

from Palestine." It still calls upon the "Arab nation, peoples, and governments" to assist Palestinian Arabs "in pursuing its armed revolution until the liberation of its homeland."[111]

Despite Arafat's duplicity, Oslo did open the door for Jordan's historic 1994 peace treaty with Israel—an enduring agreement that brought full diplomatic relations and lasting peace between the two nations.

"NO" TO EVERYTHING IN 2000

It was an offer he couldn't refuse—but he did. Israeli prime minister Ehud Barak offered Yasser Arafat almost everything Palestinians wanted in July 2000 when President Bill Clinton hosted the Israeli and Palestinian leaders at Camp David for two weeks of talks. Just about the only thing Barak didn't put on the table was a pledge Jews would vacate Israel and turn out the lights as they left.

Speaking slowly to ensure Arafat understood, Bill Clinton read him the long list of Israeli concessions: Palestinian control

Wikepedia, public domain

Avi Ohayon/Israeli Government Press Office

Avi Ohayon/Israeli Government Press Office

***Left:** Israeli Prime Minister Ehud Barak (left), President Clinton (center) and President of the Palestinian Authority Yasser Arafat (right) at the opening of the Camp David Summit.*

over all of Gaza, 92 percent of the West Bank, all of East Jerusalem, and half of the Old City of Jerusalem. Plus, "custodianship" over the Temple Mount, the return of Arab refugees to the new Palestinian states and a huge aid program on their behalf.[112]

In exchange, Israel only asked for Arafat's pledge to end the conflict and make no further claims on Israel.

Arafat said no.

"He just kept saying no to every offer, never making any counterproposals of his own," Barak said two years later, when out of office. He said Palestinian leaders reject the idea of two states for two people—the widely touted two-state solution—and seek "the destruction of Israel as a Jewish state."[113]

Arafat died in 2004, but his successors in Gaza and the West Bank (biblical Judea and Samaria), take the same position. "Palestine from the river to the sea, from the north to the south, is our land and we will never give up one inch or any part of it," Hamas leader Khalaed Mashaal declared in 2012.[114]

And Palestinian president Mahmoud Abbas told the Fatah Revolutionary Council in 2015, "What we will not agree to is a Jewish state. In principle, if [a pending French proposal] specifies this [a Jewish state], we will not accept it."[115]

EYE-TO-EYE DIPLOMACY

Former Israeli Ambassador to the U.S. Michael Oren tells in his book, *Ally*, about a revealing 2010 encounter between Vice President Joe Biden and Abbas. Meeting in Ramallah, Oren recounts, "the vice president asked the Palestinian president to look him in the eye and promise that he could make peace with Israel. Abbas refused."[116]

Left-leaning Israeli historian Benny Morris now sees the long saga of Jew-Arab relations as one of consistent Arab refusal to accept Israel's existence as a nation. He calls the 1948 war "a jihad—an Islamic holy war" and says Arab leaders want all of Palestine:

> The secular leaders—if you can call them that—like Yasser Arafat and President Mahmoud Abbas, are not prepared to accept a formula of two states for two peoples. So as not to scare the goyim, they project a vagueness about it, but they think in terms of expulsion and elimination.[117]

But even if Israel's Persian and Arab enemies, on instructions from their anti-Semitic faith, breathe out threats of annihilation,

Right: *Palestinian Authority President Mahmoud Abbas declared in 2015 Palestinians will never accept Israel as a Jewish state.*

Amos Ben Gershom/Israeli Government Press Office

Israel's Arava Desert descends from the Dead Sea to Eilat and is home, incredibly, to successful farmers.

Israel has a friend in high places. Whatever Allah may say, the God of Abraham, Isaac and Jacob is a friend and champion to the Jews. While He scattered them nearly 2,000 years ago, He has now regathered them. And He has great plans ahead for His still chosen people.

Rugged mountains in Israel's south, near Eilat.

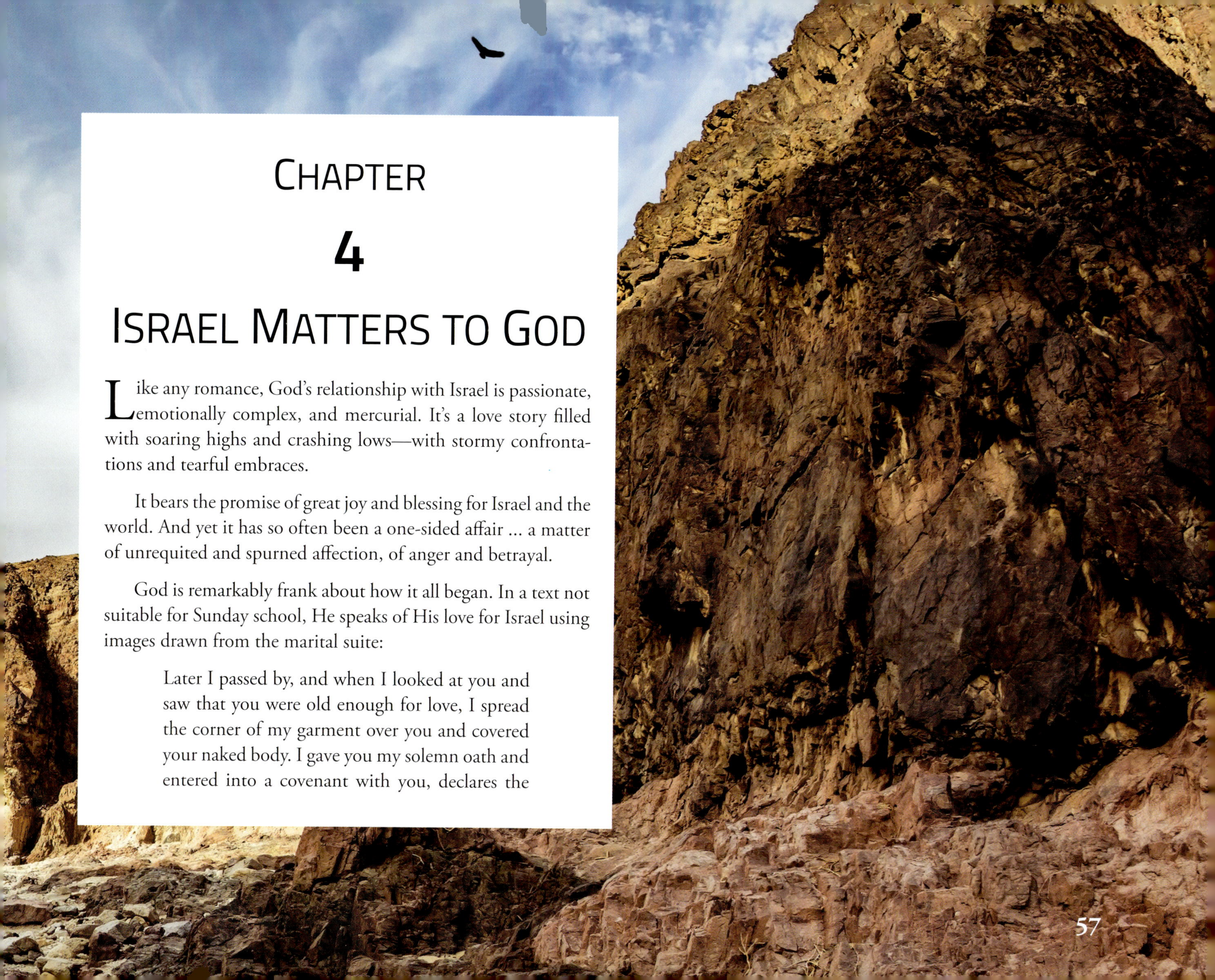

CHAPTER 4

ISRAEL MATTERS TO GOD

Like any romance, God's relationship with Israel is passionate, emotionally complex, and mercurial. It's a love story filled with soaring highs and crashing lows—with stormy confrontations and tearful embraces.

It bears the promise of great joy and blessing for Israel and the world. And yet it has so often been a one-sided affair ... a matter of unrequited and spurned affection, of anger and betrayal.

God is remarkably frank about how it all began. In a text not suitable for Sunday school, He speaks of His love for Israel using images drawn from the marital suite:

> Later I passed by, and when I looked at you and saw that you were old enough for love, I spread the corner of my garment over you and covered your naked body. I gave you my solemn oath and entered into a covenant with you, declares the

Left: *"Jesus weeps over Jerusalem," 1892 painting by Enrique Simonet.*

> Sovereign Lord, and you became mine. (Ezekiel 16:8)

But all was not well. Israel transgressed, committing spiritual adultery by pursuing idols and enraging her Husband. "I am filled with fury against you, declares the Sovereign Lord, when you do all these things, acting like a brazen prostitute!" (Ezekiel 16:30).

Love Never Gives Up

Yet His anger did not extinguish His love. Like a smitten husband who cannot forget his bride, God appeals to Israel to repent. "Return, faithless people," declares the Lord, "for I am your husband..." (Jeremiah 3:14). To illustrate His own longsuffering love for Israel, God tells the prophet Hosea to both reconcile with and redeem his wife, a prostitute:

> Go, show your love to your wife again, though she is loved by another man and is an adulteress. Love her as the Lord loves the Israelites, though they turn to other gods.... (Hosea 3:1)

Put simply, God will not forsake His beloved. "For your Maker is your husband," the Lord tells Israel through the prophet

Right: *Ancient olive trees are still cultivated in the Garden of Gethsemane on the Mount of Olives.*

Isaiah (54:5). And He will not abandon His bride:

> "For a brief moment I abandoned you, but with deep compassion I will bring you back. In a surge of anger I hid my face from you for a moment, but with everlasting kindness I will have compassion on you," says the LORD your Redeemer. (Isaiah 54:7-8)

WEEPING OVER JERUSALEM

This love affair with Israel is revealed, too, in the life of Jesus. The prophet Jeremiah wept over the sins of Judah, declaring, "Oh, that my head were a spring of water and my eyes a fountain of tears!" (Jeremiah 9:1). Because it's not entirely clear in the Hebrew text whether God or Jeremiah is speaking, some scholars read this as God's own lament and not just Jeremiah's. It's ambiguous, but in the New Testament, there is no uncertainty. When Jesus, who is God in human flesh, "approached Jerusalem and saw the city, he wept over it" (Luke 19:41). The Greek word translated "wept" here carries the idea that Jesus burst into tears upon seeing Jerusalem and likely did so with audible weeping.[118]

The Dead Sea from Masada on a cloudless day.

Dnalor 01, Wikimedia Commons, (CC-BY-SA 3.0)

Left: *Frieze from the Arch of Titus shows the spoils of war taken from the Temple after Rome destroyed Jerusalem in 70 AD.*

"If you, even you, had only known on this day what would bring you peace," Jesus pronounced as he looked out on Jerusalem. "But now," He added, "it is hidden from your eyes" (Luke 19:42). With His own excruciating death just days away, Jesus foretold the grim future awaiting His unwilling people. And He did so with tears wetting His face:

> The days will come upon you when your enemies will build an embankment against you and encircle you and hem you in on every side. They will dash you to the ground, you and the children within your walls. They will not leave one stone on another, because you did not recognize the time of God's coming to you. (Luke 19:43-44)

Knowing the price His people would pay for rejecting Him as Messiah, Jesus spoke in tender anguish at what was to come:

> Jerusalem, Jerusalem, you who kill the prophets and stone those sent to you, how often I have longed to gather your children together, as a hen gathers her chicks under her wings, and you were not willing. Look, your house is left to you desolate. (Matthew 23:37-39)

Judaean Desert as viewed from Mount Scopus in Jerusalem.

CENTURIES OF SUFFERING

Desolation did, indeed, follow. Cruel Rome crushed Jerusalem in 70 A.D., killing as many as one million Jews, and leveling the Temple. Huge stones, believed to have been thrown off the Temple Mount, can still be seen piled below. Roman soldiers "ran every one through whom they met with, and obstructed the very lanes with their dead bodies, and made the whole city run down with blood," reports the Jewish historian Josephus.[119]

Exile, along with unmatched suffering, became the lot of the Jews in the centuries ahead. Joseph ha-Kohen's sixteenth century chronicle of Jewish affliction, *The Valley of Tears*, is one long "martyrology," writes David Baron, a Jewish believer in Jesus and prolific author on God's enduring purpose for the Jewish people. He terms ha-Kohen's account

> the record of an almost unbroken chain of unparalleled sufferings—a chronicle of massacres, oppressions, banishments, fiendish tortures, spoliations and degradations, which have been inflicted upon the Jews for the most part by so-called Christian nations.[120]

Right: *"The Destruction of Jerusalem in 70 AD", an engraving by Louis Haghe of a painting by David Roberts. Roman general Titus burned Jerusalem and destroyed the Temple, fulfilling Jesus' prophecy.*

Caves in hillside near Dead Sea where David hid from King Saul.
AmyLuPhoto.com

Top Left: *Ruins of the Fortress of Masada, which fell to Rome in 73 AD.*
Bottom: *David Baron (1855-1926), author and Jewish believer in Jesus.*

But Jesus' lament for Jerusalem also foretold restoration to come. Mere days before His death, Jesus declared to the Jews, "I tell you, you will not see me again until you say, 'Blessed is he who comes in the name of the Lord'" (Matthew 23:39). That greeting—taken from Psalm 118:26—rang out from the crowds who waved palm branches and hailed Jesus on Palm Sunday when He entered Jerusalem on a donkey. The festive throng greeted Him in hopes He was about to throw off the Roman yoke and set up His earthly kingdom, ruling as Messiah from Jerusalem. Instead, He was coming to die, as a "lamb to the slaughter" and an "offering for sin."[121] But that truth was hidden from them and some who celebrated Him on Sunday may have turned against Him after His arrest and mock trial, joining the mob on Friday to call for His crucifixion.

In the long centuries ahead, Jerusalem fell under Roman, Byzantine, Muslim, Crusader, Mamluk, Ottoman, and British control. Finally, after 1,900 years, the Jewish nation awoke and returned to its ancestral land. Israel was reborn as a nation state in 1948, and in 1967 Israel unexpectedly took Jerusalem. There, to Jerusalem, is where Jesus will return. When He does, we have His word that His chosen people will see and greet Him as their Messiah, shouting, once more, "Blessed is he who comes in the name of the Lord."

Welcomed at Last

Two millennia ago, Jesus "came to his own homeland, yet his own people did not receive him" (John 1:11 CJB). The reverse scenario will unfold at His return. A day is coming when Jesus will return to his "own homeland" and to "his own people"—but this time they will receive Him, welcoming Him as their Messiah, proclaiming "Blessed is He who comes in the name of the Lord."

"And so all Israel will be saved," as Paul declares in Romans 11, where he asserts God's continuing purpose for his people, "whom he foreknew." Citing the prophet Isaiah, Paul looks forward to a day when

> The deliverer will come from Zion;
> he will turn godlessness away from Jacob.
> And this is my covenant with them
> when I take away their sins. (Romans 11:26-27)

The last chapter of this long and turbulent romance is yet to be written.

That is why no one should doubt that Israel matters to God. He is "very jealous for Jerusalem and Zion" (Zechariah

Top Right: *Israeli Army Chief Chaplain Rabbi Shlomo Goren blows a shofar at the Western Wall to mark the liberation of Judaism's holiest site on June 7, 1967, during the Six-Day War.*

David Rubinger/Israeli Government Press Office

The Negev with the Dead Sea visible in the distance.

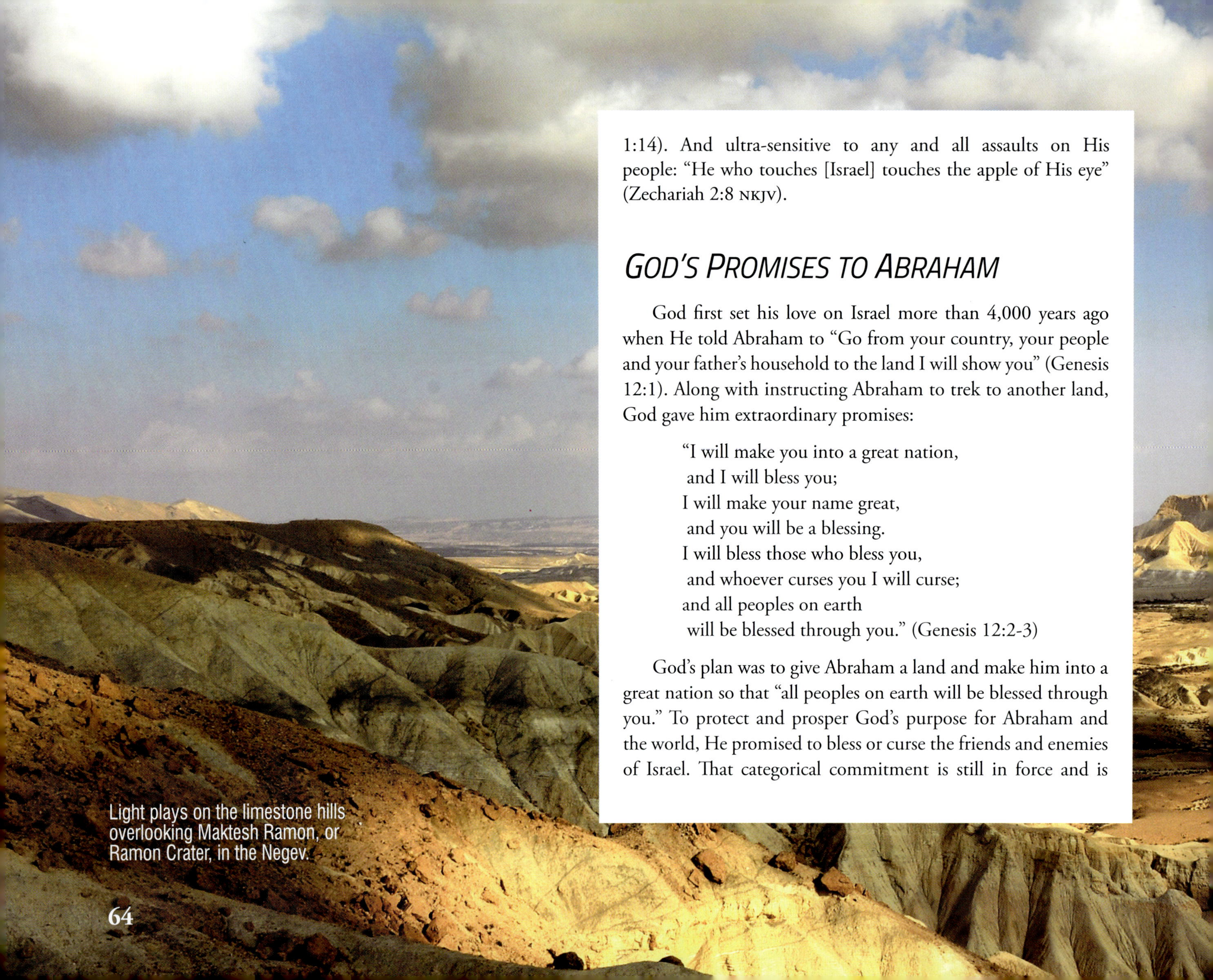

1:14). And ultra-sensitive to any and all assaults on His people: "He who touches [Israel] touches the apple of His eye" (Zechariah 2:8 NKJV).

GOD'S PROMISES TO ABRAHAM

God first set his love on Israel more than 4,000 years ago when He told Abraham to "Go from your country, your people and your father's household to the land I will show you" (Genesis 12:1). Along with instructing Abraham to trek to another land, God gave him extraordinary promises:

> "I will make you into a great nation,
> and I will bless you;
> I will make your name great,
> and you will be a blessing.
> I will bless those who bless you,
> and whoever curses you I will curse;
> and all peoples on earth
> will be blessed through you." (Genesis 12:2-3)

God's plan was to give Abraham a land and make him into a great nation so that "all peoples on earth will be blessed through you." To protect and prosper God's purpose for Abraham and the world, He promised to bless or curse the friends and enemies of Israel. That categorical commitment is still in force and is

Light plays on the limestone hills overlooking Maktesh Ramon, or Ramon Crater, in the Negev.

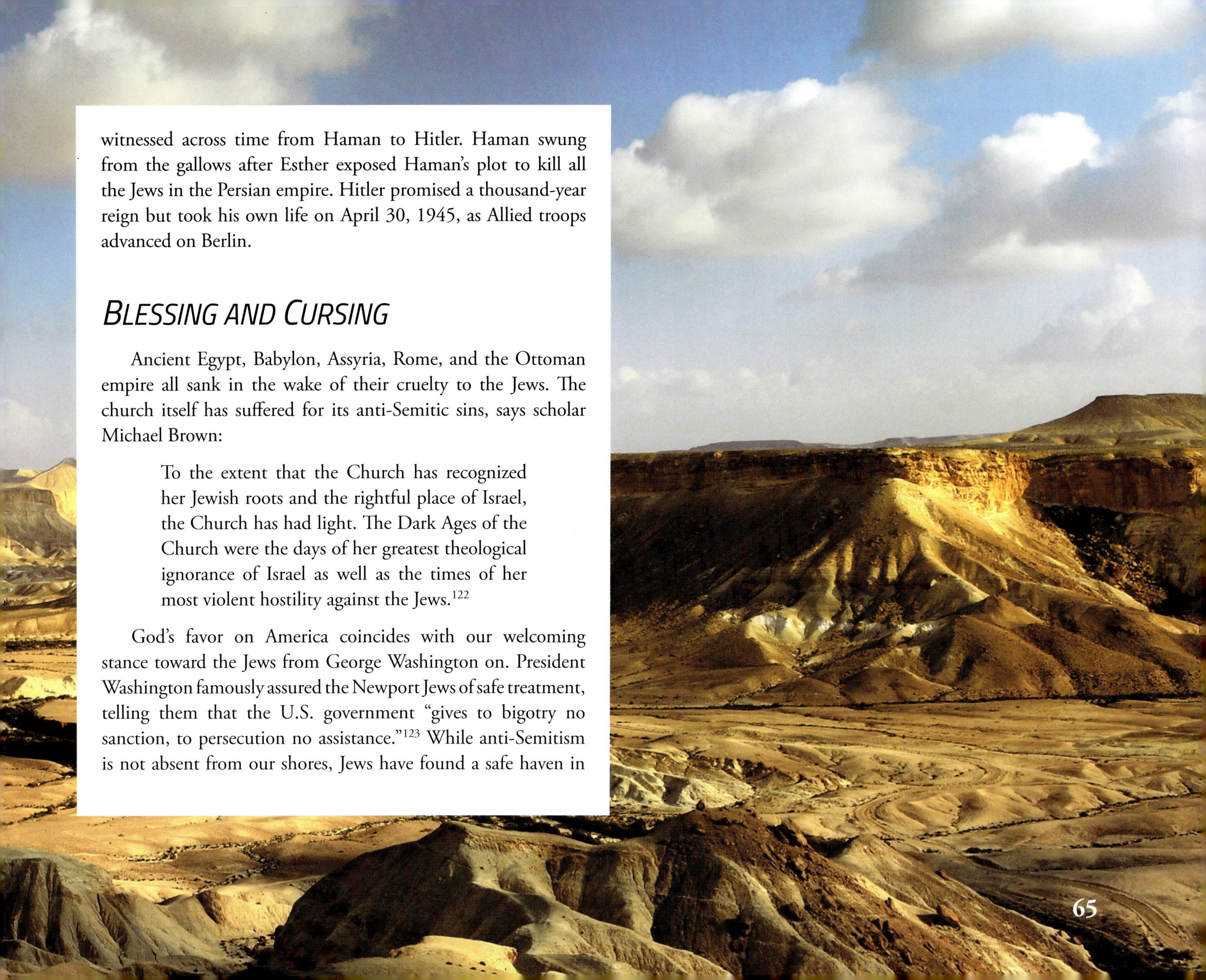

witnessed across time from Haman to Hitler. Haman swung from the gallows after Esther exposed Haman's plot to kill all the Jews in the Persian empire. Hitler promised a thousand-year reign but took his own life on April 30, 1945, as Allied troops advanced on Berlin.

Blessing and Cursing

Ancient Egypt, Babylon, Assyria, Rome, and the Ottoman empire all sank in the wake of their cruelty to the Jews. The church itself has suffered for its anti-Semitic sins, says scholar Michael Brown:

> To the extent that the Church has recognized her Jewish roots and the rightful place of Israel, the Church has had light. The Dark Ages of the Church were the days of her greatest theological ignorance of Israel as well as the times of her most violent hostility against the Jews.[122]

God's favor on America coincides with our welcoming stance toward the Jews from George Washington on. President Washington famously assured the Newport Jews of safe treatment, telling them that the U.S. government "gives to bigotry no sanction, to persecution no assistance."[123] While anti-Semitism is not absent from our shores, Jews have found a safe haven in

Left: *George Washington, America's first president. Painting by Gilbert Stuart.*

America. The U.S. is home to 5.7 million Jews, second only to the Jewish homeland, Israel, with a Jewish population of almost 6.4 million.

God's promise to bless or curse people based on how they treat Abraham and his descendants is still in force. So is His land promise to Abraham. God pledged the land of Israel, without conditions, to the father of the Jews nearly 4,000 years ago: "The whole land of Canaan ... I will give as an everlasting possession to you and your descendants after you; and I will be their God" (Genesis 17:8).

The land God gave Abraham placed His people at the crossroads of the world, well-positioned to bless the nations as emissaries of the light of God. Located on a land bridge between three continents, Israel was centrally located between the major powers of the ancient world, including Egypt, Greece, Babylon, Assyria and Persia. "The land of Canaan is the most advantageously posited of any spot of ground on the face [of the earth], to be the place from whence the truth should shine forth, and true religion spread around into all parts of the world," said early American theologian and philosopher Jonathan Edwards.[124]

Jesus Christ, the seed of Abraham, the son of David, is the

Spectacular contrasting colors in the Arava Desert south of the Dead Sea.

Right: American theologian Jonathan Edwards (1703-1758).

greatest blessing made possible to the world by the Jewish people. But now that He has come and established His body, the church, on the earth, some believe God's plan for the Jewish people—and their time to live as His people in the promised land—has come to a close.

Unconditional Promise

But God placed no conditions on His promise to Abraham and his descendants. The land was an "everlasting possession" given in perpetuity to God's people because, as the psalmist declares:

> He remembers his covenant forever, the promise
> he made, for a thousand generations, the
> covenant he made with Abraham,
> the oath he swore to Isaac.
> He confirmed it to Jacob as a decree,
> to Israel as an everlasting covenant:
> "To you I will give the land of Canaan as the
> portion you will inherit." (Psalm 105:8-11)

But what if Israel sins and violates the covenant God made with Abraham? Will that void the agreement, so to speak, and prompt

Red rocks in the Arava Desert with the Dead Sea beyond.

Trail winds through the rock-encrusted Arava Desert.

***Left:** "Moses Smashing the Tablets of the Law," by Rembrandt.*

God to seek another covenant partner? Moses told the Israelites with crystal clarity that very real consequences—extravagant blessing or dreadful curses—would result from their obedience or disobedience to God's commands. But not utter rejection.

In a litany that seems to go on forever, Moses details the punishments, pain and sorrow Israel would endure for their sins. The catalogue of woe in Deuteronomy 28 includes exile back to Egypt—a harsh edict Rome fulfilled after sacking Jerusalem by sending thousands of Jews to work as slaves in the mines and quarries of Egypt.[125] But even in exile, God will not disown and cast off His people—as He declares in categorical terms:

> Yet in spite of this, when they are in the land of their enemies, I will not reject them or abhor them so as to destroy them completely, breaking my covenant with them. I am the LORD their God. But for their sake I will remember the covenant with their ancestors whom I brought out of Egypt in the sight of the nations to be their God. I am the LORD. (Leviticus 26:44-45)

In short, God will never abandon His people no matter what they do—or have done. The Bible declares and history confirms that when God's people are unfaithful to Him they

Right: *"Jeremiah Lamenting the Destruction of Jerusalem," Rembrandt.*

will be punished. Chapter 28 of the Book of Deuteronomy sets forth the blessings and curses. But God's promise has never been revoked and He will remain faithful even when His people are not. Remember, right when the Jewish people were about to commit the supreme sin of rejecting the Messiah by calling for His death by crucifixion, Jesus looked into the future to when He would, once again, enter Jerusalem and be greeted as Messiah by His own people. Instead of disowning them for their sin, Jesus weeps over His people's desolation to come and promises a future reunion.

Judged, but Not Rejected

Six-hundred years before Christ the sins of Judah had also ripened for judgement. God was sending the armies of Babylon to capture Jerusalem, destroy the temple and take His people into exile. But in the midst of judgment, God promised to "restore the fortunes of Jacob's tents," saying "the city will be rebuilt on her ruins" (Jeremiah 30:18). And right at the point of judgment, God goes to extreme lengths to declare His permanent and inviolable bond with His people:

This is what the Lord says,

View from Masada fortress to Dead Sea and Jordan's mountains.

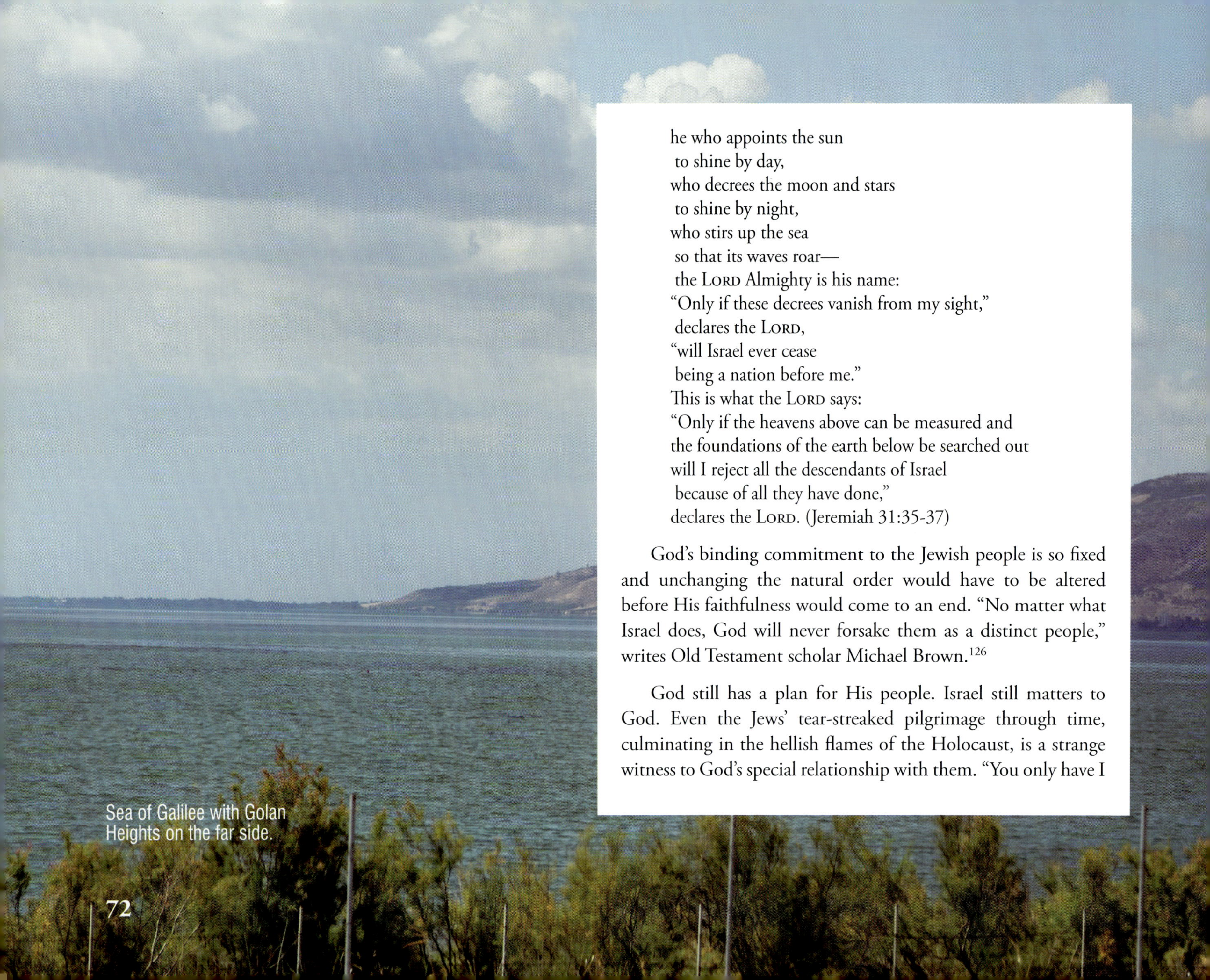

he who appoints the sun
 to shine by day,
who decrees the moon and stars
 to shine by night,
who stirs up the sea
 so that its waves roar—
 the LORD Almighty is his name:
"Only if these decrees vanish from my sight,"
 declares the LORD,
"will Israel ever cease
 being a nation before me."
This is what the LORD says:
"Only if the heavens above can be measured and
the foundations of the earth below be searched out
will I reject all the descendants of Israel
 because of all they have done,"
declares the LORD. (Jeremiah 31:35-37)

God's binding commitment to the Jewish people is so fixed and unchanging the natural order would have to be altered before His faithfulness would come to an end. "No matter what Israel does, God will never forsake them as a distinct people," writes Old Testament scholar Michael Brown.[126]

God still has a plan for His people. Israel still matters to God. Even the Jews' tear-streaked pilgrimage through time, culminating in the hellish flames of the Holocaust, is a strange witness to God's special relationship with them. "You only have I

Sea of Galilee with Golan Heights on the far side.

known of all the families of the earth," God declares in Amos 3:2, "Therefore I will punish you for all your iniquities." Orthodox Jewish author Meir Simcha Sokolovsky makes this point as well:

> The uniqueness of the Jewish People—the Chosen People—is evident not only in the miracles and the marvels which are an integral part of its history, but also in its chronicles of unmatched suffering and travail. No other nation in the world has been so persecuted, so beleaguered by evil decrees, so victimized by libels, so repeatedly expelled from so many lands as the Jewish nation.... This alone would constitute clear proof that the suffering and agonies which have been visited upon the Jewish people are not mere chance, but the inevitable consequence of the unique relationship between God and his people Israel, whom he has chosen to draw near to himself, meticulously meting out both its reward and punishment.[127]

Modern Miracle

But if the extreme suffering endured by the Jewish people bears witness to their unique status as God's chosen people, how much more their regathering as a nation? The birth of modern

The upper Galilee's green landscape in northern Israel.

***Left:** Zionist pioneer Theodor Herzl, along with most Zionist leaders, favored a secular Jewish society in Palestine.*

Israel in 1948 is a miracle. How else did 650,000 Jews defeat the combined military might of Egypt, Jordan, Lebanon, Syria and Iraq—and do so with a lightly equipped army and an almost non-existent air force? The sheer improbability of the Jewish people's survival in exile, their return to their ancient homeland and their growth, after less than 70 years into a vibrant state with a dynamic economy and one of the world's strongest militaries points to the hand of God. Just as God said it would:

> When I gather the people of Israel from the nations where they have been scattered, I will be proved holy through them in the sight of the nations. Then they will live in their own land, which I gave to my servant Jacob. (Ezekiel 28:25)

And yet Zionism, the nationalistic movement to liberate the Jewish people, was not, first and foremost, a religious enterprise. Theodor Herzl, the visionary who spearheaded the Zionist movement in Europe, rejected theocratic rule. "We shall keep our priests within the confines of their temples," Herzl said in his Zionist declaration, *The Jewish State*.[128] And historian Ken Spiro observes, "Early Zionist leaders knew, of course, that religion had preserved Jewish identity in the ghettos and shtetls

Right: *Jewish soldiers in hills of Jerusalem during Israel's War of Independence.*

of Europe, but in the modern Jewish state, they felt there would be no need for it."[129]

During the drafting of Israel's 1948 statehood declaration, the 13-member National Administration committee debated whether to include the phrase, "placing our trust in the Almighty" in Israel's founding document. One member protested, saying he and other Jews ought not be forced to affirm belief in God against their will. Ultimately, the committee settled on the phrase, "placing our trust in the 'Rock of Israel,'" a masterpiece of ambiguity because its interpretation was "left to everyone's individual conscience and conviction."[130]

Ben-Gurion: "I Don't Personally Believe..."

David Ben-Gurion, the Jewish Agency head and Zionist leader, participated in that discussion and later expressed his own disbelief in God—and his reverence for the Bible:

> Since I invoke Torah so often, let me state that I don't personally believe in the God it postu-

Israeli

Forested hillsides in the upper Galilee.

David Eldan/Israeli Government Press Office

Left: *Yigael Yadin, IDF Chief of Staff (left), and David Ben-Gurion (right) search in the Bible for the first appointment of a chief of staff in Jerusalem.*

> lates.... I am not religious, nor were the majority of the early builders of Israel believers. Yet their passion for this land stemmed from the Book of Books ... [The Bible is] the single most important book in my life.[131]

Today, Israeli society has a strongly secular cast. Nearly half of all Jews in Israel describe themselves as secular while another 29 percent are "traditional," occupying the "broad middle ground between Orthodoxy and secularism." The balance is ultra-Orthodox (9 percent) and "modern orthodox" (13 percent).[132]

Just half of Jews in Israel say they believe in God with absolute certainty. Another 27 percent believe but are less certain and 23 percent either don't believe in God or don't know if He exists.[133] Fully half of Israeli Jews say they never pray and one-third never attend synagogue; 39 percent attend infrequently, either monthly, yearly or seldom.[134]

Liberal policies on homosexuality and abortion divide secular and orthodox Jews in Israel. Tel Aviv has become a target for the LGBT agenda from around the world. Israel also has one of the world's most permissive abortion laws. The Jewish state makes abortion legal up to the point of delivery and forces taxpayers

Right: *Israelis march in a gay pride parade in Tel Aviv.*

to fund abortions for women between ages 20 and 33.[135] It also subsidizes abortions for women under 20 and over 40.[136] Just over 20,000 abortions were committed in Israel in 2014.[137] At the same time, pro-life Israelis are working to save the unborn from abortion. One leading pro-life group in Israel, EFRAT, has helped save the lives of more than 64,000 children since its founding in 1977.

All this shows that many in Israel have not made peace with the God of Israel—some do not even believe He exists. Because of that, some Christians question whether modern Israel's return to the land is, indeed, the work of God. After all, Moses told Israel in Deuteronomy that God would "gather you again from all the nations where he scattered you" after they returned to Him in obedience (Deuteronomy 30:2-3). How, then, could He return His people in unbelief?

On the other hand, if God, by His decree, scattered Israel 2,000 years ago, how could they possibly return, except by His providential aid? "He who scattered Israel," Jeremiah declared, "will gather them and will watch over his flock like a shepherd" (Jeremiah 31:10).

Writing in 1925, before the birth of modern Israel, Jewish biblical scholar David Baron rejoiced at the growing number of

Moshe Milner/Israeli Government Press Office

Sylvan vistas in the upper Galilee in northern Israel.

Israeli Tsvika/Israeli Government Press Office

Uriel Sinai/Israeli Government Press Office

Jezreel Valley, Israel's breadbasket, viewed from Mount Gilboa in northern Israel.

Top Left: *Soviet immigrants arrive at Ben Gurion Airport in 1991.*

Bottom Left: *Reception ceremony for new immigrants from the U.S. at Ben Gurion Airport.*

Jewish immigrants to Palestine. "The return in unbelief," Baron said, "is the necessary precursor to the resumption of God's dealings with them as a nation...."[138]

"The physical restoration comes first, but not because of Israel's deeds," asserts Michael Brown, considered the world's foremost Messianic Jewish apologist. "The spiritual restoration follows, once they are again in the Land."[139]

First Physical, Then Spiritual Restoration

When God declares through Ezekiel His intent to return Israel to their land, He also makes clear it will not happen because of His people's merit, but for His name's sake—and that their return will lead to spiritual restoration as well:

> "This is what the Sovereign Lord says: It is not for your sake, people of Israel, that I am going to do these things, but for the sake of my holy name, which you have profaned among the nations where you have gone.... For I will take

> you out of the nations; I will gather you from all the countries and bring you back into your own land. I will sprinkle clean water on you, and you will be clean.... I will give you a new heart and put a new spirit in you; I will remove from you your heart of stone and give you a heart of flesh.... I want you to know that I am not doing this for your sake, declares the Sovereign LORD. Be ashamed and disgraced for your conduct, people of Israel!" (Ezekiel 36:22-32)

Just as Ezekiel prophesied, Jews from "among the nations" and the "four corners of the earth" have made aliyah to Israel. Baron gave his own firsthand witness to the global return taking place even before Israel's statehood:

> I have personally, in the course of my seven different visits to the land since 1890, met Jews from all parts—from the east and the west; from India and the burning plains of Southern Arabia, and from the extreme north of Siberia and the Caucasus; and have heard them speaking in nearly all languages under heaven.[140]

Israel's Law of Return grants citizenship to all Jews who seek to live in Israel, which has absorbed nearly 3.2 million immigrants since 1948. Arrivals represent some 70 different nationalities, claim the authors of *Start-up Nation*.[141] The former Soviet Union

Ruins of Roman aqueduct.

Golden sunrise seen from Masada looking out on Dead Sea.

Ruins of the ancient Roman city, Caesarea, on the Mediterranean between Haifa and Tel Aviv.

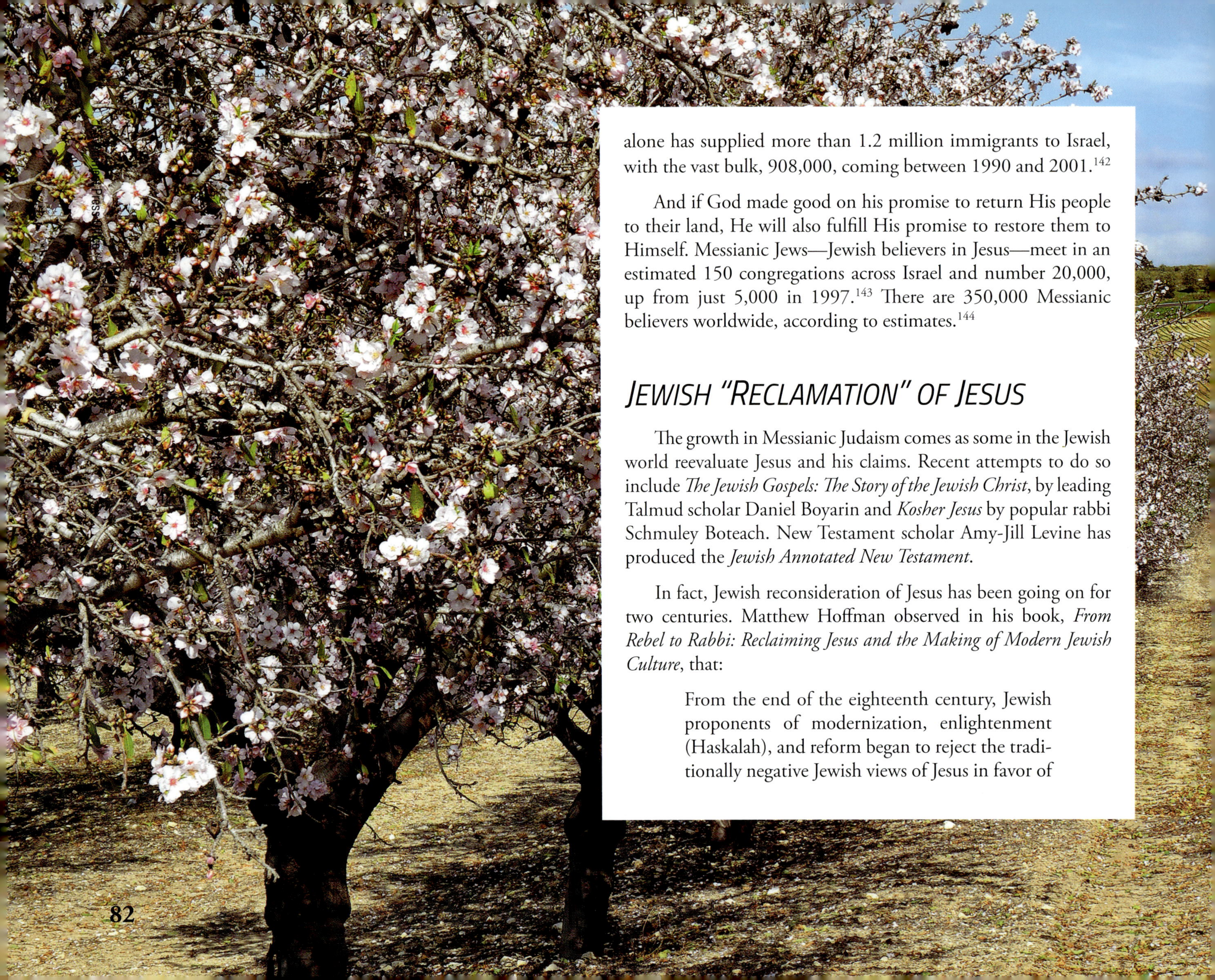

alone has supplied more than 1.2 million immigrants to Israel, with the vast bulk, 908,000, coming between 1990 and 2001.[142]

And if God made good on his promise to return His people to their land, He will also fulfill His promise to restore them to Himself. Messianic Jews—Jewish believers in Jesus—meet in an estimated 150 congregations across Israel and number 20,000, up from just 5,000 in 1997.[143] There are 350,000 Messianic believers worldwide, according to estimates.[144]

JEWISH "RECLAMATION" OF JESUS

The growth in Messianic Judaism comes as some in the Jewish world reevaluate Jesus and his claims. Recent attempts to do so include *The Jewish Gospels: The Story of the Jewish Christ*, by leading Talmud scholar Daniel Boyarin and *Kosher Jesus* by popular rabbi Schmuley Boteach. New Testament scholar Amy-Jill Levine has produced the *Jewish Annotated New Testament*.

In fact, Jewish reconsideration of Jesus has been going on for two centuries. Matthew Hoffman observed in his book, *From Rebel to Rabbi: Reclaiming Jesus and the Making of Modern Jewish Culture*, that:

> From the end of the eighteenth century, Jewish proponents of modernization, enlightenment (Haskalah), and reform began to reject the traditionally negative Jewish views of Jesus in favor of

> increasingly sympathetic appraisals of him. This complex and intriguing trend in modern Jewish history has come to be known by scholars as the Jewish reclamation of Jesus.[145]

John T. Pawlikowski, a priest who teaches at the Catholic Theological Union, noted much the same in 2008:

> The "Jesus question" is definitely making a comeback on the agenda in certain Jewish circles, much more than it was even a decade ago. The new Jewish quest for Jesus, however, is now being done much more in collaboration with Christian scholarship than was the case in the late nineteenth and early twentieth centuries. Where it will lead remains an open question.[146]

It may lead to a very bright future for the Jews, as Paul discloses in Romans 11. A leading Pharisee who persecuted Jewish followers of Jesus until a blinding light from heaven redirected his life, Paul had "great sorrow and unceasing anguish" for "my people, those of my own race" (Romans 9:2,3) who rejected Jesus. Even so, Paul insists God has not forsaken His people:

> I say then, has God cast away His people? Certainly not! For I also am an Israelite, of the seed of Abraham, *of* the tribe of Benjamin. God has not cast away His people whom He foreknew. (Romans 11:1-2 NKJV)

Almond trees blossom in the winter in Israel and are the first trees to bloom.

Not only has he not discarded His people, a great spiritual ingathering is to come. God will bring salvation to the Jews, completing the process He began with their return to the land of Israel by giving them a "new heart" and a "new spirit," as prophesied by Ezekiel. "And so all Israel will be saved," as Paul proclaims in Romans 11:25.

When that happens, it will bring extraordinary blessing to the world. It will be, Paul writes, "life from the dead":

> Again I ask: Did they stumble so as to fall beyond recovery? Not at all! Rather, because of their transgression, salvation has come to the Gentiles to make Israel envious. But if their transgression means riches for the world, and their loss means riches for the Gentiles, how much greater riches will their full inclusion bring! ... For if their rejection brought reconciliation to the world, what will their acceptance be but life from the dead? (Romans 11:11-12, 15)

This promise remains in the future, but Israel is already blessing the world. It is making life better, easier, and healthier for millions with an explosion of scientific innovation across almost every field of human endeavor. It's a foretaste of what's ahead when, at long last, the Jewish people embrace their Jewish Messiah.

Aloe plants in the ancient city of Caesarea.

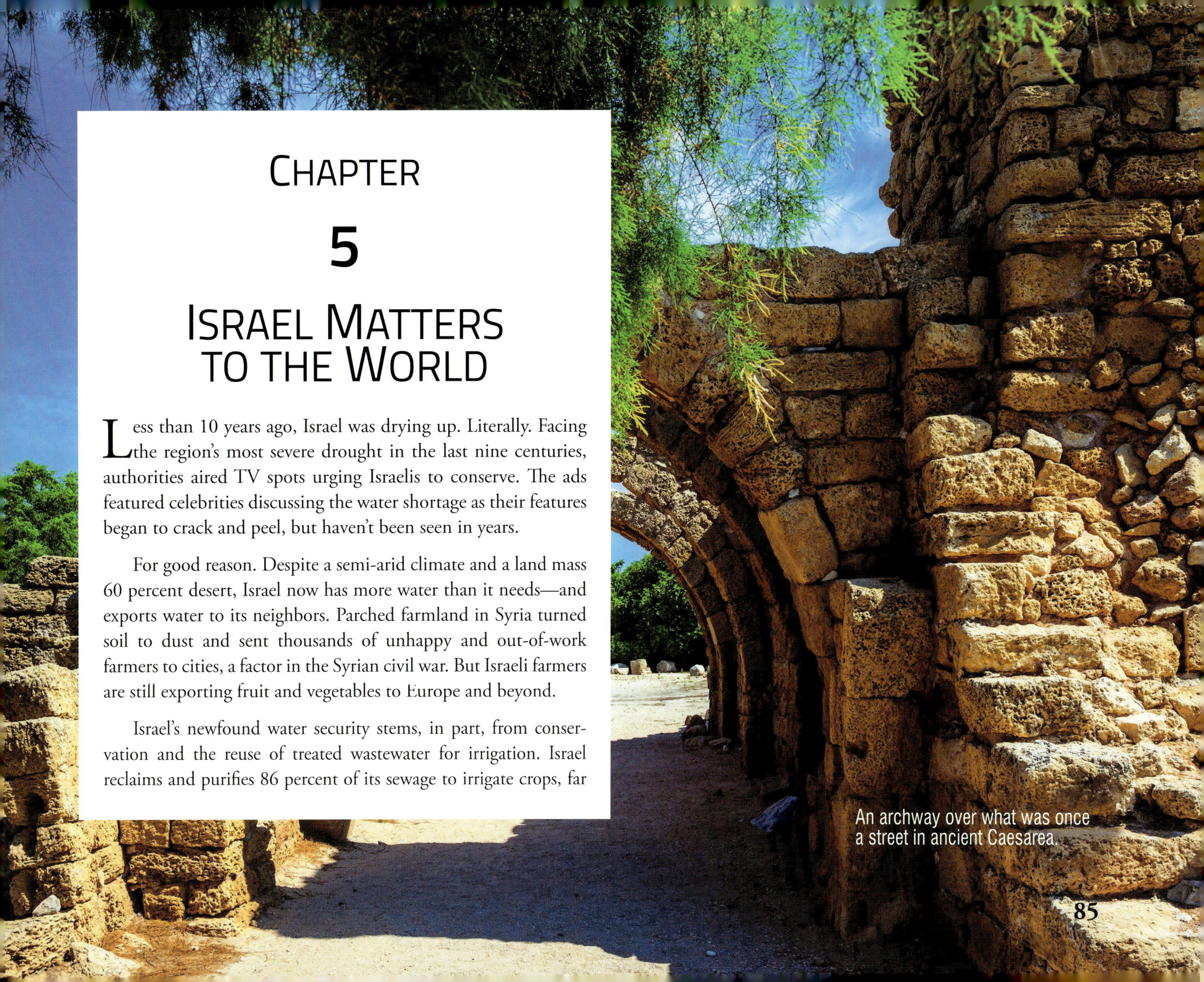

CHAPTER 5

ISRAEL MATTERS TO THE WORLD

Less than 10 years ago, Israel was drying up. Literally. Facing the region's most severe drought in the last nine centuries, authorities aired TV spots urging Israelis to conserve. The ads featured celebrities discussing the water shortage as their features began to crack and peel, but haven't been seen in years.

For good reason. Despite a semi-arid climate and a land mass 60 percent desert, Israel now has more water than it needs—and exports water to its neighbors. Parched farmland in Syria turned soil to dust and sent thousands of unhappy and out-of-work farmers to cities, a factor in the Syrian civil war. But Israeli farmers are still exporting fruit and vegetables to Europe and beyond.

Israel's newfound water security stems, in part, from conservation and the reuse of treated wastewater for irrigation. Israel reclaims and purifies 86 percent of its sewage to irrigate crops, far

An archway over what was once a street in ancient Caesarea.

Kobi Gideon/Israel Government Press Office

Left: *Racks of reverse osmosis desalination filters at Israel's Granot desalination plant.*

Rugged mountains in Arava Desert, south of the Dead Sea.

more than any other nation. But the silver bullet for Israel's water woes is the advent of made-in-Israel desalination plants. With the first plant commissioned in 2005, Israel now has five seawater desalination plants up and running. These massive water works turn Mediterranean seawater into fresh drinking water in 40 minutes and meet 55 percent of Israel's domestic water supply needs.[147]

No Other Country Has Done This

"Israel overcame seemingly insurmountable obstacles," exclaims Seth M. Siegel, author of the *New York Times* bestseller, *Let There Be Water: Israel's Solution for a Water-Starved World*. "No other country with a growing population, growing economy and falling level of rainfall has been able to achieve anything remotely like what Israel has done," he asserts.[148]

To do it, Israel had to overcome imposing technical barriers. Reverse osmosis desalination has in the past been an expensive and energy-intensive process because it takes tremendous force to push seawater through microscopic pores in filtration membranes and remove salt molecules. Add to that the problem of bio-fouling around the membranes, which requires dangerous cleaning chemicals, posing possible environmental problems.

***Right:** Israel's Granot desalination plant, helping Israel become a water-exporting nation.*

But those challenges have been met and Israeli desalination plants now produce water chemical free and at one third the cost in the 1990s. Israel's Sorek plant near Tel Aviv, the most efficient facility to date, sells 1,000 liters—enough water for one person for one week—to Israel's water authority for just 58 cents.[149]

"We produce water," Israeli Prime Minister Benjamin Netanyahu enthused in Kenya during a diplomatic tour to Africa. "We've had a substantial decline in rainfall since the establishment of modern Israel. And our population has grown ten times and our GDP per capita has grown 40 times. We should have a big water problem but we don't. We have a water surplus because we've developed ingenuity to overcome this."[150]

Netanyahu pronounced Israel's desire to share its water know-how "with our African friends,"[151] something Israel is already doing for drought-stricken California. In December 2015, Israeli firm IDE opened the largest desalination plant in the Western Hemisphere near San Diego. IDE is now engaged in planning 10 more facilities in the United States, three in California.

The need for a drought-free water supply is enormous—not just in California, but across the world. Up to two-thirds of the global population—some four billion people—face water scarcity

Kobi Gideon/Israel Government Press Office

Wadis—dry stream beds—cut through Arava Desert and suddenly fill with rushing water when rain falls.

Above: *Israel's central water filtration plant is the fourth largest in the world, and one of the most complex and advanced.*

Below: *Israel's national water carrier supplies water from the Sea of Galilee to the nation's mid-section and south using open canals, pipes, tunnels, reservoirs and pumping stations.*

ChameleonsEye / Shutterstock, Inc.

Amos Ben Gershom/Israeli Government Press Office

Israel's arid Negev receives just 8-10 inches of rain annually.

at least one month a year. A half billion people endure water scarcity year round, according to the journal *Science Advances.*[152]

Israeli firms are addressing the crisis, providing some $2 billion annually in water technology exports. And the motivation is more than money. "It was an honor that we could help poor people and poor nations and improve the quality of their lives," said Moshe Gablinger, now retired, of the work he did as an executive at an Israeli water engineering firm. "It was almost like a commandment from the Bible, this feeling we had of wanting to help people all over the world," he said of projects done in underdeveloped countries.[153]

Using Water to Build Bridges

Because it has a surplus, Israel is now positioned to do "water diplomacy"—using Israeli water technology to mend relations and help meet the needs of its neighbors. One project is a cooperative venture with Jordan to build a $900 million desalination plant that will share the water produced between Israel, Jordan, and the Palestinian Authority. By the time the project is complete in 2020, "these old foes will be drinking from the same tap," as a *Scientific American* writer observed.[154]

Israel's water revolution shows how it is reshaping the Middle East and improving the lives of millions. It also points to how Israel shook off—at least in part—its socialist heritage, trans-

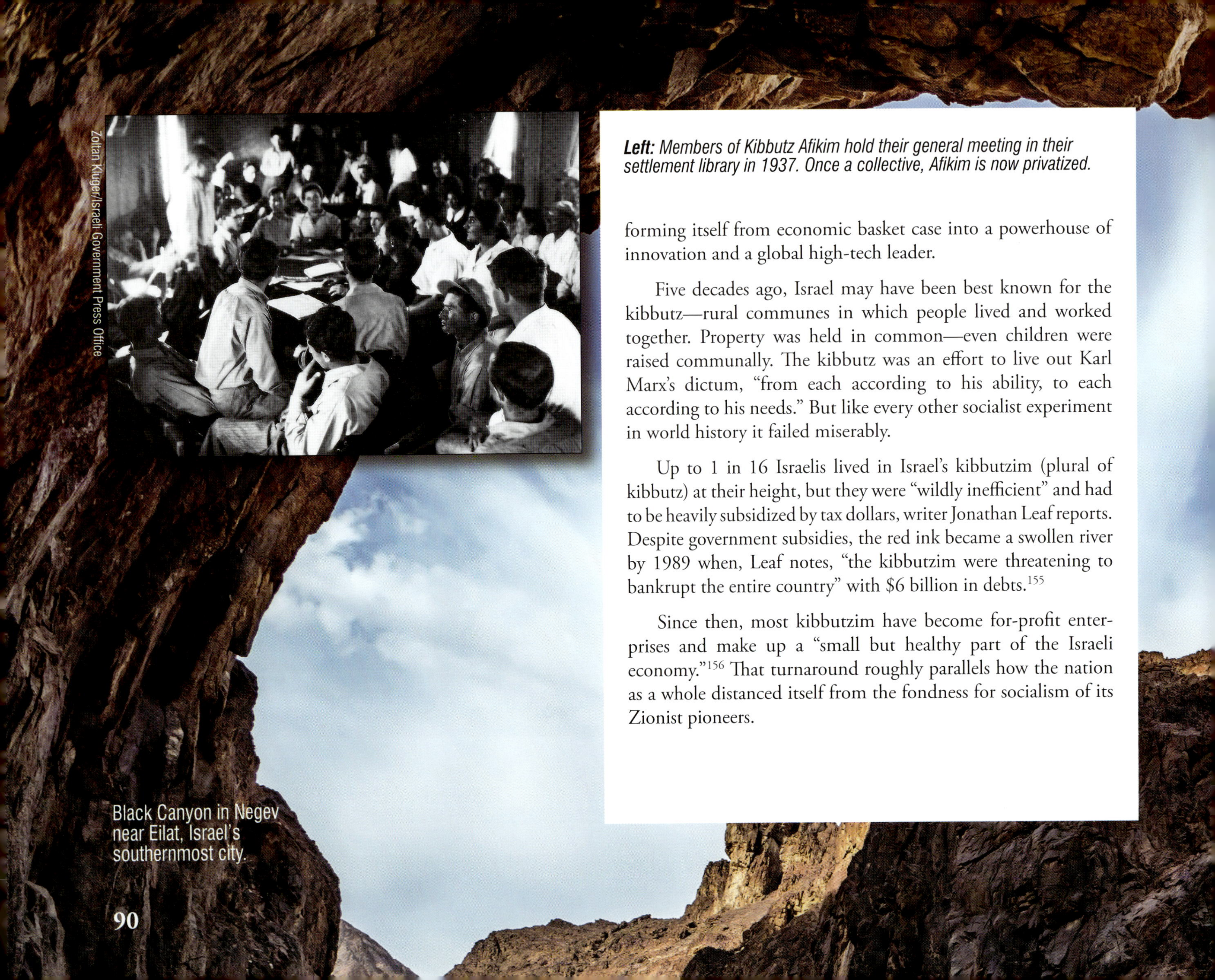

Left: *Members of Kibbutz Afikim hold their general meeting in their settlement library in 1937. Once a collective, Afikim is now privatized.*

forming itself from economic basket case into a powerhouse of innovation and a global high-tech leader.

Five decades ago, Israel may have been best known for the kibbutz—rural communes in which people lived and worked together. Property was held in common—even children were raised communally. The kibbutz was an effort to live out Karl Marx's dictum, "from each according to his ability, to each according to his needs." But like every other socialist experiment in world history it failed miserably.

Up to 1 in 16 Israelis lived in Israel's kibbutzim (plural of kibbutz) at their height, but they were "wildly inefficient" and had to be heavily subsidized by tax dollars, writer Jonathan Leaf reports. Despite government subsidies, the red ink became a swollen river by 1989 when, Leaf notes, "the kibbutzim were threatening to bankrupt the entire country" with $6 billion in debts.[155]

Since then, most kibbutzim have become for-profit enterprises and make up a "small but healthy part of the Israeli economy."[156] That turnaround roughly parallels how the nation as a whole distanced itself from the fondness for socialism of its Zionist pioneers.

Black Canyon in Negev near Eilat, Israel's southernmost city.

***Right:** Israeli Prime Minister Benjamin Netanyahu launched Israel's exodus out of socialism.*

SELLING OFF SOCIALISM

One major reason is Benjamin Netanyahu. In his first term as Israeli prime minister, Netanyahu set out to do in Israel what Margaret Thatcher tried to achieve in Britain. He told Wall Street investors in 1996 he was planning to slash regulations, sell-off state-owned businesses, and put an end to government-run cartels. It wouldn't be easy, he admitted, calling Israel's entrenched socialist system "one of the most rigid, centralized and bureaucratic economic structures in the world."[157] As late as the 1990s, George Gilder notes, Israel's government still owned "four major banks, 200 corporations, and much of the land." It also took 56 percent of total earnings each year in taxes.[158]

Gilder, author of *The Israel Test*, credits Netanyahu, who also served as Israel's finance minister from 2003 to 2005, as the "force driving the Israelis decisively out of their socialist past into the modern world of finance." By 2009, Gilder asserts, Israel had "accomplished the most overwhelming transformation in the history of economics, from a nondescript laggard in the industrial world to a luminous first."[159]

Kobi Gideon/Israeli Government Press Office

Lake Hula, in the Hula Valley in northern Israel, is an annual stop-off for birds migrating to Africa.

Left: *Workers inside the Teva Pharmaceuticals plant in Jerusalem.*

Startup Nation

Today, the kibbutz is largely forgotten and Israel is best known as the "Startup Nation" for its entrepreneurial drive and a long list of stunning contributions to human well-being in everything from water technology to agriculture to biopharmaceuticals to software to microchips and more.

Thanks to its turn toward capitalism, Israel's economy has more than doubled since 2000, with a 2015 GDP of $296 billion, 36th in the world.[160] Not bad for a nation of 8.5 million established in 1948. Israel now ranks 18th on the UN's Human Development Index—a measure of human longevity, education, and standard of living[161]—and boasts a GDP per capita of $35,436,[162] triple what it was in 1990. While the Jewish state struggled with rocketing inflation in the 1980s, hitting 445 percent in 1984, inflation is now a non-issue, coming in at -1.0 in 2015.[163] And unemployment is just 4.7 percent as of July 2016.[164]

Despite its small population, Israel has more companies listed on the tech-heavy Nasdaq than every other country, except the U.S. and China. "On a per capita basis," *Forbes* reports, "Israel boasts more venture capital, more startups and more scientists and tech professionals than any other country in the world."[165] Israel ranked 14th in the world in number of patents in 2015.[166]

Right: *Office building in Herzliya Pituach, an entrepreneurial hotspot north of Tel Aviv.*

It ranks first in medical device patents and second for medical device solutions.[167]

Israel is home to the world's largest manufacturer of generic drugs, the $20 billion giant, Teva. Once its acquisition of Allergan's generic drug subsidiary, Anda Inc, is complete, Teva will supply one in six prescriptions in the U.S.[168] Israel is also a global leader in military equipment exports with international sales of $5.7 billion in 2015,[169] ranking it eighth in the world, according to the Stockholm International Peace Research Institute.[170] Israel is also one of the world's leading exporters of polished and rough diamonds, with sales to other nations of nearly $7.2 billion in 2015.[171]

SURGERY WITHOUT SCALPELS

One of the most striking displays of Israeli innovation is incision-free surgery using MR-guided focused ultrasound. First used to remove uterine fibroids, the Israeli-developed technique just won FDA approval to treat essential tremor, the most common movement disorder affecting some 10 million Americans. That promises to transform the lives of millions of people whose shaky hands impair their ability to drink a glass of water, thread a needle, or sign their names. And the treatment comes without scalpel or anesthesia.

Hafakot / Shutterstock, Inc.

Beautiful Yarkon Park just minutes from downtown Tel Aviv.

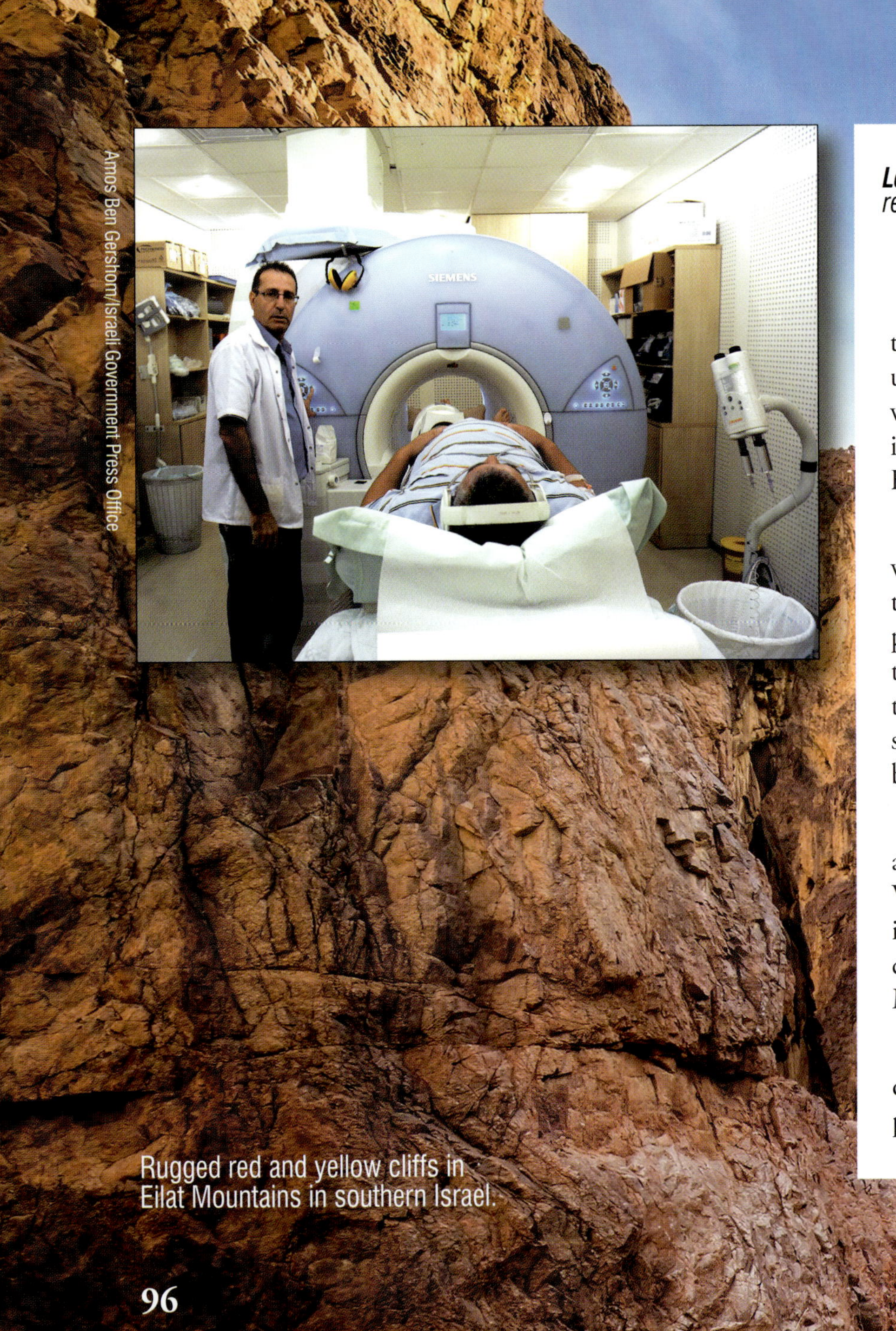

Amos Ben Gershon/Israeli Government Press Office

Rugged red and yellow cliffs in Eilat Mountains in southern Israel.

Left: *Israeli-developed MR-guided focused ultrasound is used to remove uterine fibroids and treat essential tremor.*

John Watterson, a retired history professor, lived with a tremor in his hands since he was 13. His signature before he underwent the procedure in a trial at the University of Virginia was a shaky, barely readable scrawl. But immediately afterwards it was clear and legible. "That was miraculous," Watterson said. His wife, Yvonne, called it "the happiest moment of my life."[172]

Israeli firm Insightec developed its Exablate Neuro system, which treats essential tremor noninvasively by targeting the thalamus with focused acoustical waves that heat and destroy problem tissue—all under MR guidance. Patients are awake throughout and can provide feedback to the physician during the procedure. Insightec is also using MR-guided focused ultrasound technology to give prompt relief to patients with painful bone cancers.

Such treatments are just the beginning. "The technology allows us to treat almost any tumor inside the body," says Kobi Vortman, Ph.D., vice chairman of InSightec, which he founded in 1999. Brain tumors, prostate cancer, liver tumors, breast cancer, even stroke are all candidates, he says, for treatment using MR-guided focused ultrasound.

"The way I see it and dream about it," says Vortman, "is doing a huge change in medicine and helping millions of people globally."[173]

AMAZING BREAKTHROUGHS

If Israel went looking for a "corporate motto," GE's retired ad slogan, "We bring good things to life" should be first on the list. Israeli innovation is making life better for millions every day, just as God promised when He told Abraham, "in you all the families of the earth shall be blessed" (Genesis 12:3 NKJV). The Jewish people have blessed the world above all by giving us the Messiah, Jesus Christ, but God's promise to Abraham includes material blessings made possible by Jewish ingenuity and drive.

Israel "concentrates the genius of the Jews," write George Gilder. "Efflorescent in the desert, militarily powerful, industrially preeminent, culturally cornucopian, technologically paramount, it has become a vanguard of human achievement."[174] Indeed, Israeli inventors, engineers, and entrepreneurs have given the world a long list of amazing breakthroughs and advances, as the following small sample details.

Rewalk enables paraplegics to walk, even compete in a 10K race. This battery-powered "wearable robotic exoskeleton" powers paralyzed limbs, enabling people with spinal cord injuries to stand, walk, turn, even go up and down stairs. Adam Gorlitsky lost his ability to walk after an auto accident, but did a 10K race with help from Rewalk, finishing in seven hours. "I feel like this technology changes the world," the Charleston, South Carolina, man said.[175]

PillCam is a digestible capsulized mini-camera which gives doctors and patients the option of a non-invasive endoscopy or

Herman Chanania/Israeli Government Press Office

Left: *Drip irrigation has helped Israel conserve water while expanding agricultural yield sixteen-fold.*

colonoscopy. Just an inch long, it comes equipped with a miniature video camera, its own lights and a recording device worn by the patient to receive images sent wirelessly by the PillCam. The patient simply swallows the capsule and the PillCam does the rest, moving through the close quarters and tight turns of the digestive tract over 8-12 hours and capturing images as it goes.

Babysense monitors a baby's respiration to prevent crib death. Using sensors located below the mattress, Babysense activates an audible and visual alarm if breathing stops or becomes irregularly slow. Sold in 35 countrics, thc manufacturer claims it has helped protect more than 600,000 infants from crib death.

WoundClot is a unique gauze-like material designed in Israel to stop hemorrhaging in minutes without the use of compression. Self-activating, WoundClot is applied over the trauma site and is capable of absorbing 2,500 percent of its weight in fluids while forming a gel membrane that adheres to the wound. Originally designed for the battlefield, it speeds the natural clotting process, remains biologically active for 24-36 hours, and dissolves within seven days.

Drip irrigation, pioneered in Israel, has helped the Jewish state reduce its water use by 10 percent since 1948 while expanding agriculture yield sixteen-fold.[176] Launched in the 1960s, Israeli firm Netafim is now active in 110 countries over five continents and is the world's leading provider of drip irrigation systems.[177]

***Right:** Tasty cherry tomatoes with long shelf lives are an Israeli innovation.*

Drip irrigation uses a network of valves, pipes, tubing and emitters to drip water and reach plant roots. Netafim claims up to 50 percent less water is used via drip irrigation, which when used to deliver fertilizer, too, increases crop productivity up to 200 percent.[178] Huge gains in a hungry and water-scarce world.

Cherry Tomatoes. "Israeli know-how is everywhere," Israeli Prime Minister Benjamin Netanyahu told the UN in a 2015 speech. Along with all the high-tech wonders out of Israel, add the "delicious cherry tomato," Netanyahu announced to the famously anti-Israel body. "That too was perfected in Israel, in case you didn't know."[179] While shoppers once purchased green tomatoes and waited for them to ripen, Israeli agricultural firm, Hazera, developed tasty cherry tomatoes with a long shelf life. Picked when red, the bite-sized salad toppers last 23 days.[180]

Nanography. First Israeli entrepreneur Benny Landa took printing into the computer age by introducing the digital press in 1993. Landa's invention did away with film and printing plates, making it possible to do economical short-run, on-demand and variable data printing. HP acquired his firm, Indigo Digital Press, in 2002, and now he is on to the next "big thing" by introducing nanography—a new printing technology using ultra-small, or nano-sized, pigments. Nanography gives printers, for the first time, the low cost-per-page and high productivity of traditional offset printing with the versatility and short-run economics of digital printing.

Scene from Banias Nature Reserve in northern Israel.

Ein Borek, a resort and hotel destination on the Dead Sea.

Moshe Milner/Israeli Government Press Office

Left: *Israeli entrepreneur and inventor Benny Landa developed digital printing and nanography.*

"We see it as a breakthrough technology that could enable us to transform our mainstream printing that we currently produce with offset presses," said Robert Keane, president of Cimpress, the parent company of Vistaprint, and the world's largest web-to-print firm.[181]

Landa credits the "magic" of Israel and its unique populace for making his new technology possible. "It's in every Israeli's blood that life has to do not just with yourself but with Zionism and a higher purpose," the inventor and philanthropist said. "When they leave the army to go into business, they bring that same indefinable fervor. It's the magic that made Indigo successful and it's the magic that will make us successful. I couldn't have done this anywhere else."[182]

Iron Dome is a high-tech wonder Israel uses to knock enemy missiles out of the sky. It almost didn't get built. When Brig. Gen. Danny Gold, then head of research and development for the Israeli Defense Ministry, first suggested a ground-based missile interceptor system to protect Israeli civilians from enemy rockets, many called it science fiction or said its development cycle would be too long—perhaps 15-20 years. A solution was needed right away because Israel's neighbors were turning the small Jewish state into a free-fire zone. Some 4,000 Hezbollah rockets hit northern Israel in 2006, killing 44 Israeli civilians.

A growth of flowers by fallen piillars in Caesarea.

Top Right: *Iron Dome missile launches to intercept rocket fired from Gaza in 2014.*

Bottom Right: *Iron Dome missiles destroy Hamas-fired rockets in the sky above the city of Ashdod.*

And Palestinians launched 8,000 projectiles from Gaza toward Israeli cities between 2000 and 2008.

Gold started the program in 2005, gaining key political backing and funding along the way. Ultimately, urgency and ingenuity—along with some $405 million dollars[183]—took the project from concept to completion in a mere six years. Built by Israel's Rafael Advanced Defense Systems, Iron Dome first destroyed Hamas rockets in 2011. Today, the Israel Defense Forces (IDF) claims a 90 percent kill rate of incoming missiles. That gives Israelis a protective canopy and a measure of comfort when sirens sound.

Waze is a free turn-by-turn navigation app with real-time traffic updates. Launched in Israel in 2008, it helps a reported 50 million drivers avoid congestion and accidents, steer clear of police traps, and find the fastest routes. Google bought Waze in 2013 for a stunning $966 million[184] and is now using the app in a pilot ride-sharing service that may pose a future challenge to Uber. Waze illustrates Israel's global leadership in mobile apps development. IVC Research Center lists 1,040 Israeli app firms in Israel,[185] which explains why Israel is also now known as the "StartApp nation."

Nehemiya Gershon/Israel Defense Forces

Haim Zach/Israeli Government Press Office

Lonely acacia tree grows beneath towering cliffs in the Eilat Mountains.

Amos Ben Gershom/Israeli Government Press Office

***Left:** Worker at ECI Telecom, founded in 1961 as the Electronics Corporation of Israel.*

USB flash drives, the hand-held memory sticks that give you plug-and-play data storage and backup for your computer, phone and tablet were invented in Israel. Entrepreneur Dov Moran's firm, M-Systems, first produced the file-storage solution in 1999, selling his firm to SanDisk seven years later for $1.6 billion. Sometimes called "thumb drives," USB flash drive storage capacity was a mere 8 MB to 32 MB at first, but now reaches 200 GB. This one device worked a revolution in computing. By using the USB interface and providing ultra-fast data transfer and backup, USB flash drives quickly took the place of floppy disk drives and optical discs, now dinosaurs of the computer age.

Cell Phones. With 4.5 billion in use worldwide, cell phones are a ubiquitous feature of modern life and Israeli know-how has played a huge role. "There is nary a smartphone in the world without at least some made-in-Israel tech," reports the *Times of Israel*.[186] Engineers at Motorola's R&D facility in Israel developed the technology employed for cell phone communications[187] and Israeli innovation continues to improve cell phones, today. For example, Apple is designing and manufacturing its own iPhone chips at its facility in Herzilya, Israel, the firm's second largest research development facility in the world.[188] In addition, the unique dual lens camera Apple introduced on the iPhone7 comes

Banias Nature Reserve in northern Israel offers wooded trails, Israel's largest waterfall, and ruins of ancient cities.

Right: *Intel workers, in sterile suits, supervising the manufacturing process at Intel plant in Jerusalem.*

Israeli Government Press Office

from an Israeli startup Apple purchased.[189] And the technology used to optimize memory storage in Apple products comes from Israel, too.[190] Looking ahead, one report indicates that iPhone8 is now under development in, where else, Israel.[191]

Microprocessors. Intel established its first overseas chip design office in Haifa in 1974. Since then, Intel Israel has designed some of Intel's best-selling chips, including the 8088 chip in 1980 (a processor IBM used to launch the era of "personal computing"), the Pentium processor with MMX technology, and Intel Centrino Mobile Technology.[192] More recently, Intel Israel designed the Skylake sixth generation processor family. Unveiled in August 2015, the processors give computer owners, Intel says, a huge jump in performance, battery life and graphics.

Intel's Israeli team "saved the company" in the early 2000s, an analyst said, by insisting on a new and disruptive chip design. "Had midlevel developers in the Haifa plant not challenged their corporate superiors, Intel's global position today would be much diminished," write *Start-up Nation* co-authors Dan Senor and Saul Singer.[193]

An unnamed eBay executive told Senor and Singer the fate of many hi-tech firms rests on Israeli talent: "Google, Cisco, Microsoft, Intel, eBay ... the list goes on. The best-kept secret is

Top Left: *Intel manufacturing plant in Kiryat Gal, about 10 miles from Gaza's northern border.*

Bottom Left: *Israeli Prime Minister Benjamin Netanyahu with Google chief Eric Schmidt.*

that we all live and die by the work of our Israeli teams."[194]

Tech-titan Microsoft placed its first R&D Center outside the U.S. in Israel in 1991. "If you do the math, Microsoft is almost as much an Israeli company as it is an American company," Microsoft CEO Steve Ballmer said in 2008.[195] Microsoft Israel played a significant role in designing numerous iterations of the Windows operating system and the face recognition software used in the motion sensing device, Kinect.

"For a relatively small country, Israel has a super role in technological innovation," Eric Schmidt, executive chairman of Google parent company Alphabet, told a Tel Aviv audience in 2016. "I can't think of a place where you could see this diversity and the collection of initiatives, aside from Silicon Valley," Schmidt said. "That is a pretty strong statement."[196]

Aid to Injured Syrians

But technology, science and software are not the only means by which Israel betters the world. The Jewish state also has a long tradition of international humanitarian aid. That includes technical assistance to underdeveloped countries and relief for

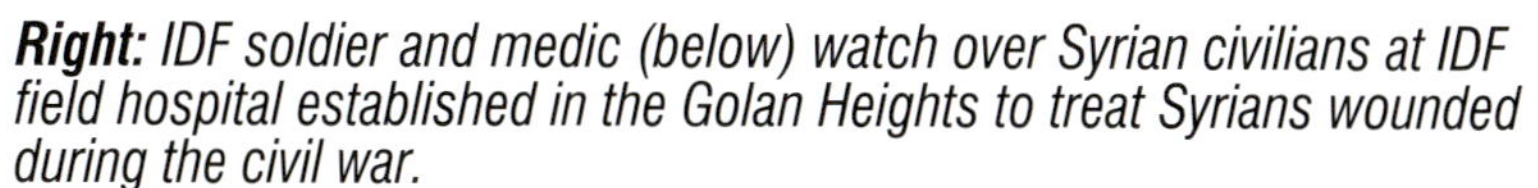

***Right:** IDF soldier and medic (below) watch over Syrian civilians at IDF field hospital established in the Golan Heights to treat Syrians wounded during the civil war.*

nations hit by natural disasters, or facing medical emergencies. And when it comes to aid, Israel doesn't discriminate. Everyone qualifies—best friends and bitter enemies.

The Israeli government airlifted 80 tons of relief supplies to the U.S. in 2005, just days after Hurricane Katrina devastated New Orleans and battered the Gulf Coast, claiming more than 1,800 lives. Relief personnel showed up from Israel to provide medical and psychological care, as well, and assist in search and rescue. "America has always been there for Israel, and Israel is there for America," said Israeli Ambassador Daniel Ayalon.[197]

Israel is also binding the wounds of Syrian civilians just across its border where a multi-sided civil war has raged since 2011. The IDF takes in wounded Syrians at a field hospital it maintains on the border with Syria,[198] transferring patients who need more extensive care to medical facilities inside Israel. That's how six-year-old Yasmine, a Syrian girl severely wounded in the cross-fire between warring Syrian factions, arrived at Haifa's Rambam Medical Center in early 2016.

After two weeks at the hospital, Yasmine had almost recovered from her injuries when tests revealed blood cancer.[199] Her caregivers refused to release her without treating her for that, as well. Because Yasmine needed a matching bone marrow donor

Kobi Gideon, Government Press Office

Kobi Gideon, Government Press Office

Detail from rock face in Caesarea Philippi, an ancient Roman city near Mount Hermon, now an archaeological site.

***Left:** Kenya Prime Minister Jomo Kenyatta with Israeli Foreign Minister Golda Meir in 1963 at ceremony for new Israel embassy building in Nairobi.*

and her family lived in an enemy nation, Israeli security forces stepped in. In what may be one of the world's first humanitarian "snatch and grab" operations, security personnel secretly entered Syria to locate her family, identify a donor and smuggle the individual back into the Jewish state.

After seven months of treatment, Yasmine recovered and left the hospital for Syria, along with her mother. "I would be lying," her mother acknowledged, "if I said I expected the good treatment and generosity and these countless acts of rare humanitarianism."[200]

Israeli generosity towards Syrians in need so amazed one Syrian refugee he created a website, www.thankyouamisrael.com, to voice his gratitude and document Jewish aid to Syrians. "I grew up with statements like, 'These people are your enemies. The Jews are evil,'" Aboud Dandachi, a Sunni Muslim, told Ynetnews.com. "And then I saw that the Jews are the most humane and generous people of this era."[201]

Repairing the World

The Israeli impulse to serve others in need stems from "the ancient Jewish tradition of 'Tikun Olam,'" said Foreign Ministry Director General Dore Gold. Sometimes translated, to "repair

Lush Israeli summer garden.

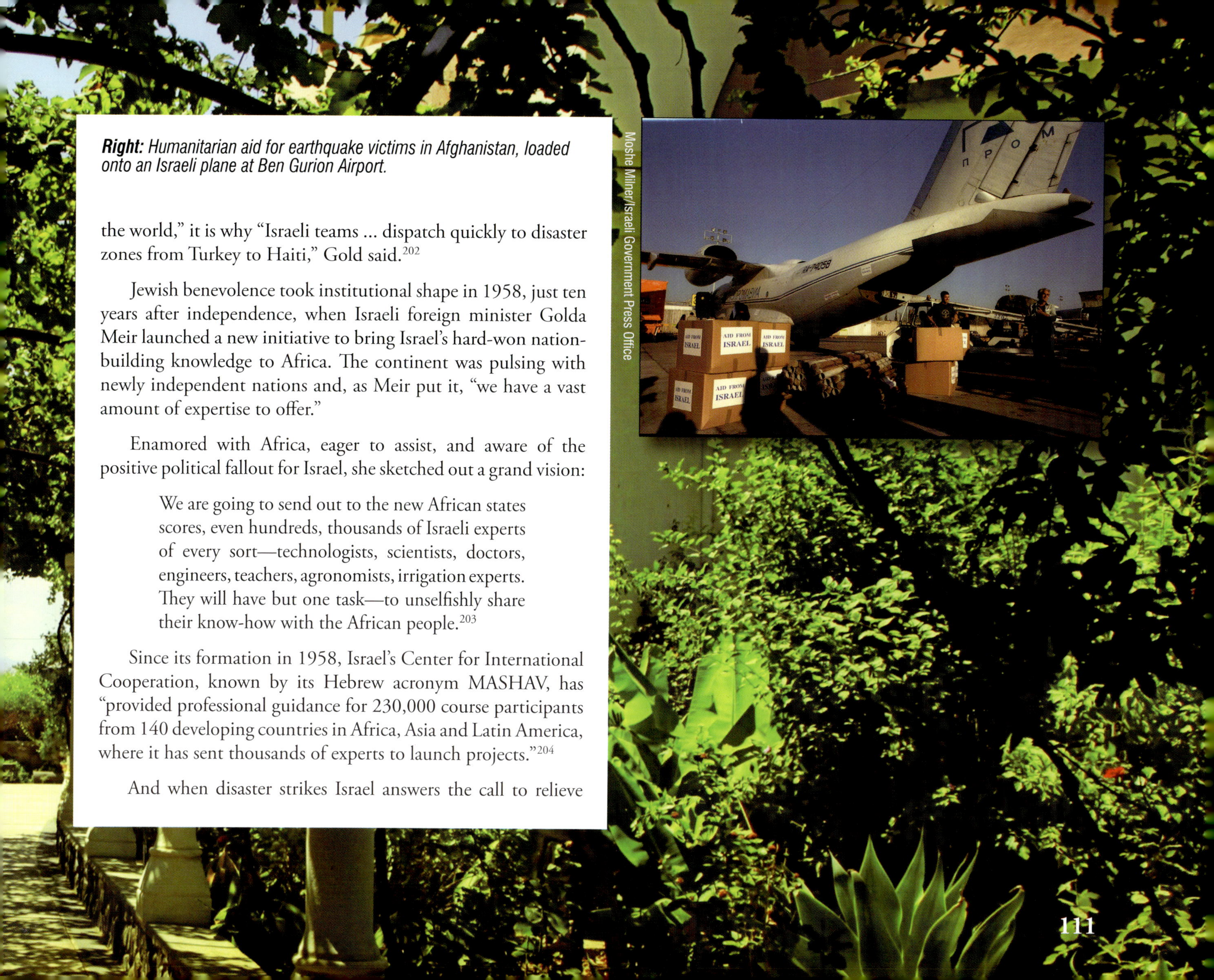

***Right:** Humanitarian aid for earthquake victims in Afghanistan, loaded onto an Israeli plane at Ben Gurion Airport.*

Moshe Milner/Israeli Government Press Office

the world," it is why "Israeli teams ... dispatch quickly to disaster zones from Turkey to Haiti," Gold said.[202]

Jewish benevolence took institutional shape in 1958, just ten years after independence, when Israeli foreign minister Golda Meir launched a new initiative to bring Israel's hard-won nation-building knowledge to Africa. The continent was pulsing with newly independent nations and, as Meir put it, "we have a vast amount of expertise to offer."

Enamored with Africa, eager to assist, and aware of the positive political fallout for Israel, she sketched out a grand vision:

> We are going to send out to the new African states scores, even hundreds, thousands of Israeli experts of every sort—technologists, scientists, doctors, engineers, teachers, agronomists, irrigation experts. They will have but one task—to unselfishly share their know-how with the African people.[203]

Since its formation in 1958, Israel's Center for International Cooperation, known by its Hebrew acronym MASHAV, has "provided professional guidance for 230,000 course participants from 140 developing countries in Africa, Asia and Latin America, where it has sent thousands of experts to launch projects."[204]

And when disaster strikes Israel answers the call to relieve

Israeli Government Press Office

Left: IDF soldier and his dog search for survivors of 1998 terrorist bombing of American embassy in Nairobi, Kenya.

human misery and help rebuild. A short list of Israel's humanitarian and relief initiatives in the recent past include:

Nepal: The day after an 8.1 magnitude earthquake killed more than 6,200 people in Nepal in 2015, Israel sent a medical delegation of 122 people and 95 tons of relief and medical supplies. The IDF also provided a 260-person search-and-rescue team to locate survivors under the rubble.[205]

Philippines: Typhoons wreaked havoc in the Philippines in 2009, 2013, and 2014. Each time Israel dispatched relief and medical missions, providing tons of relief supplies, setting up IDF field hospitals, and providing search and rescue.

Haiti: Israel was first to arrive in Haiti immediately after an earthquake devastated the impoverished nation in 2010. The team of more than 200 Israelis set up a field hospital and treated more than 1,110 patients.

Japan: A team of 50 people, along with 18 tons of aid arrived from Israel after a magnitude 9.0 earthquake struck the island nation in 2011.

Turkey: After a 7.2 magnitude earthquake killed 432 people, Israel was the first to send the prefabricated housing and tents requested by Ankara.

Indonesia: Israel sent an El Al plane loaded with 75 tons of relief supplies to help Indonesians recover after a tsunami barreled ashore on December 26, 2005.

"Providing aid and assistance is part of who we are," said Maj. Gen. Eyal Eizenberg, Commander of the IDF Home Front Command. "In the places where there is no one, we will be there.... It's a huge honor to represent the State of Israel and an even bigger honor to help save lives and assist those in need."[206]

And when it comes to providing emergency medical care in the field, no one does it better. The UN—a frequent harsh critic of Israel—gave its top designation to the Israeli army's field hospital team in 2017. The honor made Israel the only nation in the world to garner "Type 3" status from the UN's World Health Organization (WHO).

A medical village of up to 30 tents, the IDF's Medical Corps field hospital offers 86 beds and four operating rooms. It can be assembled in 12 hours almost anywhere and has the functional capacity, *The Times of Israel* reports, of an "advanced, permanent" hospital. The head of the IDF Medical Corps calls the field hospital a "national treasure." Equipped with WHO's highest ranking, Israel will get "preferential access to disasters in the future," a WHO official explained.[207]

IsraAID, one of Israel's best-known private relief organizations, has sent teams to bring life-saving aid in just about every international humanitarian crisis since its founding in 2001. It mobilizes medics, search and rescue units, post-trauma experts

Remains of ancient Roman seacoast city Caesarea Maritima.

and community mobilizers to meet needs when disaster hits. Since its founding, IsraAID teams have responded to crises in 35 countries, helping some 1 million people and distributing more than 1,000 tons of relief and medical supplies.

Comic Relief

Israel is the one nation that sends "therapeutic clowns" to provide cheer and comfort in the face of medical and humanitarian emergencies. Israel's Dream Doctors project, a private initiative, has dispatched medical clowns with aid teams working in Thailand, Indonesia, Haiti, and Nepal. Dream Doctors cite research showing "the presence of a medical clown helps reduce the anxiety of the child patient and family, lessens pain and alleviates depression, and sometimes makes it unnecessary to use sedation."[208]

When a Nepalese boy, his foot already amputated, had to wait until his parents arrived for additional surgery, a Dream Doctors clown delivered smiles and laughter with a wheelchair race and water fights using medical syringes.

"The key is to take a patient's mind off their pain and immediate situation and transfer them to a magical world of fantasy and fun," a medical official told Israel21c.org. "The Dream Doctors do just that and more, and are proving that even the trauma of a devastating earthquake may be temporarily moved aside to make way for smiles and laughter."[209]

Tel Aviv skyscrapers hug Mediterranean coastline at night.

Dream Doctors Project

***Right:** Medical clowns stage wheelchair race to cheer patients injured by 2015 Nepal earthquake.*

"Eye from Zion" a volunteer Israeli organization that gives free medical care wherever it is needed, visited Kyrgyzstan in 2015 and provided surgical care that gave sight to 90 adults and children. Many of those treated in the predominantly Muslim nation were able to see for the first time.[210]

Save a Child's Heart provides cardiac surgery to children with almost no chance of living to adulthood, due to congenital heart defects. Founded in 1995, the medical group has saved the lives of 4,000 children from some 44 countries. Many patients are from Iraq, Morocco, Jordan and the West Bank (biblical Judea and Samaria). One patient was the nephew of Marwan Barghouti, a Palestinian leader in the second intifada who was convicted for murder and is now serving five life sentences.[211]

It's not unusual for Israel to provide medical care to its enemies. Critics blast Israel for its "illegal occupation," calling it an "apartheid nation," but Israeli health providers give care to Jew and Arab alike. Gaza is ruled by the terrorist group Hamas, yet thousands of Gaza residents obtain care each year in Israeli hospitals.[212]

A few weeks after Hamas fired more than 1,000 rockets into Israel during its 2014 war against the Jewish state, a Tel Aviv hospital treated the daughter of top Hamas leader Ismail Haniyeh.[213] The former prime minister of Gaza, Haniyeh issues fiery denunciations of Israel. He advocated violence against Israel in a 2012 speech,

declaring: "The gun is our only response to [the] Zionist regime.... no compromise should be made with the enemy."[214]

By contrast, Israeli Prime Minister Benjamin Netanyahu phoned Palestinian leader Mahmoud Abbas on July 22, 2016, with his condolences after Abbas' brother died from cancer in Qatar. A Tel Aviv hospital had earlier treated Abbas' brother.[215]

Prodigious in the products it brings to the world and a looked-to source of relief, expertise, and smiles, Israel is making life better for millions. More than 2,700 years ago, Isaiah prophesied that "In days to come Jacob shall take root, Israel shall blossom and put forth shoots and fill the whole world with fruit (Isaiah 27:6). It's a prophecy coming true before our eyes.

CHAPTER 6

ISRAEL MATTERS TO AMERICA

The "Father of Zionism" was a lifelong Methodist who came to Christ at age 10. If that's a surprise, consider this. He also wrote a national bestseller, *Jesus is Coming*, in 1878. It spoke of the "glorious future restoration in store for Israel"[216] and sold several million copies, coming out in 48 languages,[217] including Yiddish and Hebrew.[218]

The author, William E. Blackstone, was a bald man with mutton chops and kind eyes. He called himself "God's little errand boy," and became wealthy as a Chicago real estate investor, retiring in mid-life to become a lay-pastor, missionary, and author. "One of the most influential and admired religious figures of his generation,"[219] Blackstone (1841-1935) was a tireless champion of Jewish return to Palestine. He spent decades in the Zionist cause, enlisting the powerful and wealthy on behalf of Jewish

Quiet Jordan River near the Sea of Galilee.

Sweeping vista of the Jezreel Valley,
Israel's fertile agricultural heartland.

Biola University

Left: *Methodist lay minister and "Father of Zionism," William E. Blackstone.*

return and urging Presidents Benjamin Harrison, Theodore Roosevelt and Woodrow Wilson to boost Jewish restoration to Palestine.

Blackstone traveled to Istanbul in 1888 where he saw thousands of suffering Russian Jews seeking refuge and then went on to Palestine where he visited Jewish settlements. Burdened by the plight of Russian Jews who faced horrific pogroms and banishment under the Czar, Blackstone gathered Christian and Jewish leaders in Chicago on November 24-25, 1890, for a historic "Conference on the Past, Present and Future of Israel." Attendees unanimously approved a resolution of "sympathy with the oppressed Jews of Russia," asking President Harrison to seek an international conference on restoring the Jews to Palestine.[220]

RICH AND POWERFUL SIGN ON

But Blackstone took things a step further. On his own, he drafted a petition to the President urging a national homeland for Jews in Palestine. And using the talents that made him a wealthy businessman, Blackstone persuaded many of America's rich and powerful to add their names to his petition. The 413 signatories included John D. Rockefeller, J. Pierpont Morgan, the Chief Justice of the U.S. Supreme Court, the Speaker of the House, three governors, 22 state and federal judges, and the mayors of New York, Chicago, Boston, Philadelphia, and Baltimore. Add to that the editors and publishers of 93 newspapers and periodicals, seven college presidents, and more than 200 Protestant and Catholic leaders.[221]

Not surprisingly, the long list of notable Americans captured White House attention and Blackstone traveled to Washington to give his "Blackstone Memorial" to the President in person on March 5, 1891. He added a personal letter telling President Harrison the time was ripe to act on behalf of the Jews:

> [T]here seem to be many evidences to show that we have reached the period in the great roll of centuries, when the everlasting God of Abraham, Isaac and Jacob, is lifting up His hand to the Gentiles (Isa 49:22) to bring His sons and his daughters from far, that he may plant them again in their own land, Ezekiel 34, etc. Not for twenty-four centuries, since the days of Cyrus, King of Persia, has there been offered to any mortal such a privileged opportunity to further the purposes of God concerning His ancient people.[222]

Blackstone concluded with the words of Gen 12:3, "I will bless them that bless thee."

Golden glow shimmers off sandy hills in Samaria.

Rainbow graces Kafr Kannas, an Arab town in northern Israel linked to ancient Cana, where Jesus made water into wine.

Right: *President Benjamin Harrison interceded on behalf of Russian Jews suffering severe persecution in the 1890s.*

While President Harrison did not agree to an international conference, his administration took up the cause of Russian Jewry. It communicated, Harrison said, "with much earnestness, to the government of the Czar, its serious concern because of the harsh measures now being enforced against the Hebrews in Russia."[223] And that brought some relief to Russian Jews. Blackstone's petition "had a direct effect in the repeal by Russia of the expulsion edicts that had driven hundreds of thousands of Russian Jewish refugees to America and elsewhere," asserts Hyman Meites, a Russian Jew who came to Chicago in 1891.[224]

A quarter-century later Blackstone helped persuade President Woodrow Wilson to support the Balfour Declaration and a national homeland in Palestine for the Jews. For his efforts, Louis Brandeis, a key leader of American Zionism and U.S. Supreme Court Justice, and Nathan Straus, owner of R. H. Macy and wealthy philanthropist, lauded him as "the Father of Zionism."[225] The Chicago Jewish community planted a grove in his name in the Jerusalem Forest.[226]

AMERICAN ZIONISM

This zealous Methodist is just one among many advocates for Jewish return in U.S. history. The Jewish Telegraphic Agency applauded America in 1935 for its "generous and unstinted support given to the cause of Zionism." That support, the Jewish news service insisted, reached across American society: "With rare exceptions the public press of the Republic, its pulpit, its educators and intellectual leaders, its industrialists and labor leaders, have generously upheld the Jewish rights to their ancient Homeland."[227]

More than any other nation, the United States has been a friend to the sons of Abraham. From the Puritans onward, America has been a uniquely pro-Israel nation. Even today, for reasons spiritual, strategic and commercial, Israel matters to America.

Blackstone's *Jesus is Coming* reached a mass audience and "influenced the thinking of many Christian leaders, powerfully shaping evangelical Christianity into the friend of Israel that it is today," asserts Blackstone scholar Paul W. Rood.[228] A generation earlier, another American "proto-Zionist" did much the same. New York University Hebrew professor George Bush made the case for the coming restoration and conversion of the Jews in his popular 1844 study of Ezekiel 37, *The Dry Bones of Israel Revived*.

Top Left: *U.S. President Woodrow Wilson supported the Balfour Declaration and a Jewish homeland in Palestine.*

Right: *American Zionist leader and Supreme Court Justice Louis Brandeis.*

In it, Bush, a well-known author in both America and Europe,[229] described the coming "restoration from the thralldom and oppression which has so long ground them [the Jews] to the dust ... elevating them to a rank of honorable repute among the nations of the earth."[230] Ezekiel's vision of a valley strewn with dry bones that dramatically reassemble, take on flesh, and come to life is a symbolic representation, Bush asserted, of

> ... a very feeble and gradual beginning of a course of events, which is to issue in the most stupendous results. The dispersed and downcast remnant shall, one after another, turn their faces to Zion, and in sparse and scattered bands find their way to the land of their fathers. Thus shall "bone come to his bone;" one Jew shall meet another, entering from different quarters of the globe upon the predestined soil of Palestine.[231]

A distant ancestor of two presidents, Bush is honored at the Friends of Zion Museum in Jerusalem as a "prophet of Zionism before the Zionist movement."[232]

Beautiful sunrise on the Negev.

Verdant and well-watered by rainfall off the Mediterranean, seen in distance, Mt. Carmel is the "evergreen mountain."

Top Left: *French writer Alexis de Tocqueville observed that Christianity reigned triumphant in early 19th century America.*

Bottom Left: *President Abraham Lincoln supported Jewish restoration to Palestine.*

"Palestine Mania"

Blackstone and Bush are just two of many Jewish restoration proponents who dotted America's religious landscape in the nineteenth century—an era when Christianity "reign[ed] without any obstacles, by universal consent," as French visitor Alexis de Tocqueville remarked in the 1830s.[233] During this time, "restorationism was a mainstream American idea, and so was the obsession with Jerusalem," historian James Carroll asserts.[234]

"So much has been said for generations of the Jews regaining possession of Jerusalem, that it is agreeable to think that they are likely to do so at last," the *New York Times* observed in 1879.[235] Abraham Lincoln told a White House visitor in 1863 that "restoring the Jews to their national home in Palestine…is a noble dream and one shared by many Americans."[236] Lincoln harbored the wish, himself, to visit Palestine. According to one source, he told his wife before his assassination at Ford's Theater, "there was no city on earth he so much desired to see as Jerusalem."[237]

PURITAN PATTERN

But America's nineteenth century "Palestine mania," as historian Michael Oren termed it, is no anomaly. It belongs to a long tradition stretching back to the Puritans and remains true today. "Generations of Christians in this country, representing a variety of dominations [sic], laymen and clergy alike, have embraced the concept of renewed Jewish sovereignty in Palestine," asserts Oren.[238]

In the seventeenth century, leading colonial Puritan divines John Cotton (1584-1652) and Increase Mather (1639-1723), the first president of Harvard, "called for the destruction of the Ottoman Empire to make way for the Jews' return," writes Oren.[239] Mather predicted the Jews would be "brought into their own land again" and "make the greatest Nation upon the whole earth."[240] Puritan theologian and pastor Jonathan Edwards (1703-1758), the first president of Princeton, believed "the Jews will return to their own land again" and spoke of their acceptance of Jesus as Messiah.[241] As did Richard Bulkley (1583-1659), a Puritan minister who founded Concord, Massachusetts.[242]

***Right:** Both Jonathan Edwards, top right, the first president of Princeton, and Yale president Ezra Stiles, bottom right, predicted Jewish restoration to the ancient land of Israel, based on biblical texts.*

Sunlight penetrates morning fog over Dead Sea.

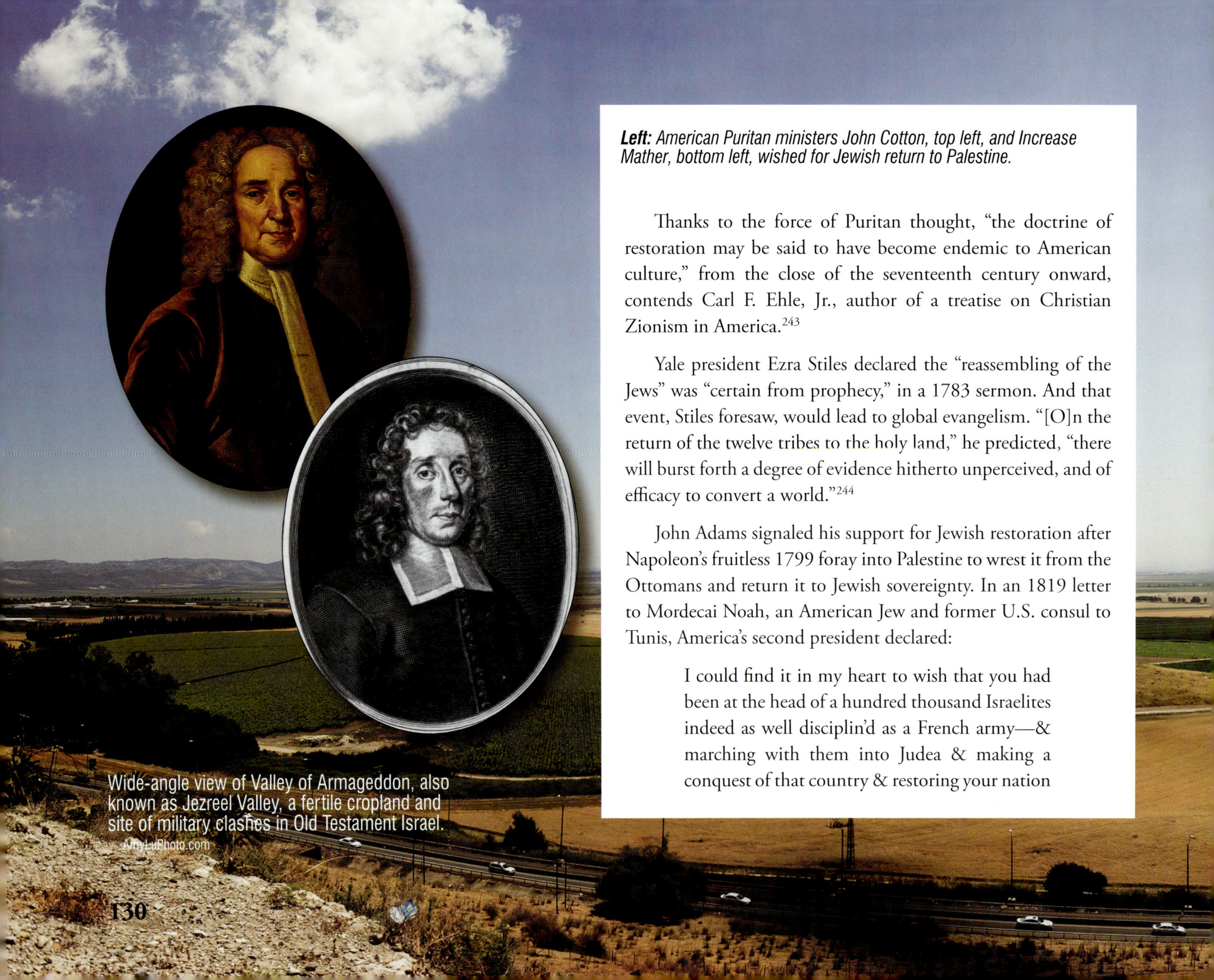

Wide-angle view of Valley of Armageddon, also known as Jezreel Valley, a fertile cropland and site of military clashes in Old Testament Israel.
AmyLuPhoto.com

Left: *American Puritan ministers John Cotton, top left, and Increase Mather, bottom left, wished for Jewish return to Palestine.*

Thanks to the force of Puritan thought, "the doctrine of restoration may be said to have become endemic to American culture," from the close of the seventeenth century onward, contends Carl F. Ehle, Jr., author of a treatise on Christian Zionism in America.[243]

Yale president Ezra Stiles declared the "reassembling of the Jews" was "certain from prophecy," in a 1783 sermon. And that event, Stiles foresaw, would lead to global evangelism. "[O]n the return of the twelve tribes to the holy land," he predicted, "there will burst forth a degree of evidence hitherto unperceived, and of efficacy to convert a world."[244]

John Adams signaled his support for Jewish restoration after Napoleon's fruitless 1799 foray into Palestine to wrest it from the Ottomans and return it to Jewish sovereignty. In an 1819 letter to Mordecai Noah, an American Jew and former U.S. consul to Tunis, America's second president declared:

> I could find it in my heart to wish that you had been at the head of a hundred thousand Israelites indeed as well disciplin'd as a French army—& marching with them into Judea & making a conquest of that country & restoring your nation

Right: *Founding Father Elias Boudinot speculated on America's providential role in restoring God's "beloved people to their own land."*

Right Lower: *President John Adams declared his support for Jewish sovereignty in "Judea."*

> to the dominion of it—For I really wish the Jews again in Judea an independent nation....[245]

AMERICA'S DIVINE PURPOSE?

Elias Boudinot, the former president of the Continental Congress, predicted "the mighty power of God" would restore the Jews "to their beloved ... Palestine."[246] A devoted Presbyterian, and founder and president of the American Bible Society, Boudinot mused in 1816 of an American role in returning Jews to their ancient homeland:

> Who knows but God has raised up these United States in these latter days, for the very purpose of accomplishing his will in bringing his beloved people to their own land.... We may, under God, be called to act a great part in this wonderful and interesting drama.[247]

Two centuries later, it is clear Boudinot was correct. God has used the U.S. to secure a homeland for the Jews and to safeguard

Left: *Wealthy businessman John Wanamaker, top left, and liberal theologian Shailer Mathews, bottom left, urged President Wilson to support Jewish restoration to Palestine.*

them in it. U.S. intervention at two crucial points in the first half of the twentieth century brought about the rebirth of Israel, giving the Jews a national home after nearly 1,900 years of exile.

The first instance came in 1917 while the British government was considering whether to support Jewish restoration to Palestine. The year prior William Blackstone had gathered signatures in support of his second petition, this one to President Woodrow Wilson, calling for an "international conference to consider the condition of the Jews and their right to a home in Palestine."[248]

Baptist, Methodist, and Presbyterian ministerial bodies in California gave their support. So did influential leaders such as theologian Shailer Mathews, Andrew D. White (president of Cornell University and a former ambassador to Russia), Newton W. Thompson (governor of California), and John Wanamaker (department store magnate and United States Postmaster General).[249] Most notably, the Presbyterian Church, U.S.A. approved the document, a factor that may have weighed favorably on President Wilson, who was raised in the home of a Presbyterian minister.

Salt-encrusted rocks along the Dead Sea shoreline.

WILSON: "WITH YOU COMPLETELY"

"I am a son of the manse, son of a Presbyterian clergyman, and therefore am with you completely and am proud to think that I may in some degree help you rebuild Palestine," Wilson declared when Zionist leader Rabbi Stephen Wise presented Blackstone's petition to Wilson on June 30, 1917.[250]

Wilson soon enlisted in the Zionist cause, permitting Louis Brandeis, the head of American Zionism, to cable British Foreign Secretary Arthur Balfour on October 13, 1917, with news of the president's "entire sympathy" for a Jewish homeland in Palestine. Less than three weeks later, Balfour sent his famous one paragraph note to Zionist leader Baron Rothschild, announcing the British government would "view with favour the establishment in Palestine of a national home for the Jewish people." Historian Paul C. Merkley asserts that without Wilson's support, "most scholars agree, the British Cabinet would never have adopted the Balfour Declaration."[251]

Thirty years later, President Harry S. Truman overruled the strenuous objections of his foreign policy advisors by approving a U.N. partition plan granting statehood in Palestine to both

Right: *President Harry S. Truman, a modern day "Cyrus" for his singular role in the rebirth of modern Israel.*

The cobalt blue Gulf of Aqaba seen from Eilat Mountains at Israel's southernmost point.

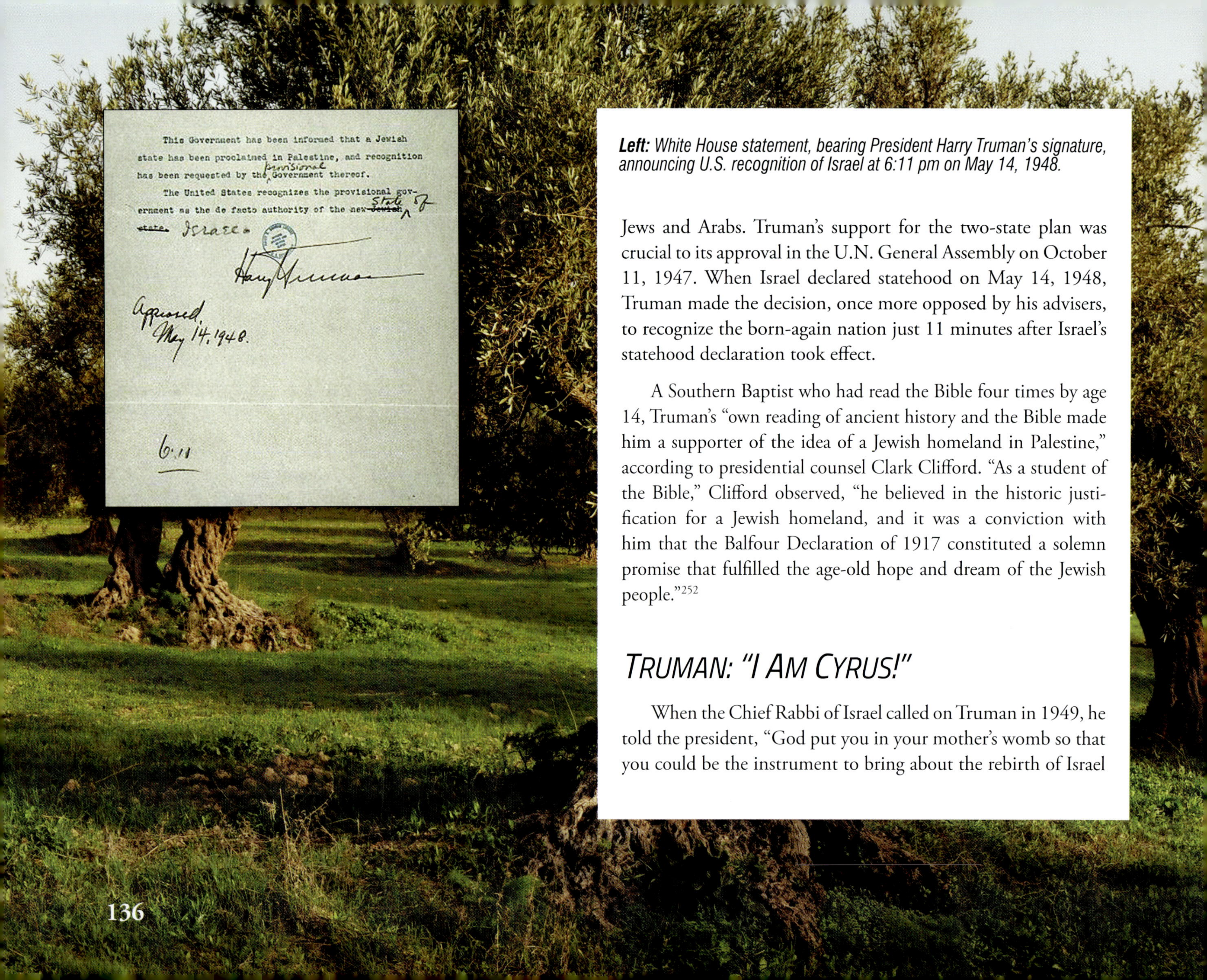

This Government has been informed that a Jewish state has been proclaimed in Palestine, and recognition has been requested by the provisional Government thereof.

The United States recognizes the provisional government as the de facto authority of the new ~~Jewish~~ State of ~~state~~ Israel.

Harry Truman

Approved,
May 14, 1948.

6.11

Left: *White House statement, bearing President Harry Truman's signature, announcing U.S. recognition of Israel at 6:11 pm on May 14, 1948.*

Jews and Arabs. Truman's support for the two-state plan was crucial to its approval in the U.N. General Assembly on October 11, 1947. When Israel declared statehood on May 14, 1948, Truman made the decision, once more opposed by his advisers, to recognize the born-again nation just 11 minutes after Israel's statehood declaration took effect.

A Southern Baptist who had read the Bible four times by age 14, Truman's "own reading of ancient history and the Bible made him a supporter of the idea of a Jewish homeland in Palestine," according to presidential counsel Clark Clifford. "As a student of the Bible," Clifford observed, "he believed in the historic justification for a Jewish homeland, and it was a conviction with him that the Balfour Declaration of 1917 constituted a solemn promise that fulfilled the age-old hope and dream of the Jewish people."[252]

TRUMAN: "I AM CYRUS!"

When the Chief Rabbi of Israel called on Truman in 1949, he told the president, "God put you in your mother's womb so that you could be the instrument to bring about the rebirth of Israel

Right: *Israeli Prime Minister David Ben-Gurion, with Abba Eban, presents a menorah to President Harry Truman in 1951.*

after two thousand years." The Chief Rabbi opened his Bible to the book of Ezra and read the words of Cyrus, the Persian potentate who issued a decree in 539 B.C., allowing the exiled Jews to return to their homeland. According to an eyewitness:

> On hearing these words Truman rose from his chair and with great emotion, tears glistening in his eyes, he turned to the Chief Rabbi and asked him if his actions for the sake of the Jewish people were indeed to he interpreted thus and the hand of the Almighty was in the matter.

The Rabbi answered that Truman "had been given the task once fulfilled by the mighty King of Persia, and that he too, like Cyrus, would occupy a place of honor in the annals of the Jewish people."[253]

Later, when a long-time friend introduced Truman at Jewish Theological Seminary in New York as "the man who helped create Israel," Truman took exception. He stepped to the podium and shot back, "What do you mean, 'helped to create?' I am Cyrus. I am Cyrus!"[254]

Fritz Cohen/Israeli Government Press Office

Grove of ancient olive trees in Israel's Judean Mountains.

Pink bougainvillea blossoms help frame the Sea of Galilee seen from the Mount of Beatitudes. (Amyluphoto.com)

DEEP SPIRITUAL TIES

Truman rejected opposition to Israel's statehood from the "'striped-pants boys' in the State Department" because of the enduring spiritual tie that binds Americans and Israelis, Christians and Jews. That deep affinity underwrites the special U.S.-Israel relationship and has been celebrated by numerous presidents since.

"I don't understand you Americans backing Israel," Soviet Premier Aleksei Kosygin remarked to Lyndon Johnson in 1967. "There are 80 million Arabs and only 3 million Jews. Why do it?" Johnson's quick answer? "Because it's right."[255]

Johnson's grandfather had charged him to "take care of the Jews, God's chosen people. Consider them your friends and help them any way you can." Johnson did so in 1938 when he worked, as a U.S. congressman, to help Jews escape Nazi Germany.[256]

"America and Israel have a common love of human freedom and they have a common faith in a democratic way of life," Johnson told a B'nai B'rith gathering in 1968. "Most if not all of you have very deep ties with the land and with the people of

Top Left: *President Lyndon Johnson.*

Bottom Left: *President Richard Nixon.*

__Top Right:__ President Gerald Ford
__Bottom Right:__ President Jimmy Carter

Israel, as I do, for my Christian faith sprang from yours...."[257]

Other presidents since have said much the same:

- **Richard Nixon:** "I can only say that the friendship that we have for this nation, the respect and the admiration we have for the people of this nation, their courage, their tenacity, their firmness in the face of very great odds, is one that makes us proud to stand with Israel...."
- **Gerald R. Ford:** "My commitment to the security and future of Israel is based upon basic morality as well as enlightened self-interest. Our role in supporting Israel honors our own heritage."
- **Jimmy Carter**: "The United States ... has a warm and a unique relationship of friendship with Israel that is morally right. It is compatible with our deepest religious convictions, and it is right in terms of America's own strategic interests. We are committed to Israel's security, prosperity, and future as a land that has so much to offer the world."
- **Ronald Reagan:** "Since the foundation of the State of Israel, the United States has stood by her and helped her to pursue security, peace, and economic growth. Our

Israel's Judean Desert, between Jerusalem and the Dead Sea, turns red and gold at sunset.

Top Left: *President Ronald Reagan*
Bottom Left: *President George H. W. Bush*

friendship is based on historic moral and strategic ties, as well as our shared dedication to democracy."

- **George H. W. Bush:** "The friendship, the alliance between the United States and Israel is strong and solid—built upon a foundation of shared democratic values, of shared history and heritage that sustain the moral life of our two countries."

- **Bill Clinton:** "Our relationship would never vary from its allegiance to the shared values, the shared religious heritage, the shared democratic politics which have made the relationship between the United States and Israel a special—even on occasion a wonderful—relationship."

- **George W. Bush:** "Both our countries are founded on certain basic beliefs, that there is an Almighty God who watches over the affairs of men and values every life. These ties have made us natural allies, and these ties will never be broken."

- **Barack Obama:** "A strong and secure Israel is in the national security interest of the United States not simply because we share strategic interests.... America's commitment to Israel's security flows from a deeper place—and that's the values we share."[258]

Top Right: *President Bill Clinton*
Bottom Right: *President George W. Bush*

- **Donald J. Trump:** "When I become president, the days of treating Israel like a second-class citizen will end on day one.... And we will send a clear signal that there is no daylight between America and our most reliable ally, the state of Israel."

Notwithstanding his warm words, President Obama is outside the presidential pattern of friendly and supportive U.S. relations with Israel. Beyond Obama's frosty relationship with Israeli Prime Minister Benjamin Netanyahu, the Obama administration, as *Jerusalem Post* writer Caroline Glick comments, "has systematically leaked Israel's most closely guarded secrets to the media."[259] In one instance, the White House disclosed the nations which agreed to give Israel fly-over rights to attack Iran. Obama opposed stronger sanctions against Iran and dismissed Israel's strenuous objections to the nuclear deal with Iran, a nation which openly seeks Israel's destruction.

And in the waning days of his presidency, Obama betrayed Israel at the UN Security Council when the U.S. abstained from, rather than veto, an anti-Israel resolution which blasted Israel for its so-called settlement activity. The resolution, approved 14-0 two days before Christmas and Hanukkah 2016, called the building of Jewish homes "a flagrant violation" of interna-

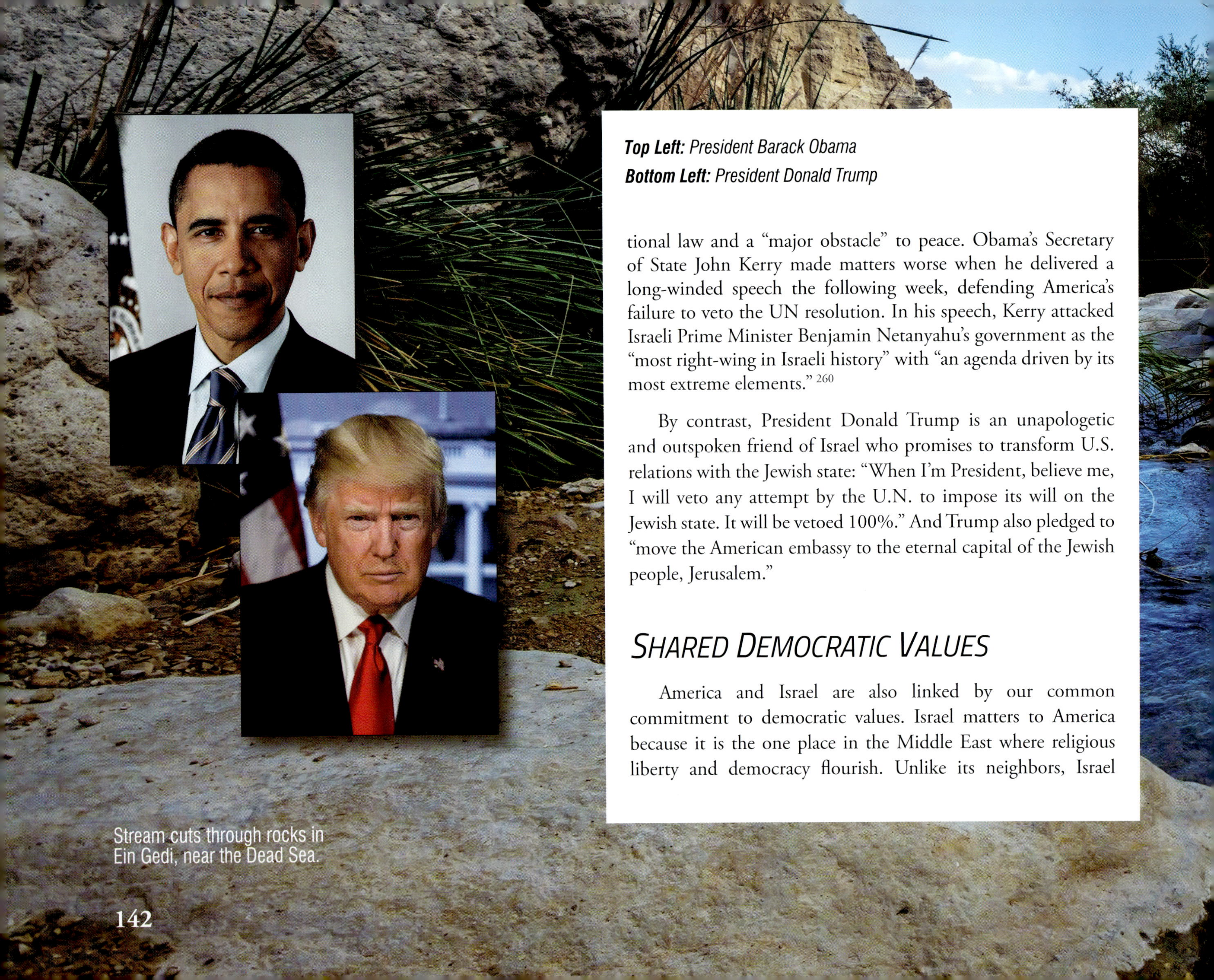

***Top Left:** President Barack Obama*

***Bottom Left:** President Donald Trump*

tional law and a "major obstacle" to peace. Obama's Secretary of State John Kerry made matters worse when he delivered a long-winded speech the following week, defending America's failure to veto the UN resolution. In his speech, Kerry attacked Israeli Prime Minister Benjamin Netanyahu's government as the "most right-wing in Israeli history" with "an agenda driven by its most extreme elements." [260]

By contrast, President Donald Trump is an unapologetic and outspoken friend of Israel who promises to transform U.S. relations with the Jewish state: "When I'm President, believe me, I will veto any attempt by the U.N. to impose its will on the Jewish state. It will be vetoed 100%." And Trump also pledged to "move the American embassy to the eternal capital of the Jewish people, Jerusalem."

Shared Democratic Values

America and Israel are also linked by our common commitment to democratic values. Israel matters to America because it is the one place in the Middle East where religious liberty and democracy flourish. Unlike its neighbors, Israel

Stream cuts through rocks in Ein Gedi, near the Dead Sea.

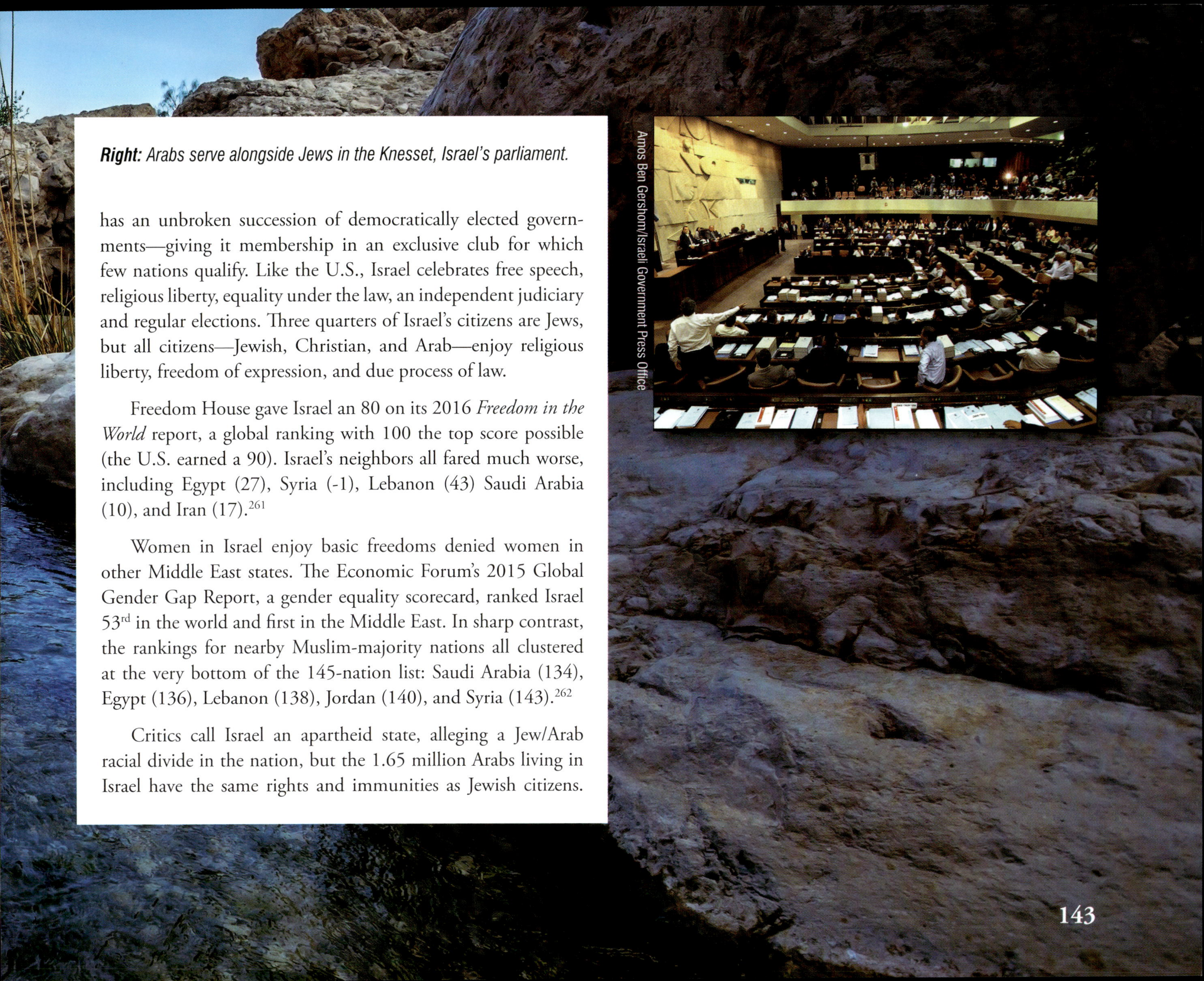

Right: *Arabs serve alongside Jews in the Knesset, Israel's parliament.*

has an unbroken succession of democratically elected governments—giving it membership in an exclusive club for which few nations qualify. Like the U.S., Israel celebrates free speech, religious liberty, equality under the law, an independent judiciary and regular elections. Three quarters of Israel's citizens are Jews, but all citizens—Jewish, Christian, and Arab—enjoy religious liberty, freedom of expression, and due process of law.

Freedom House gave Israel an 80 on its 2016 *Freedom in the World* report, a global ranking with 100 the top score possible (the U.S. earned a 90). Israel's neighbors all fared much worse, including Egypt (27), Syria (-1), Lebanon (43) Saudi Arabia (10), and Iran (17).[261]

Women in Israel enjoy basic freedoms denied women in other Middle East states. The Economic Forum's 2015 Global Gender Gap Report, a gender equality scorecard, ranked Israel 53rd in the world and first in the Middle East. In sharp contrast, the rankings for nearby Muslim-majority nations all clustered at the very bottom of the 145-nation list: Saudi Arabia (134), Egypt (136), Lebanon (138), Jordan (140), and Syria (143).[262]

Critics call Israel an apartheid state, alleging a Jew/Arab racial divide in the nation, but the 1.65 million Arabs living in Israel have the same rights and immunities as Jewish citizens.

Arabs serve in the Knesset, Israel's parliament, and a Christian Arab sits on Israel's Supreme Court.

Israeli Arabs are content to live as citizens of the Jewish state, as well. Some 83 percent of Arabs say they prefer to live in Israel rather than move elsewhere, according to a 2015 poll.[263] In addition, Israeli Arabs enjoy a life expectancy of 79 years, 10 years longer than that for the Arab world as a whole. And per capita income for Israeli Arabs is 50 percent higher than for Arabs in Arab countries.[264] Israel is a wonderful place to live ... a free and open country," asserts Israeli Arab journalist Khaled Abu Toameh. "I would rather live in Israel as a second class citizen," he says, "than as a first class citizen in Cairo, Gaza, Amman or Ramallah."[265]

Strategic Partner

Another crucial reason Israel matters to America is the Jewish state's vital role as a U.S. strategic partner in the world's most restless and volatile region. A democratic stronghold with one of the globe's most lethal and efficient armed forces, Israel is a potent check on Arab-Muslim ambitions. It has acted twice to keep its neighbors out of the nuclear club, having bombed nuclear facilities in Iraq and Syria. It may be forced to attempt that again within the next decade if Iran takes the path to nuclear weapons Obama gave it in his deal with the rogue terrorist state.

Gorgeous sunrise on a cloudless morning in Israel. (Victoria Vitkovska)

Right: *The F-35 Joint Strike Fighter, developed with Israeli collaboration.*

Despite strains to the alliance, Israel remains a reliable and stable friend to the U.S. It votes with the U.S. at the United Nations and is a long-standing ally in the Middle East. It mobilized in 1970, at Richard Nixon's request, to defend Jordan against Syria. And despite the threat to civilians from incoming Iraqi Scud missiles during the 1991 Gulf War, Israel agreed not to retaliate, complying with a presidential request from George H. W. Bush.[266]

U.S. and Israeli forces engage in regular joint training operations and cooperate in the development of military technology used by both nations. Israel serves as a strategic location for some $800 million in war materiel prepositioned for when conflict flares. Secretary of State Alexander M. Haig defined Israel's enormous value to the U.S. more than 30 years ago with a striking metaphor still true today. "Israel is the largest American aircraft carrier in the world that cannot be sunk, does not carry even one American soldier, and is located in a critical region for American national security."[267]

The price tag on a new aircraft carrier is $13 billion, which puts the $3.8 billion America sends to Israel annually for military spending in some perspective. Especially when one recognizes that much of the aid is reinvested in the U.S., creating jobs

Left: *A mine resistant ambush protected all-terrain vehicle with composite armor supplied by Plasan, a kibbutz-owned Israeli firm.*

for American workers. The current aid agreement calls for 74 percent of U.S. aid to Israel to be spent in the U.S. The new 10-year agreement with Israel, which begins in 2019, requires all aid funds to be spent in the U.S. after the first five years.[268]

The close U.S.-Israeli strategic relationship supplies the U.S. military with dazzling, leading-edge military equipment such as the "Iron Fist Light Configuration." The U.S. Army purchased the Israeli made active protection system for its armored personnel carriers in 2015. Iron Fist protects against anti-tank rockets and anti-tank guided missiles using "radar and electro-optics ... [to] jam the GPS systems of incoming projectiles causing them to malfunction and fall to the ground."[269]

Another life-saving made-in-Israel innovation is the armor used to protect U.S. military vehicles in Iraq and Afghanistan. Manufactured at a kibbutz in Israel, the plastic composite armor protects against IEDs and ambush without adding greatly to vehicle weight. "Two days ago, my patrol was ambushed by insurgents using 7.62mm PKM Machineguns," a sergeant in Iraq told the manufacturer. "None of the rounds penetrated the armor of the vehicle, including one that would have impacted with my head." A Marine whose armored vehicle hit an IED in

Right: *F-35 helmet developed by Israel's Elbit Systems and Rockwell Collins gives pilots 360-degree situational awareness via video feed projected on its visor.*

Afghanistan said his unit "walked away smiling, laughing, and lived to fight another day."[270]

Because of the U.S. and Israel's special relationship, the two nations have collaborated in the development of weapons and defense systems like the F-35 Joint Strike Fighter and the Iron Dome missile interceptor. Among its features, the F-35 uses pilot helmets jointly developed by Israel's Elbit Systems and the U.S. firm Rockwell Collins to display flight information on the helmet's visor. The helmet-mounted display system (HMDS) also enables pilots to "look through" the plane and see their surroundings via six infrared cameras on the aircraft.[271]

The U.S. has invested $1.3 billion since 2011 for production of Israel's Iron Dome.[272] The anti-missile system uses interceptor rockets produced both in Israel and in the U.S. by Raytheon, the world's largest maker of guided missiles. Iron Dome is now a candidate for use by the American military. In 2016, the U.S. Army conducted an Iron Dome test in New Mexico during which the anti-missile system successfully downed an unmanned drone.

America's strategic partnership with Israel also provides the U.S. with an extraordinary wealth of intelligence. During the

Date palm plantation. Jewish settlers restored date palms to Palestine in the early 20th century.

Kobi Gideon/Israeli Government Press Office

Setting sun lights up Judean Desert with golden glow.

Left: *Prime Minister Benjamin Netanyahu and Chairman of Microsoft Bill Gates.*

Cold War, Israel gave captured Soviet weapons systems to the U.S. More recently, Israeli intelligence intercepted terror group communications, informing U.S. and British intelligence services that a terrorist bomb brought down a Russian passenger plane over the Sinai Peninsula on October 31, 2015, killing 224 people.[273]

"The ability of the U.S. Air Force in particular, and the Army in general, to defend whatever position it has in NATO owes more to the Israeli intelligence input than it does to any other single source of intelligence, be it satellite reconnaissance, be it technology intercept, or what have you," said Maj. Gen. George J. Keegan Jr., former head of U.S. Air Force intelligence. Remarkably, he said the intelligence gleaned from Israeli spies was worth "five CIAs."[274]

Thriving Commercial Relationship

A crucial ally, Israel is a vital commercial partner as well. The chairman of Israel's largest bank calls the U.S. "Israel's most important trading partner."[275] The U.S. is also Israel's largest trade partner with total annual commerce between the two nations of $38 billion. Israel buys $13.5 billion annually in U.S. goods and services and sends $24.5 billion in goods and services back to the U.S. each year.[276] Israeli firms bring jobs to

the U.S., too. U.S. affiliates of Israeli-owned firms employed 23,200 American workers and invested $551 million in research and development in 2012.[277]

Israel's high-tech sector—the so-called "Silicon Wadi"—is vital to the U.S. economy. Some 250 multinational firms have established research and development centers in Israel, many of them well-known American tech firms like Intel, Microsoft, Google, and Apple. IVC Research Center reports that these foreign firms employ two-thirds of research and development workers in Israel. The Israelis who serve these firms provide "mission critical work," asserts an American eBay executive. "It's much more than just outsourcing call centers to India or setting up IT services in Ireland. What we do in Israel is unlike what we do anywhere else in the world."[278]

Intel Israel employs some 10,000 people at six locations "because we're after the talent and the creativity of the Startup Nation," Intel Israel president Maxine Fassberg said in 2015. "Israel is crucial to Intel," she added. "Intel cannot do without the geniuses here in Israel."[279]

Spiritual ties, common democratic values, shared security interests, and a burgeoning commercial partnership. It's why Israel and the Jewish people matter to America—and have for centuries.

CHAPTER 7

ISRAEL MATTERS TO THE CHURCH AND TO YOU

If you've ever wondered why Easter Sunday falls on differing dates each year, the answer is easy: anti-Semitism. Surprised? Skeptical? Well, consider what Roman Emperor Constantine said in 325 A.D.

After the Council of Nicea imposed an empire-wide rule for dating Easter—one still followed today—Constantine explained why. The emperor, who convened the famous church council, said the change was made to divorce Easter from the Jewish Passover—even though Christ's death, burial and resurrection took place during Passover Week. It was, he said, a unanimous conclusion:

> [I]t seemed to everyone a most unworthy thing that we should follow the custom of the Jews in the celebration of this most holy solemnity, who, *polluted wretches!*, having stained their

Ruins of Crusader fortress near Caesarea Maritima turn crimson at sunset.

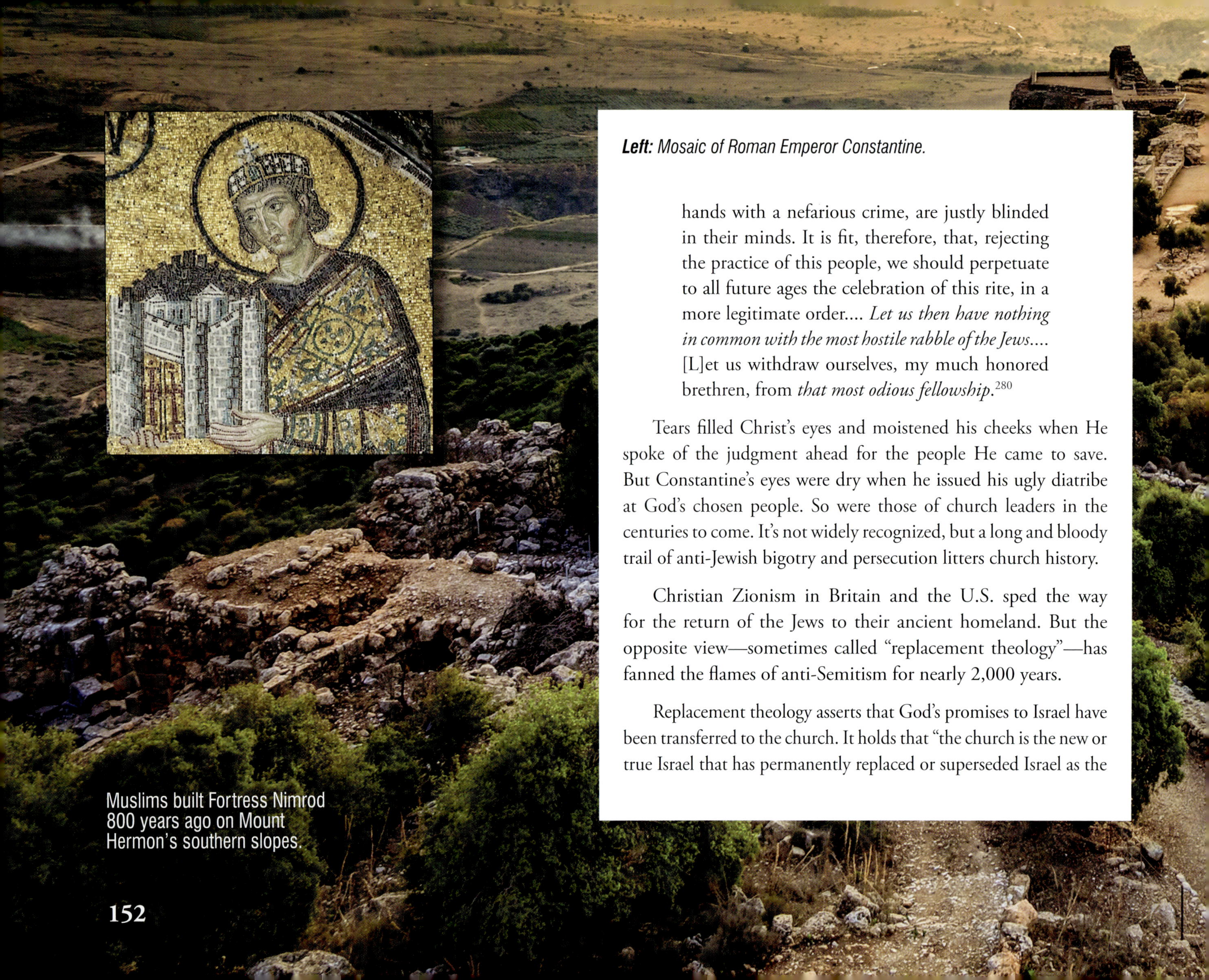

Muslims built Fortress Nimrod 800 years ago on Mount Hermon's southern slopes.

Left: Mosaic of Roman Emperor Constantine.

> hands with a nefarious crime, are justly blinded in their minds. It is fit, therefore, that, rejecting the practice of this people, we should perpetuate to all future ages the celebration of this rite, in a more legitimate order.... *Let us then have nothing in common with the most hostile rabble of the Jews....* [L]et us withdraw ourselves, my much honored brethren, from *that most odious fellowship.*[280]

Tears filled Christ's eyes and moistened his cheeks when He spoke of the judgment ahead for the people He came to save. But Constantine's eyes were dry when he issued his ugly diatribe at God's chosen people. So were those of church leaders in the centuries to come. It's not widely recognized, but a long and bloody trail of anti-Jewish bigotry and persecution litters church history.

Christian Zionism in Britain and the U.S. sped the way for the return of the Jews to their ancient homeland. But the opposite view—sometimes called "replacement theology"—has fanned the flames of anti-Semitism for nearly 2,000 years.

Replacement theology asserts that God's promises to Israel have been transferred to the church. It holds that "the church is the new or true Israel that has permanently replaced or superseded Israel as the

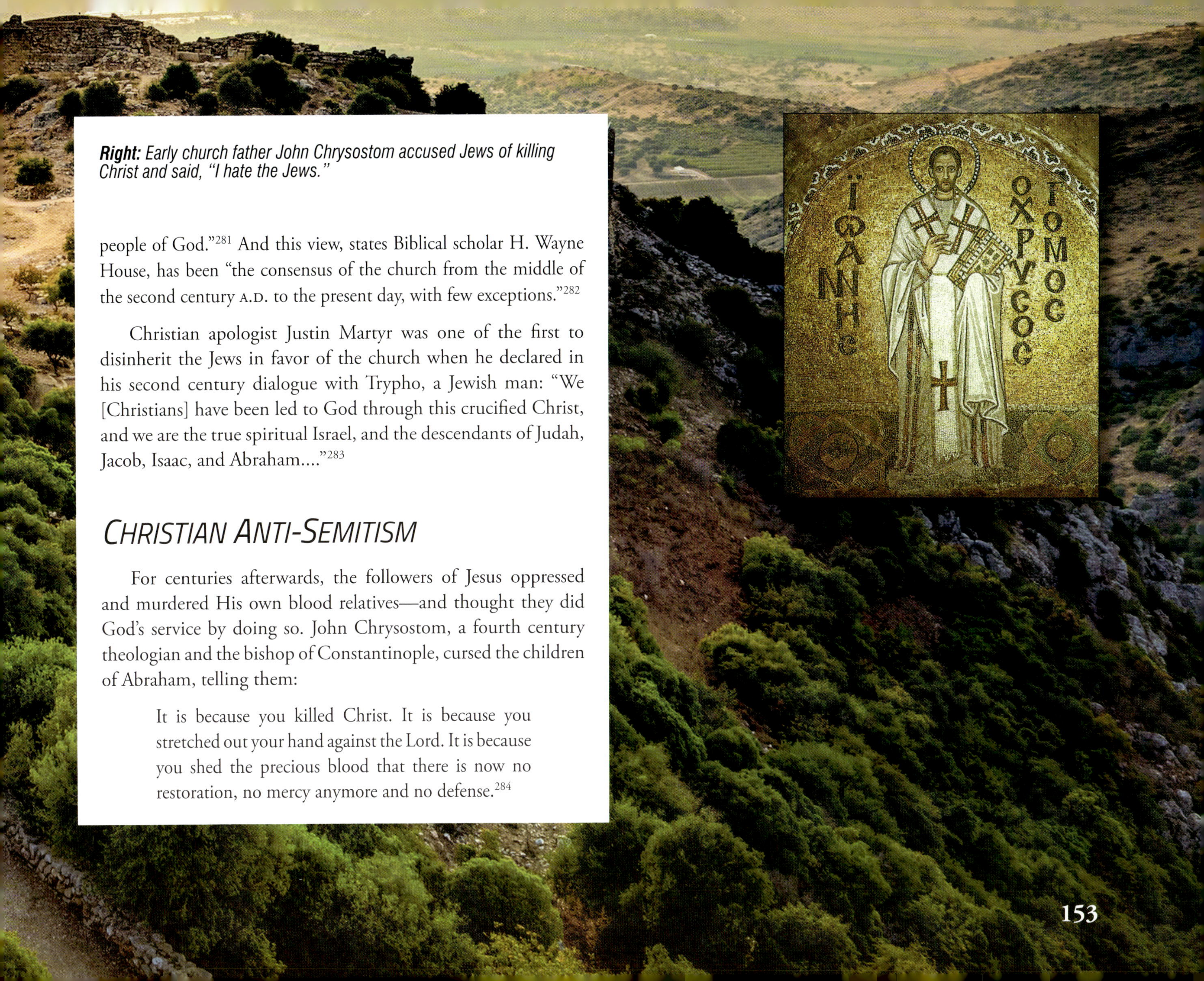

Right: *Early church father John Chrysostom accused Jews of killing Christ and said, "I hate the Jews."*

people of God."[281] And this view, states Biblical scholar H. Wayne House, has been "the consensus of the church from the middle of the second century A.D. to the present day, with few exceptions."[282]

Christian apologist Justin Martyr was one of the first to disinherit the Jews in favor of the church when he declared in his second century dialogue with Trypho, a Jewish man: "We [Christians] have been led to God through this crucified Christ, and we are the true spiritual Israel, and the descendants of Judah, Jacob, Isaac, and Abraham...."[283]

CHRISTIAN ANTI-SEMITISM

For centuries afterwards, the followers of Jesus oppressed and murdered His own blood relatives—and thought they did God's service by doing so. John Chrysostom, a fourth century theologian and the bishop of Constantinople, cursed the children of Abraham, telling them:

> It is because you killed Christ. It is because you stretched out your hand against the Lord. It is because you shed the precious blood that there is now no restoration, no mercy anymore and no defense.[284]

Top Left: *Crusader conquest of Jerusalem depicted on the doors of the Milan Cathedral.*

Bottom Left: *Montfort Crusader Castle in upper Galilee in northern Israel. Built in 12th century.*

Chrysostom considered the synagogue "worse than a brothel," a "den of scoundrels and the repair of wild beasts" and "a place of meeting for the assassins of Christ." None too surprisingly, he also said, "I hate the synagogue.... I hate the Jews for the same reason."[285] Catholic historian Malcolm Hay comments that, "For many centuries the Jews listened to the echo of those three words of St. John Chrysostom, the Golden-Mouthed: 'God hates you.'"[286]

Michael Brown, author of *Our Hands Are Stained with Blood*, provides a summary of Jewish woe under Christian rule:

> During the long, dark years of the Middle Ages, Jews were frequently given the option of baptism or expulsion, baptism or torture, baptism or death. Every type of degrading law was passed against them: They were forbidden to work good jobs; after all, they were an accursed people, assassins of Christ, so how could they be allowed to prosper? They were forced to listen to humiliating public sermons aimed at their conversion—wasn't this the holy obligation of the Church? Their children were kidnapped

Right: *Crusader castle Mirabel in central Israel. Israel has more crusader castles than any other nation.*

> and baptized as "Christians," thus saving them from the fires of hell. They were rounded up and beaten as a highlight of Easter celebrations, since they deserved it as murderers of the Lord. And in the fervor and fanaticism of the Crusades, as the riffraff of Europe gathered to "liberate" the Holy Land from the Muslim infidels, a great new discovery was made: There were infidels that could be killed in their own backyard! Why wait for the Holy Land? And so the hideous slogan was born: "Kill a Jew and save your soul!"[287]

And once in the Holy Land, some Crusaders committed more mayhem, torching a Jerusalem synagogue during the First Crusade (1069-99 A.D.). They burned the Jews within alive, "circling the screaming, flame-tortured humanity singing 'Christ We Adore Thee!' with their Crusader crosses held high."[288]

Church councils from the fourth to the fifteenth century prohibited Jews from holding public office, owning Christian servants, constructing new synagogues, and forced them to wear special clothes and live in ghettoes.[289]

The Lateran Council of 1215, which gathered church leaders from across western Christianity, ruled that Jews "in all Christendom and in all times" "were ordained to wear a distinctive

Seawall at Acre in northern Israel at sunset.

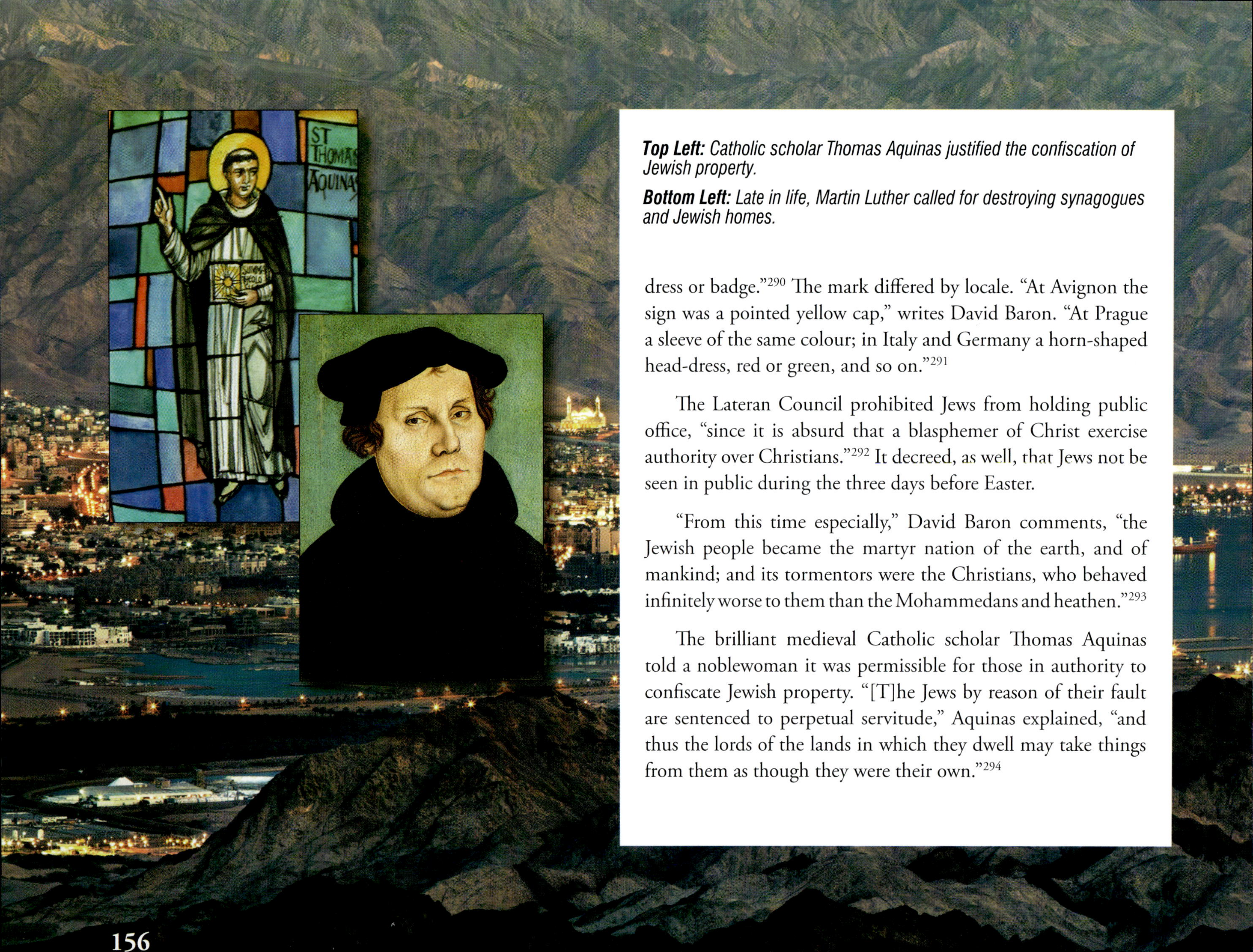

Top Left: *Catholic scholar Thomas Aquinas justified the confiscation of Jewish property.*

Bottom Left: *Late in life, Martin Luther called for destroying synagogues and Jewish homes.*

dress or badge."[290] The mark differed by locale. "At Avignon the sign was a pointed yellow cap," writes David Baron. "At Prague a sleeve of the same colour; in Italy and Germany a horn-shaped head-dress, red or green, and so on."[291]

The Lateran Council prohibited Jews from holding public office, "since it is absurd that a blasphemer of Christ exercise authority over Christians."[292] It decreed, as well, that Jews not be seen in public during the three days before Easter.

"From this time especially," David Baron comments, "the Jewish people became the martyr nation of the earth, and of mankind; and its tormentors were the Christians, who behaved infinitely worse to them than the Mohammedans and heathen."[293]

The brilliant medieval Catholic scholar Thomas Aquinas told a noblewoman it was permissible for those in authority to confiscate Jewish property. "[T]he Jews by reason of their fault are sentenced to perpetual servitude," Aquinas explained, "and thus the lords of the lands in which they dwell may take things from them as though they were their own."[294]

Luther: Set Synagogues on Fire

Martin Luther complained in 1523 that the Roman Catholic Church had "dealt with the Jews as if they were dogs and not human beings."[295] But at the end of his life, Luther wrote *The Jews and Their Lies*, outlining his plan to deal with them:

> First, their synagogues or churches should he set on fire, and whatever does not burn up should be covered or spread over with dirt so that no one may ever be able to see a cinder or stone of it. And this ought to be done for the honor of God and of Christianity in order that God may see that we are Christians.... Secondly, their homes should be broken down and destroyed. Thirdly, they should be deprived of their prayer books and Talmuds in which such idolatry, lies, cursing and blasphemy are taught. Fourthly, their Rabbis must be forbidden under threat of death ... to teach any more.[296]

Luther's chilling words, along with centuries of Christian mistreatment and oppression of Jews, set the table for Hitler's evil work to exterminate European Jewry. Holocaust historian Raul Hilberg showed that all Nazi policies—except for the extermination of the Jews—merely mimicked practices already put in place by the church centuries earlier.[297] As Hilberg wrote, "The

Night lights of Eilat, an Israeli resort city of 50,000 people on the Gulf of Aqaba.

Amos Ben Gershom/Israeli Government Press Office

With 200,000 people, Beersheba is the largest city in Israel's Negev.

Left: *Pope John Paul II praying at the Western Wall in 2000.*

German Nazis, then, did not discard the past; they built upon it. They did not begin a development; they completed it."[298]

The Roman Catholic Church repudiated anti-Semitism in 1965, rejecting the charge of "deicide" against the Jewish people and acknowledging God's election of the Jews.[299] Pope John Paul II publicly apologized for Catholic persecution of Jews in 2000 during a visit to Israel. He took numerous other actions in pursuit of Christian-Jewish reconciliation during his papacy, including the publication in 1998 of "We Remember: A Reflection on the Shoah [Holocaust]," which declared the Church's "deep sorrow for the failures of her sons and daughters in every age."[300]

Anti-Israel Christians Today

The crude and abhorrent anti-Semitism of the church is in the past, but some Protestants now adopt a harshly critical attitude toward Israel. Instead of blessing the Jews and seeking the peace of Jerusalem, mainline Protestants and some evangelicals echo Palestinian charges against the Jewish state. These Christians publish one-sided critiques that focus blame on Israel, absolve Palestinians for assaults on Jews, and soft-pedal Muslim persecution of Christians.

The World Council of Churches (WCC) is a leading advocate for the anti-Israel boycott, disinvestment and sanctions (BDS) campaign—a Palestinian initiative to delegitimize Israel and eliminate the Jewish state. The WCC, which claims to represent 500 million Christians in 348 church bodies, is the world's largest interchurch organization. It routinely denies Israel's right to exist and has endorsed the Kairos Palestine statement, which denies the Jewish people's historic link to the land of Israel.[301]

Outgoing WCC leader Samuel Kobia rebuked Israel for its "sin against God" in 2009. Kobia blamed the Jewish state for its "occupation" and "humiliation of a whole people for over six decades." At the same time, he said nothing about Islam's war on Christians, the third-class status imposed on Christians in many sharia-ruled Muslim states, and the total prohibition on Christianity in Saudi Arabia.[302]

The World Council of Churches partnered with the like-minded National Council of Churches (NCC) in 2016 to ask the U.S. to "reconsider" its military aid to Israel—funding which is vital to Israel's security. The two ecumenical groups urged "an end to the occupation and to settlements on occupied land," but did not call upon Palestinians to acknowledge Israel's right to exist as a Jewish state—something Palestinian leaders refuse to do. And the WCC/NCC statement was silent, as the Anti-Defamation League observed, about Iran, Hezbollah and ISIS—all regimes committed to Israel's annihilation.[303]

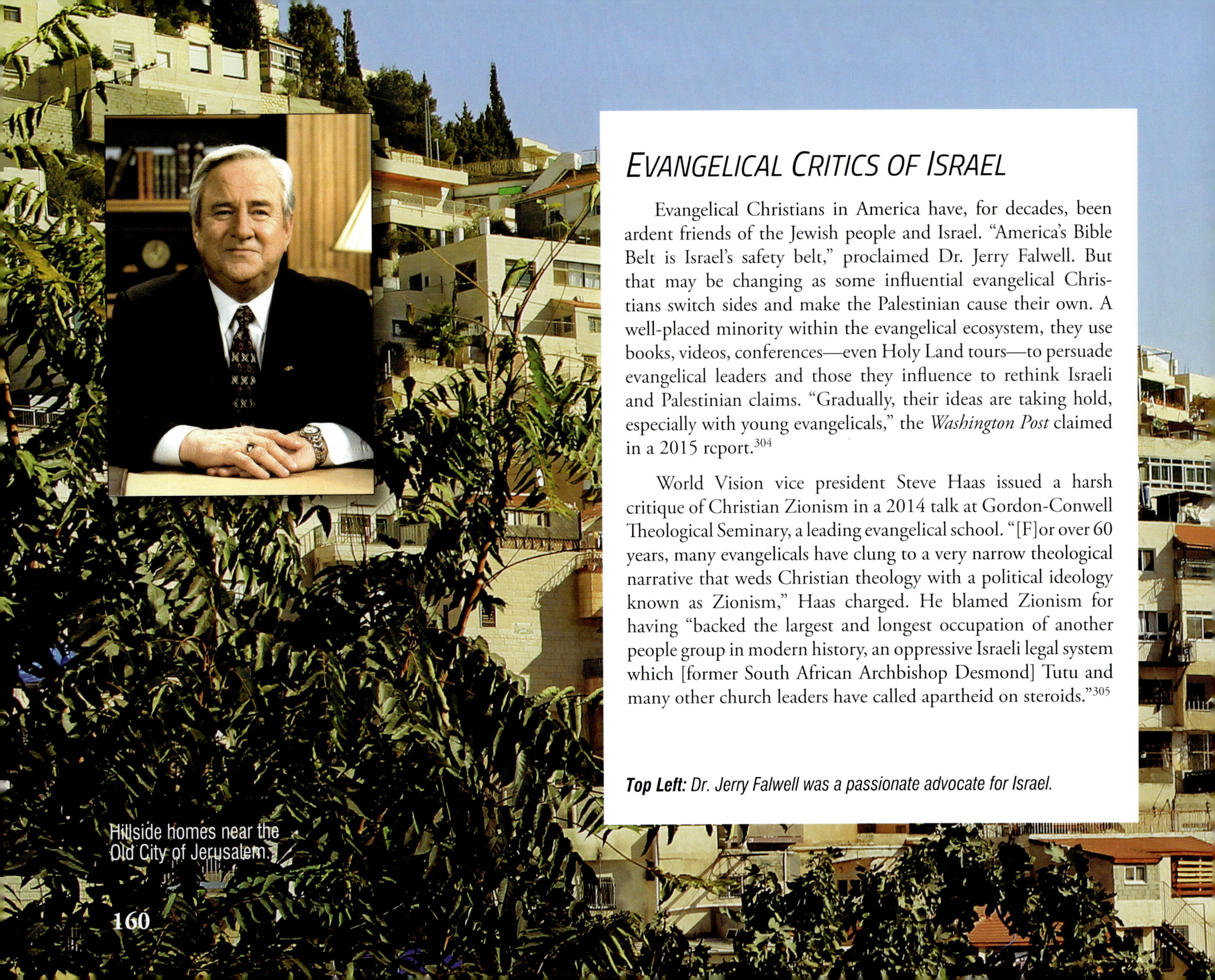

Hillside homes near the Old City of Jerusalem.

EVANGELICAL CRITICS OF ISRAEL

Evangelical Christians in America have, for decades, been ardent friends of the Jewish people and Israel. "America's Bible Belt is Israel's safety belt," proclaimed Dr. Jerry Falwell. But that may be changing as some influential evangelical Christians switch sides and make the Palestinian cause their own. A well-placed minority within the evangelical ecosystem, they use books, videos, conferences—even Holy Land tours—to persuade evangelical leaders and those they influence to rethink Israeli and Palestinian claims. "Gradually, their ideas are taking hold, especially with young evangelicals," the *Washington Post* claimed in a 2015 report.[304]

World Vision vice president Steve Haas issued a harsh critique of Christian Zionism in a 2014 talk at Gordon-Conwell Theological Seminary, a leading evangelical school. "[F]or over 60 years, many evangelicals have clung to a very narrow theological narrative that weds Christian theology with a political ideology known as Zionism," Haas charged. He blamed Zionism for having "backed the largest and longest occupation of another people group in modern history, an oppressive Israeli legal system which [former South African Archbishop Desmond] Tutu and many other church leaders have called apartheid on steroids."[305]

Top Left: *Dr. Jerry Falwell was a passionate advocate for Israel.*

Right: *Liberal evangelical Tony Campolo has addressed the pro-Palestinian Christ at the Checkpoint conference in Bethlehem.*

World Vision quickly distanced itself from his sharp attack, but it was not out of character for the billion-dollar relief organization with strong evangelical roots and a legacy of anti-Israel bias. Among other things, the aid group has sponsored the Christ at the Checkpoint conference in Bethlehem, a forum where evangelical and others attack Israel and advance the Palestinian agenda. American evangelicals who have addressed the conference include Haas, left-wing evangelical author Tony Campolo; Willow Creek co-founder Lynne Hybels; Wheaton professor Gary Burge; and Christian radio host Hank Hanegraaff.

Alex Awad, who spearheaded the conference,[306] calls Israel's founding "illegitimate" and "immoral." He charges "Christian fundamentalists" with "blindly supporting Israel," saying they "are destroying the church by tolerating and endorsing injustice."[307] The conference name, itself, suggests Jesus is a Palestinian who must submit to onerous inspections when entering Israel. In fact, Israeli checkpoints are not an instrument of oppression but a burden made necessary by Palestinian terrorism.

"Jesus was a Palestinian who was born under occupation. Jesus lived under occupation," Naim Ateek charged at a Christ at the Checkpoint conference. In a striking anti-Semitic outburst, Ateek, founder of the Jerusalem-based Sabeel Ecumenical Liberation Theology Center, not only altered Jesus' Jewish identity but

equated modern Israel, the lone Middle East democracy, with the cruel Roman Empire: "Everything he taught, everything he said, was done under occupation, exactly the way we live today."[308]

Haas, Anglican priest Stephen Sizer and Lynne Hybels led a 2011 Holy Land tour to give U.S. church leaders an understanding of the "current tragic conflict in the Holy Land."[309] Co-sponsored by World Vision and the Willow Creek Association, the tour enjoyed assistance from the Holy Land Trust, a Bethlehem-based group which supports the anti-Israel BDS movement.

NGO Monitor, a pro-Israel watchdog, charges Holy Land Trust with conducting "highly politicized tours promoting the Palestinian narrative and targeting church leaders." While espousing non-violence, Holy Land Trust executive director Sami Awad has also said non-violent protests are "not a substitute for the armed struggle."[310]

Stephen Sizer, the author of *Christian Zionism: Road Map to Armageddon?*, has denounced Christian Zionists. "There are certainly churches in Israel/Palestine that side with the occupation, that side with Zionism," Sizer said. "One of my burdens is to challenge them theologically and show that they've repudiated Jesus, they've repudiated the Bible, and they are an abomination."[311]

But terror chief Yasser Arafat is, apparently someone with whom Sizer was on friendly terms. A photo viewable on Sizer's Flickr page shows Sizer smiling broadly while standing in a shoul-

Right: *Anti-Israel billionaire George Soros has funded evangelical trips to Israel that promote the Palestinian perspective.*

der-to-shoulder embrace with Arafat, a cunning and ruthless mass-murderer who earned fame as the Soviet-trained father of modern terrorism (The Arafat/Sizer photo is at www.flickr.com/photos/stephensizer/8561122135/).[312]

Anti-Israel billionaire George Soros has sent more than $700,000 to the Telos Group,[313] which takes groups of evangelical leaders to Israel each year, treating them to pilgrimages that promote the Palestinian perspective. Armed with an anti-Israel view of the conflict, some of these influential evangelicals return to the U.S. to write and blog, and distance evangelicals from Israel.

IMPACT ON YOUNG EVANGELICALS

Anti-Israel films are challenging Christian support for the Jewish state, too. These slick productions distort the facts but reach a broad evangelical audience. The 2009 film *With God on Our Side* screened at churches and colleges, but its pro-Palestinian slant caused World Vision to pull its endorsement, saying the "film should have done a better job in presenting the Israeli perspective."[314]

Christian retailer Mart Green, a member of the family who owns Hobby Lobby, financed *Little Town of Bethlehem*, a 2010 documentary that profiles three peace advocates to give viewers

Harald Dettenborn

Medjool date palm trees in Ein Gedi. Known as the "king of dates," Medjool dates are sweet and healthy treats.

Palm branches reach toward a pale blue sky.

***Left:** Anti-Zionist videos* Little Town of Bethlehem *and* With God on Our Side *influence evangelicals with a distorted view of the Israeli/Palestinian conflict.*

a Christian, Muslim, and Jewish perspective on the Israeli/Palestinian conflict. But each figure followed in the film—Palestinian Christian Sami Awad, Palestinian Muslim Ahmad Al Azzeh, and Israeli Jew Yonatan Shapira—"tell the same story—that Palestinians are innocent victims of an oppressive Israeli occupation, much like the Roman occupation in the time of Jesus."[315]

And Awad's commitment to nonviolence is open to question. The founder of the Holy Land Trust, Awad favorably compares the peaceful U.S. civil rights movement in the 1960s with a bloody Palestinian uprising. "The First Intifada was a lot like the civil rights movement in the U.S.," Awad pronounces on the film, which was screened at some 400 colleges and other venues.[316] In fact, the First Intifada (1987-1993) was a protracted period of violence during which Palestinians used Molotov cocktails, hand grenades and guns to kill 16 Israeli civilians and 11 IDF soldiers. Some 1,100 Palestinians were killed in confrontations with Israeli security forces.[317]

Ahmad Al Azzeh, who worked as a nonviolence trainer at the Holy Land Trust when interviewed for the film, reportedly favors a "one-state solution" and the "right of return" for Palestinian refugees. But that "solution" would put an end to Israel as a Jewish state since it would merge Arabs and Jews into one nation with Palestinian Arabs in the majority.

Jonathan Weiss / Shutterstock, Inc.

Right: *Hobby Lobby chief strategist Mart Green financed the film* Little Town of Bethlehem, *which is sharply critical of Israel.*

Shapira, who served 12 years as an Israel Defense Forces pilot, now says he was "part of a terror organization."[318] An anti-Israel activist, Shapira is a member of Breaking the Silence, a group which charges Israel with "war crimes."[319] Shapira also supports the BDS movement, which seeks the elimination of Israel, and participated in two flotilla attempts to break the Israeli blockade into Gaza.[320]

These three men's views "are the only testimonies presented in the one-sided, anti-Israel documentary financed by Mart Green," writes Tricia Miller, a senior research analyst for CAMERA, the Committee for Accuracy in Middle East Reporting in America.[321]

In June 2016, CAMERA called on Green, chief strategy officer for Hobby Lobby and former Oral Roberts University chairman, to make amends. It asked him to "embark on a campaign to unwind the damage done to the reputation of the Jewish state and the dignity of Jews who claim it as their homeland."[322] Green has never denounced or distanced himself from this anti-Israel propaganda film.

The popular Christian magazine *Relevant* claims to reach 2.3 million "twenty- and thirtysomething Christians" each month through its print and online versions, podcasts and other outlets. Once a strong supporter of Israel, it often gives readers the view from Ramallah—and one factor is a Telos Group tour taken by *Relevant*'s publisher.[323]

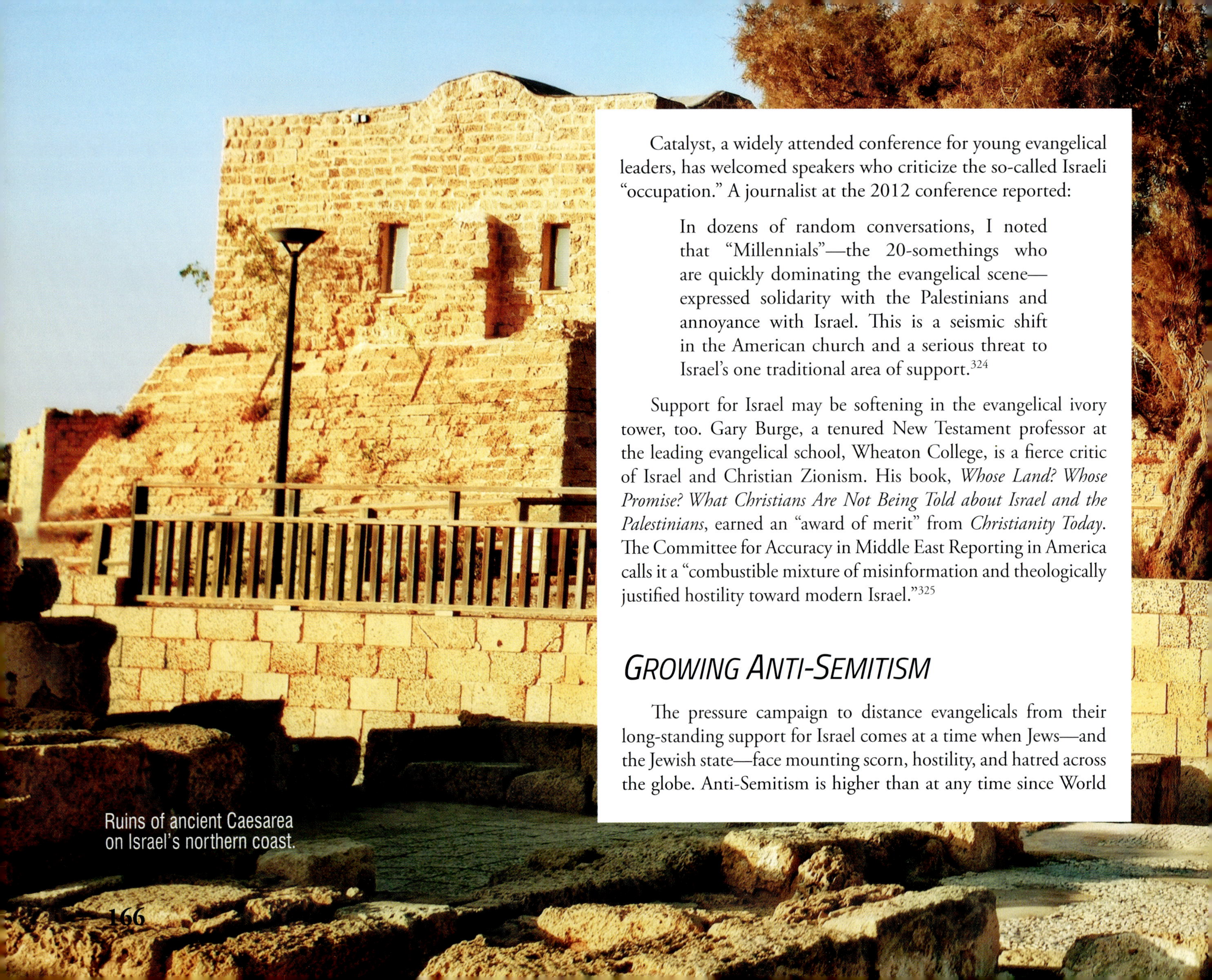

Catalyst, a widely attended conference for young evangelical leaders, has welcomed speakers who criticize the so-called Israeli "occupation." A journalist at the 2012 conference reported:

> In dozens of random conversations, I noted that "Millennials"—the 20-somethings who are quickly dominating the evangelical scene—expressed solidarity with the Palestinians and annoyance with Israel. This is a seismic shift in the American church and a serious threat to Israel's one traditional area of support.[324]

Support for Israel may be softening in the evangelical ivory tower, too. Gary Burge, a tenured New Testament professor at the leading evangelical school, Wheaton College, is a fierce critic of Israel and Christian Zionism. His book, *Whose Land? Whose Promise? What Christians Are Not Being Told about Israel and the Palestinians*, earned an "award of merit" from *Christianity Today*. The Committee for Accuracy in Middle East Reporting in America calls it a "combustible mixture of misinformation and theologically justified hostility toward modern Israel."[325]

Growing Anti-Semitism

The pressure campaign to distance evangelicals from their long-standing support for Israel comes at a time when Jews—and the Jewish state—face mounting scorn, hostility, and hatred across the globe. Anti-Semitism is higher than at any time since World

Ruins of ancient Caesarea on Israel's northern coast.

War II, reports a senior executive at B'nai B'rith International.[326] The percentage of countries where governments or social groups harassed Jews reached a seven-year high of 39 percent in 2013.[327]

"Tens of thousands of Jews [are] leaving France, Belgium and other European countries," because of radical Islam and anti-Semitism, Russia's top rabbi warned in 2016. The Jewish presence in Europe could disappear in 30 years, he predicted, unless action is taken.[328] And the head of the Jewish Agency declared in 2016, "There is no future for the Jews in France because of the Arabs, and because of a very anti-Israel position in society...."[329]

Anti-Semitism is spiking on U.S. college campuses, too, with anti-Semitic incidents up 45 percent in the first half of 2016 from the same period in 2015. "Jewish students ... report fearing for their safety and wellbeing," says the Amcha Initiative, which studied hostility toward Jews on more than 100 colleges with large Jewish populations.[330] Alan Dershowitz, a Harvard law professor and pro-Israel voice, recalls encountering "passionate hatred, ecstatic hatred," even "orgasmic hatred," from students who detested his support for the Jewish state. "When I looked into their faces, I could imagine young Nazis in the 1930s in Hitler's Germany."[331]

And hatred for the state of Israel is also soaring. A 2013 BBC poll measuring global attitudes toward 22 countries found the Jewish state ranked near the bottom. The only other nations less popular were North Korea, Pakistan, and Iran.[332] Thirty-one UN member countries—including 18 Muslim-majority nations—refuse to recognize or grant full diplomatic relations with the Jewish state.

Sage Ross

Morning sun brightens homes in Gilo, a neighborhood on Jerusalem's southeastern edge.

Left: *Harvard law professor Alan Dershowitz, who is Jewish, encountered anti-Israel rage from students at American universities.*

"[T]oday in the countries of the world, Israel is a pariah state," declared Israel's Strategic Affairs Ministry Director General Sima Vaknin in 2016, listing the Israel equals apartheid canard as one reason.[333]

A leading cause of Israel's tarnished standing on the world stage is the movement to boycott, divest and sanction Israel (BDS). Launched in 2005 by a coalition of Palestinian organizations, the BDS campaign calls on "people of conscience all over the world to impose broad boycotts" and "divestment initiatives against Israel." It urges government sanctions against the Jewish state—the lone democracy in the Middle East.

While Arab boycotts against Jewish interests are nothing new—the Fifth Palestine-Arab Congress called for a boycott in 1922 and the Arab League launched its boycott in 1945—BDS organizers lobby for the worldwide isolation of Israel. It is a global economic, political and cultural jihad against the Jewish state.

"We are in the midst of a great struggle being waged against the state of Israel, an international campaign to blacken its name," Israel Prime Minister Benjamin Netanyahu warned in 2015. "It is not connected to our actions; it is connected to our very existence."[334]

Right: *Demonstrators protest Israel and support the BDS movement to boycott the Jewish state in a 2014 march in Washington, D.C.*

Ryan Rodick Beller/Shutterstock, Inc

Three Key BDS Demands

Israel's existence is, in fact, the real "problem" the BDS movement seek to "solve." Backed by enemies of Israel like the Muslim Brotherhood, Hamas, and the Palestinian Authority, the campaign makes three sweeping demands on Israel:

1) end "its occupation and colonization of all Arab lands" and dismantle "the Wall"

2) recognize "the fundamental rights of the Arab-Palestinian citizens of Israel to full equality

3) allow "Palestinian refugees to return to their homes and properties."[335]

But meeting these demands—which, as stated, slander Israel and profoundly distort Israeli/Arab reality—would mean the end of the Jewish state. Restoring "all Arab lands" would mean giving up 100 percent of Israel since Hamas regards Israel's entire land mass as occupied Arab land and so does the Palestinian Authority. Palestinian Media Watch reports that the official Palestinian Authority TV station tells children Israeli cities are "occupied" Palestinian cities.[336]

Arab Israelis already enjoy equal rights in Israel—including the rights to free speech, vote, run for office, sit in the Knesset

***Left:** Palestinian Authority TV program announces Israeli cities are "occupied cities."*

and serve as a justice on Israel's Supreme Court. No Arab nation gives its citizens the same full spectrum of freedoms. And Israeli Arabs have enjoyed these liberties since Israel's founding.

ENDING ISRAEL

The final BDS demand, an unlimited right of return for Palestinians is a poison pill. It would create a Palestinian majority within Israel and put an end to the Jewish state. Which is what BDS advocates want.

"Definitely, most definitely we oppose a Jewish state in any part of Palestine. No Palestinian, rational Palestinian, not a sell-out Palestinian, will ever accept a Jewish state in Palestine," declares BDS leader Omar Barghouti.[337] And violence is a legitimate tool, as well, for Barghouti who justifies "resistance by any means, including armed resistance."[338]

DUTY TO DEFEND

Now is the time for more Christians to take up the defense of Israel and the Jewish people. Fortunately, evangelicals have led the way in doing so over the last four decades. A 2014 Pew

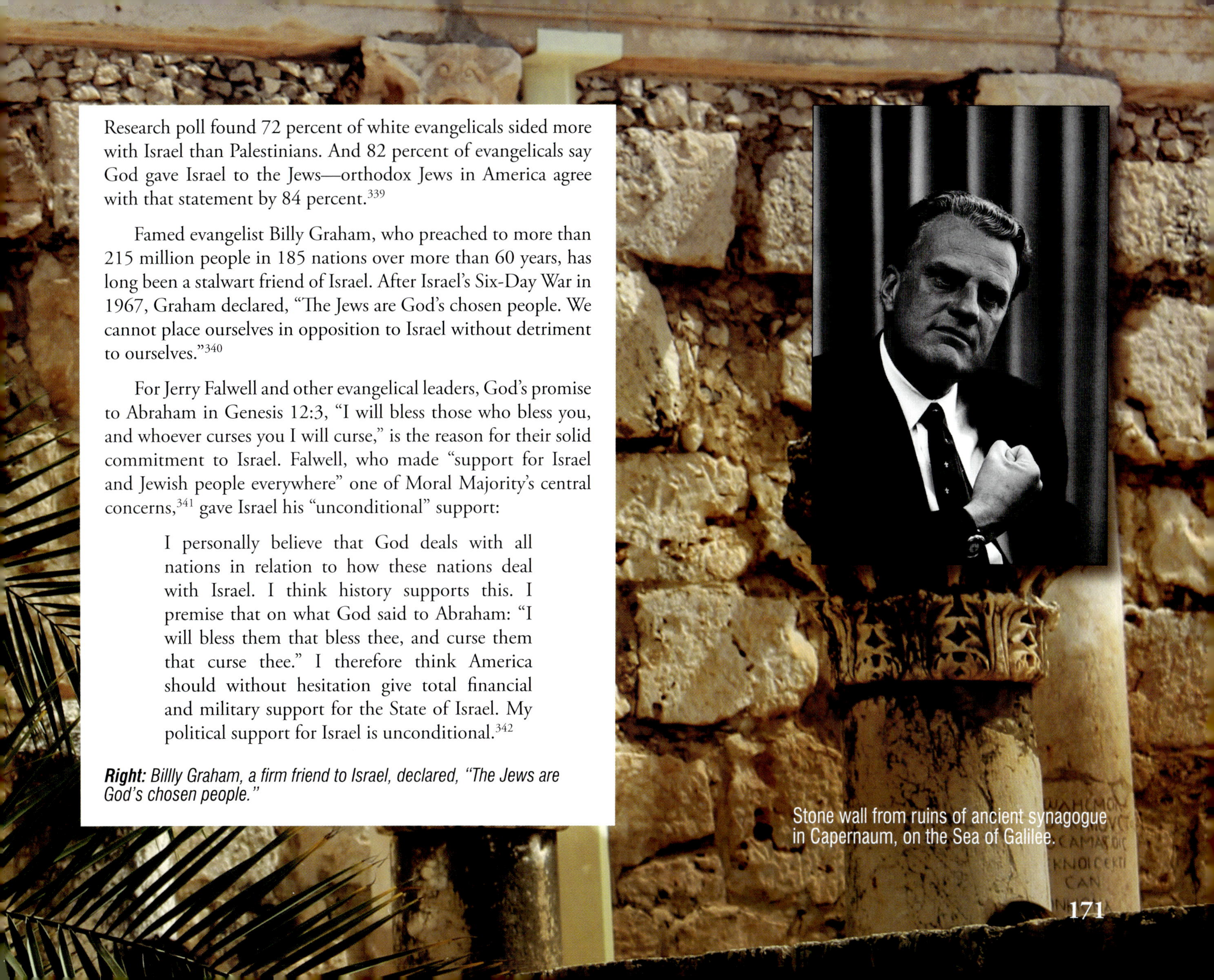

Research poll found 72 percent of white evangelicals sided more with Israel than Palestinians. And 82 percent of evangelicals say God gave Israel to the Jews—orthodox Jews in America agree with that statement by 84 percent.[339]

Famed evangelist Billy Graham, who preached to more than 215 million people in 185 nations over more than 60 years, has long been a stalwart friend of Israel. After Israel's Six-Day War in 1967, Graham declared, "The Jews are God's chosen people. We cannot place ourselves in opposition to Israel without detriment to ourselves."[340]

For Jerry Falwell and other evangelical leaders, God's promise to Abraham in Genesis 12:3, "I will bless those who bless you, and whoever curses you I will curse," is the reason for their solid commitment to Israel. Falwell, who made "support for Israel and Jewish people everywhere" one of Moral Majority's central concerns,[341] gave Israel his "unconditional" support:

> I personally believe that God deals with all nations in relation to how these nations deal with Israel. I think history supports this. I premise that on what God said to Abraham: "I will bless them that bless thee, and curse them that curse thee." I therefore think America should without hesitation give total financial and military support for the State of Israel. My political support for Israel is unconditional.[342]

Right: *Billly Graham, a firm friend to Israel, declared, "The Jews are God's chosen people."*

Stone wall from ruins of ancient synagogue in Capernaum, on the Sea of Galilee.

Moshe Milner/Israeli Government Press Office.

Lush green of Israeli fields and forests west of the Sea of Galilee.

***Left:** Israeli Prime Minister Menachem Begin, far left, meets in 1980 with evangelical leaders, including Jerry Falwell, D. James Kennedy, Adrian Rogers and Charles Stanley.*

Christian broadcaster Pat Robertson is another leading pro-Israel voice. He told an audience in Israel in 2004 the following:

> Evangelical Christians support Israel because we believe that the words of Moses and the ancient prophets of Israel were inspired by God. We believe that the emergence of a Jewish state in the land promised by God to Abraham, Isaac, and Jacob was ordained by God.[343]

John Hagee, pastor of Cornerstone Church in San Antonio, Texas, first hosted a "Night to Honor Israel" rally in 1981. Similar events have since been held in communities across America through Christians United for Israel, a million-member organization Hagee founded in 2006. Christians have a "biblical mandate to bless the Jews," Hagee says.

Christians in Defense of Israel, which I have the privilege to lead, speaks out on behalf of Israel and the shared values that link America to the Jewish state. It's my belief that Israel and America share a common bond through our history, heritage, and faith. That is why Christians must stand in solidarity with Israel and its right to exist as a sovereign nation.

Our Liberty Counsel Ambassador trips to Israel, along with our Covenant Journey program for Christian college-age students

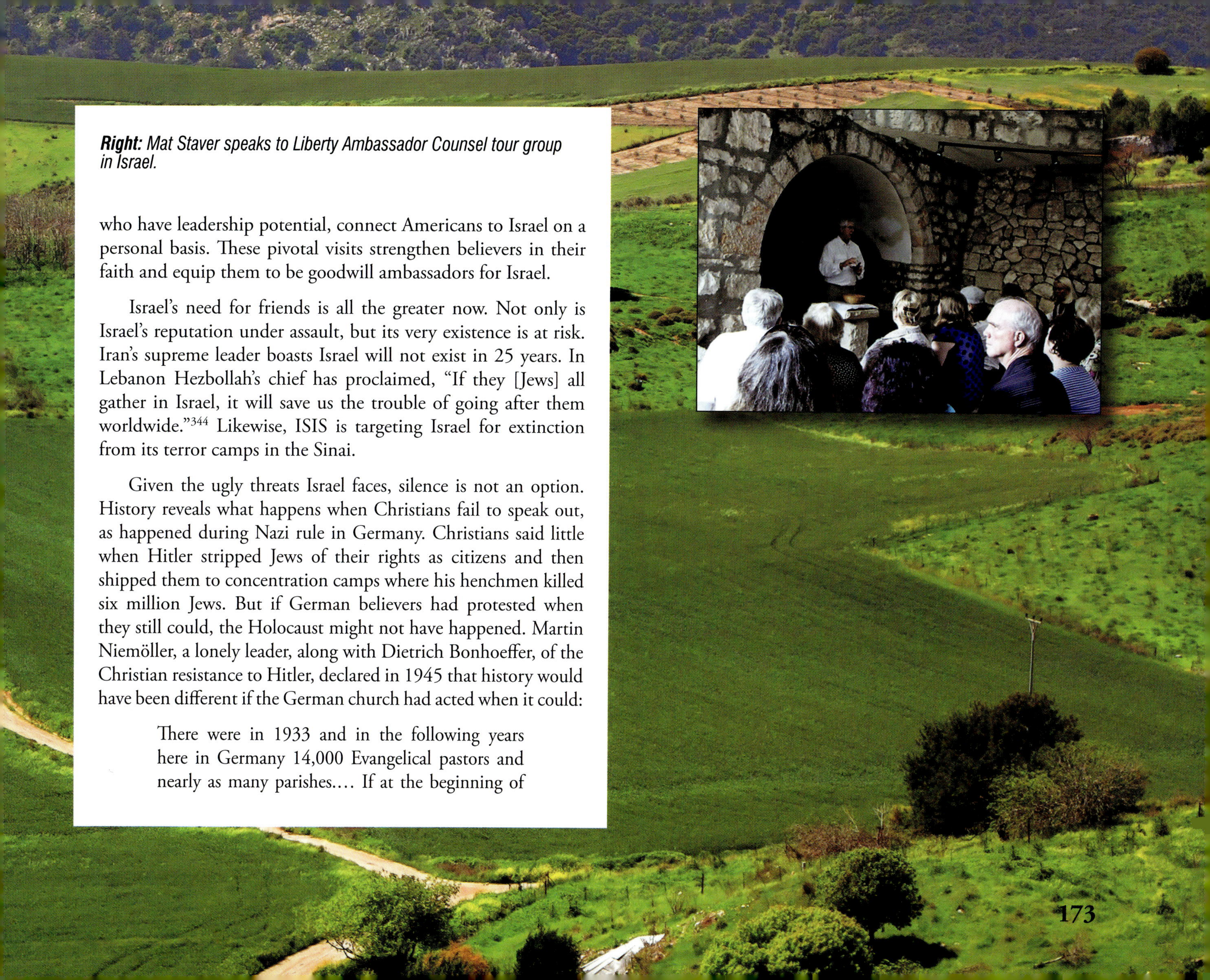

Right: *Mat Staver speaks to Liberty Ambassador Counsel tour group in Israel.*

who have leadership potential, connect Americans to Israel on a personal basis. These pivotal visits strengthen believers in their faith and equip them to be goodwill ambassadors for Israel.

Israel's need for friends is all the greater now. Not only is Israel's reputation under assault, but its very existence is at risk. Iran's supreme leader boasts Israel will not exist in 25 years. In Lebanon Hezbollah's chief has proclaimed, "If they [Jews] all gather in Israel, it will save us the trouble of going after them worldwide."[344] Likewise, ISIS is targeting Israel for extinction from its terror camps in the Sinai.

Given the ugly threats Israel faces, silence is not an option. History reveals what happens when Christians fail to speak out, as happened during Nazi rule in Germany. Christians said little when Hitler stripped Jews of their rights as citizens and then shipped them to concentration camps where his henchmen killed six million Jews. But if German believers had protested when they still could, the Holocaust might not have happened. Martin Niemöller, a lonely leader, along with Dietrich Bonhoeffer, of the Christian resistance to Hitler, declared in 1945 that history would have been different if the German church had acted when it could:

> There were in 1933 and in the following years here in Germany 14,000 Evangelical pastors and nearly as many parishes.... If at the beginning of

Dutch National Archives, and Spaarnestad Photo.

Mediterranean surf breaks on shore at sunset.

Left: *More Jews could have been saved from Hitler, Martin Niemöller said, if more Christians had stood in resistance.*

> the Jewish persecutions we had seen that it was the Lord Jesus Christ who was being persecuted, struck down and slain in "the least of these our brethren," if we had been loyal to Him and confessed Him, for all I know God would have stood by us, and then the whole sequence of events would have taken a different course. And if we had been ready to go with Him to death, the number of victims might well have been only some ten thousand.[345]

Likewise, Basilea Schlink, a German Christian leader who lived through the Third Reich, looked back with regret after the war:

> We are personally to blame. We all have to admit that if we, the entire Christian community, had stood up as one man and if, after the burning of the synagogues [on Krystallnacht], we had gone out on the streets and voiced our disapproval, rung the church bells, and somehow boycotted the actions of the S.S., the Devil's vassals would probably not have been at such liberty to pursue their evil schemes.
>
> But we lacked the ardor of love—love that is never passive, love that cannot bear it when its

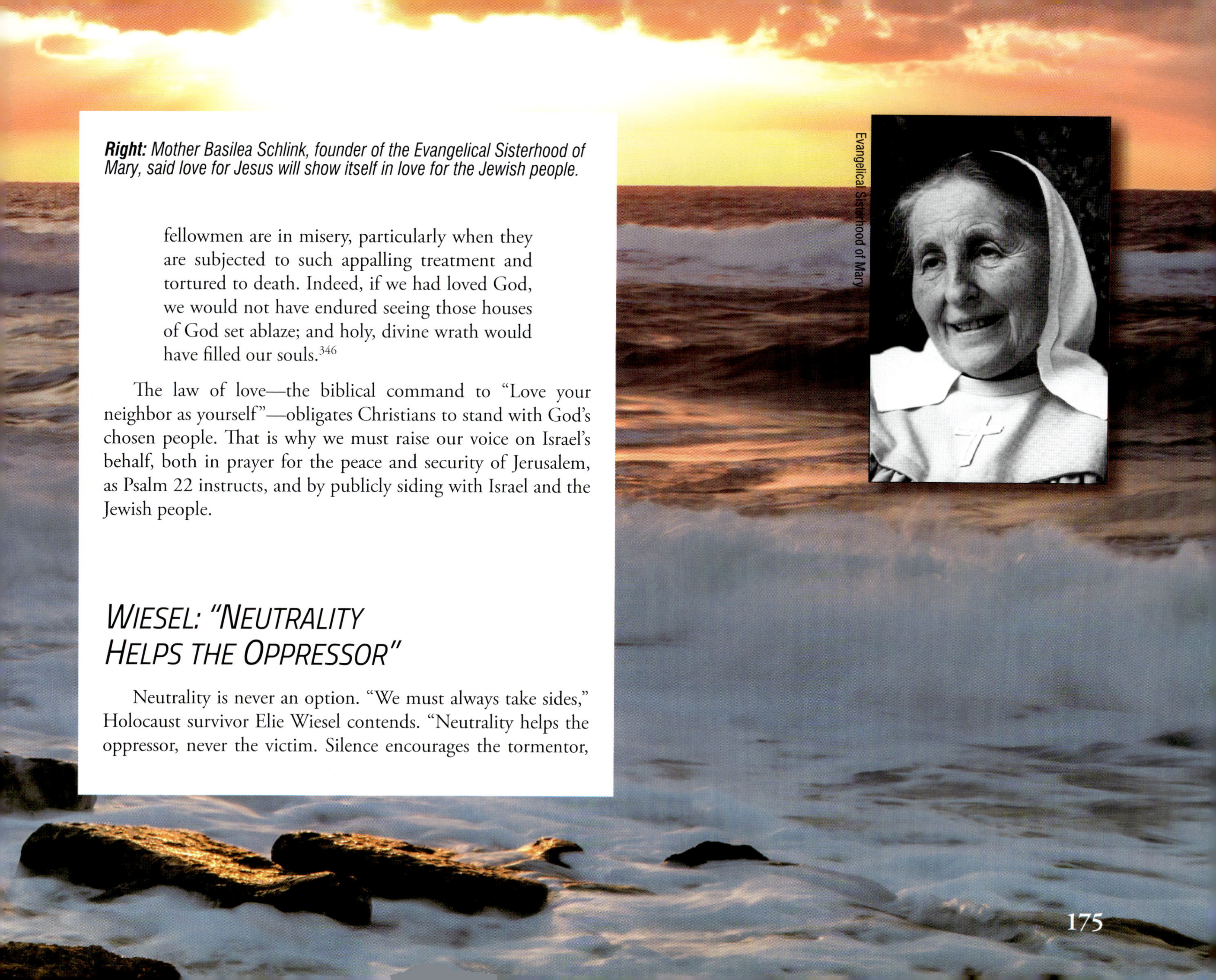

Right: *Mother Basilea Schlink, founder of the Evangelical Sisterhood of Mary, said love for Jesus will show itself in love for the Jewish people.*

> fellowmen are in misery, particularly when they are subjected to such appalling treatment and tortured to death. Indeed, if we had loved God, we would not have endured seeing those houses of God set ablaze; and holy, divine wrath would have filled our souls.[346]

The law of love—the biblical command to "Love your neighbor as yourself"—obligates Christians to stand with God's chosen people. That is why we must raise our voice on Israel's behalf, both in prayer for the peace and security of Jerusalem, as Psalm 22 instructs, and by publicly siding with Israel and the Jewish people.

Wiesel: "Neutrality Helps the Oppressor"

Neutrality is never an option. "We must always take sides," Holocaust survivor Elie Wiesel contends. "Neutrality helps the oppressor, never the victim. Silence encourages the tormentor,

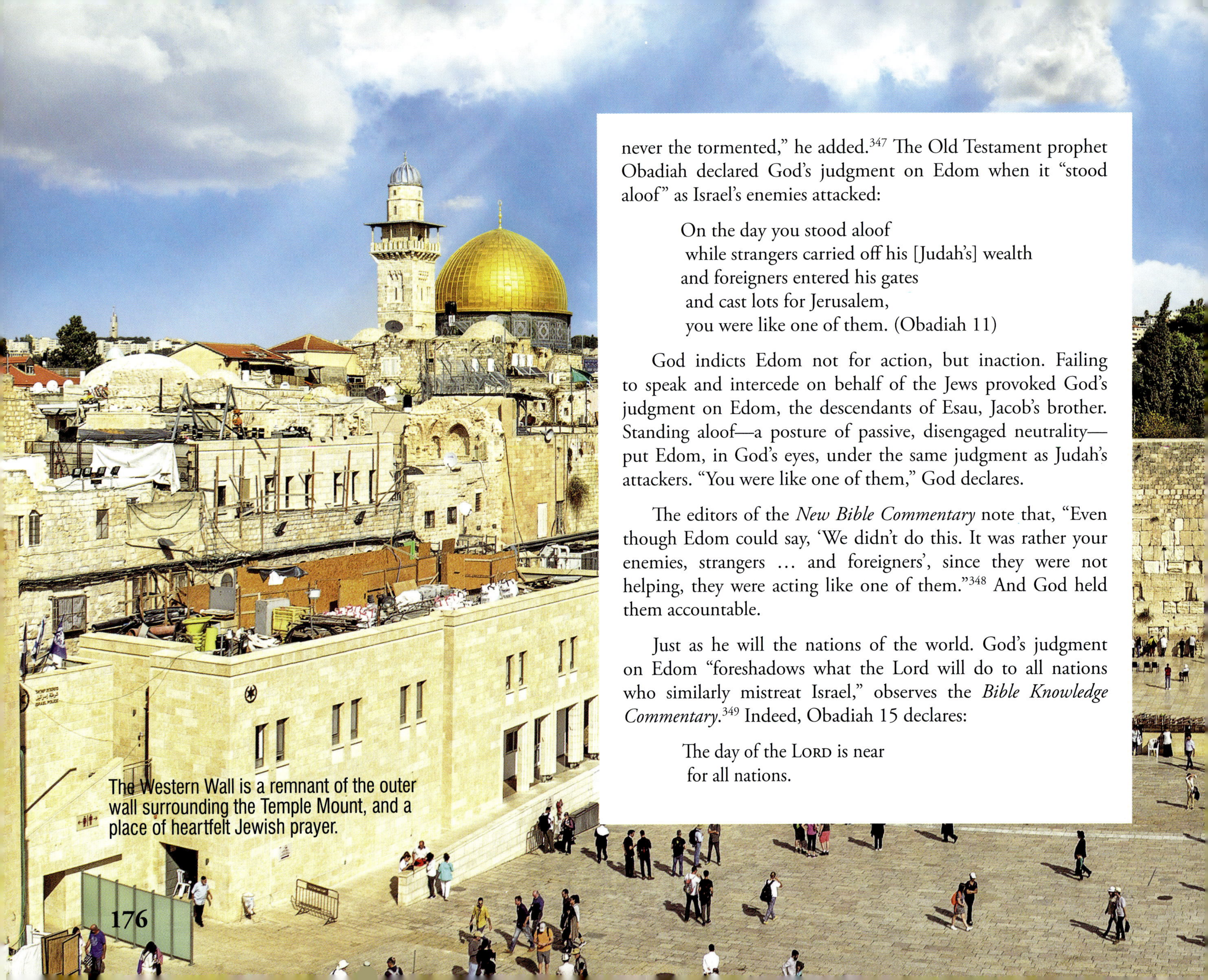

never the tormented," he added.[347] The Old Testament prophet Obadiah declared God's judgment on Edom when it "stood aloof" as Israel's enemies attacked:

> On the day you stood aloof
> while strangers carried off his [Judah's] wealth
> and foreigners entered his gates
> and cast lots for Jerusalem,
> you were like one of them. (Obadiah 11)

God indicts Edom not for action, but inaction. Failing to speak and intercede on behalf of the Jews provoked God's judgment on Edom, the descendants of Esau, Jacob's brother. Standing aloof—a posture of passive, disengaged neutrality—put Edom, in God's eyes, under the same judgment as Judah's attackers. "You were like one of them," God declares.

The editors of the *New Bible Commentary* note that, "Even though Edom could say, 'We didn't do this. It was rather your enemies, strangers … and foreigners', since they were not helping, they were acting like one of them."[348] And God held them accountable.

Just as he will the nations of the world. God's judgment on Edom "foreshadows what the Lord will do to all nations who similarly mistreat Israel," observes the *Bible Knowledge Commentary*.[349] Indeed, Obadiah 15 declares:

> The day of the Lord is near
> for all nations.

The Western Wall is a remnant of the outer wall surrounding the Temple Mount, and a place of heartfelt Jewish prayer.

> As you have done [to Israel], it will be done to you;
> your deeds will return upon your own head.

What is true for the Gentile nations is true, as well, for believers in Jesus. We, too, will be held accountable for our response to His people. In fact, how we treat Israel is a gauge of our relationship with Jesus. "If we love Jesus, we shall love the people whom He loves and always will love and who will yet be the centre and blessing of all nations," insists Basilea Schlink, founder of the Evangelical Sisterhood of Mary.[350]

One reading of Matthew 25 suggests Christ will hold all people accountable for how they treat Israel when He returns to Jerusalem and sits "on his throne in heavenly glory." With all the nations "gathered before him ... he will separate the people one from another as a shepherd separates the sheep from the goats" (v. 32). To the sheep, He announces:

> Come, you who are blessed by my Father; take your inheritance, the kingdom prepared for you since the creation of the world. For I was hungry and you gave me something to eat, I was thirsty and you gave me something to drink, I was a stranger and you invited me in, I needed clothes and you clothed me, I was sick and you looked after me, I was in prison and you came to visit me. (vv. 34-35)

And when the righteous ask the Lord when they came to his aid, He will answer: "I tell you the truth, whatever you did for *one of the least of these brothers of mine*, you did for me" (v. 40).

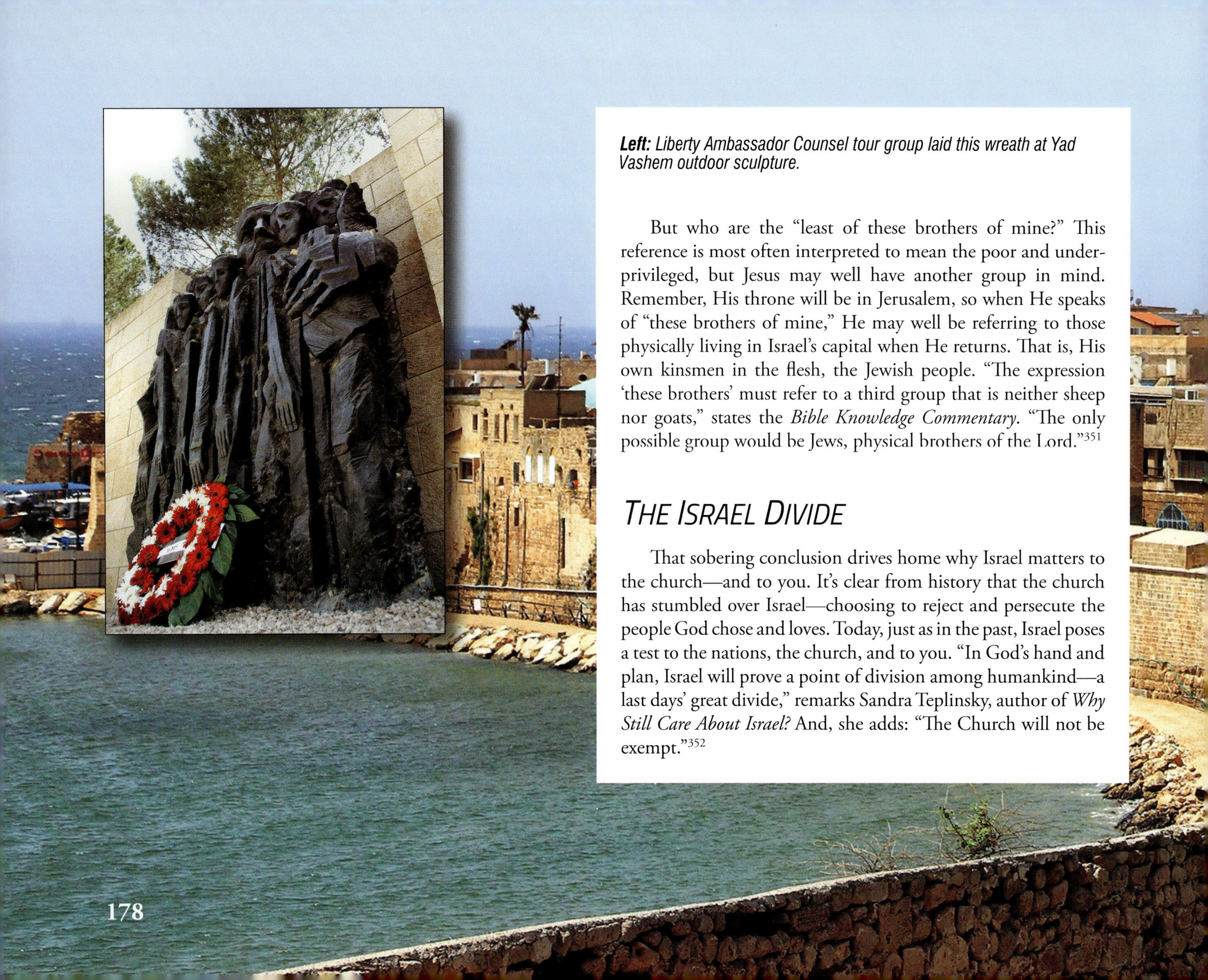

Left: *Liberty Ambassador Counsel tour group laid this wreath at Yad Vashem outdoor sculpture.*

But who are the "least of these brothers of mine?" This reference is most often interpreted to mean the poor and underprivileged, but Jesus may well have another group in mind. Remember, His throne will be in Jerusalem, so when He speaks of "these brothers of mine," He may well be referring to those physically living in Israel's capital when He returns. That is, His own kinsmen in the flesh, the Jewish people. "The expression 'these brothers' must refer to a third group that is neither sheep nor goats," states the *Bible Knowledge Commentary*. "The only possible group would be Jews, physical brothers of the Lord."[351]

The Israel Divide

That sobering conclusion drives home why Israel matters to the church—and to you. It's clear from history that the church has stumbled over Israel—choosing to reject and persecute the people God chose and loves. Today, just as in the past, Israel poses a test to the nations, the church, and to you. "In God's hand and plan, Israel will prove a point of division among humankind—a last days' great divide," remarks Sandra Teplinsky, author of *Why Still Care About Israel?* And, she adds: "The Church will not be exempt."[352]

“Be forewarned,” writes Teplinsky, “God is allowing Israel to serve as a strategic point of division. Some in the Body of Christ will stand with the sons and daughters of Jacob; some will turn away. As conflict escalates between Israel and her enemies, your stand in the end will be less about the Jewish state and more about Him.”[353]

But by standing with Israel, in compassion and courage, you can impact history and speed the advance of God’s kingdom—much as early Christian Zionists proved pivotal to the rebirth of modern Israel. “I don’t believe the Jewish state would have been possible without Christian Zionism,” Israeli Prime Minister Benjamin Netanyahu has said.[354] Just as Christians helped mid-wife the physical restoration of Israel, believers now have a role in its spiritual restoration as well. As a former Israeli Foreign Ministry official observed:

> With Christians now reaching out to the Jewish people in genuine contrition and love, we are witnessing a remarkable phenomenon ... that will, please God, usher in the final redemption of the Jewish people and of all humankind.[355]

God’s Word tells us redemption is coming. “All Israel will be saved,” Paul proclaims. “The deliverer will come from Zion; he will turn godlessness away from Jacob” (Romans 11:26). And when God’s chosen people, at long last, embrace their Messiah,

At the northernmost tip of Haifa Bay is the ancient city of Acre which appears much as it would have during the Crusades.

Paul states in Romans 11 it will be "riches for the world" and "life from the dead."

That, ultimately, is why Israel matters.

You can be a part of making it happen. Pray for the peace of Jerusalem. Bless and defend Israel—and call upon God to hasten her coming redemption.

Epilogue

How You Can Bless Israel

What should Christians do to love and honor Israel? How can you bless Israel?

First and foremost, by reaching out with compassion and conviction to share Jesus with the Jewish people—and by supporting Jewish evangelism. "The best way to bless Israel is with Yeshua the Messiah (Jesus Christ)," proclaims One for Israel, a group of Israeli Jews who believe in Jesus.

God's priority is for the Good News to go "first to the Jew, then to the Gentile" (Romans 1:16), but missionary activity and church resources have reversed the pattern, allocating scant time and resources to reaching the lost sheep of the house of Israel. Learn how to share the Jewish Messiah with the Jewish people and pray that God will open their hearts and minds to the Gospel.

Your prayers for the "peace of Jerusalem" are another way to bless Israel. Ask God to protect and shield Israel from terror attacks and from neighbors, such as Iran, which seek Israel's demise. Pray also for peace with Palestinian Arabs and for a just,

Israeli farms below the Golan Heights in northeast Israel.

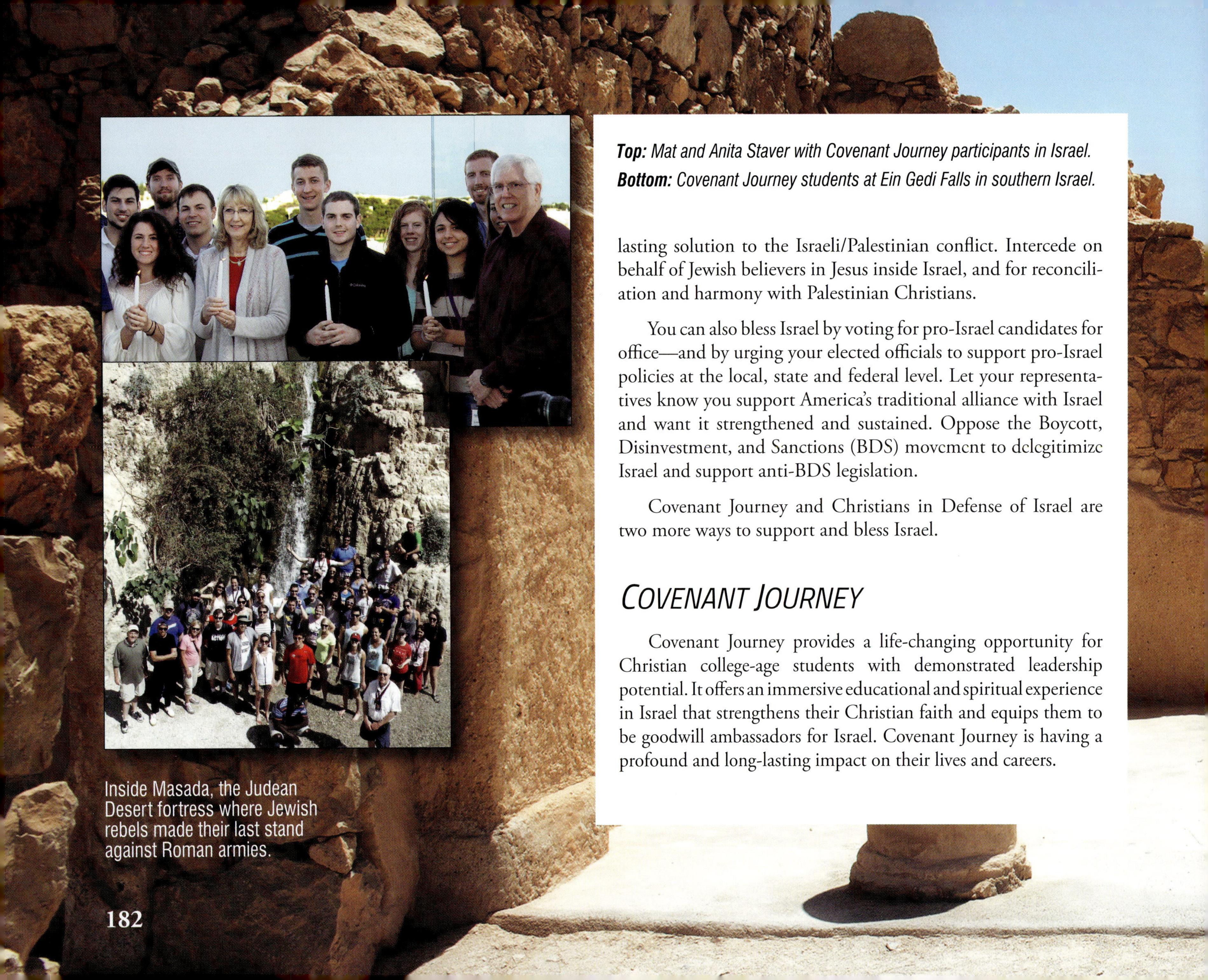

Top: *Mat and Anita Staver with Covenant Journey participants in Israel.*
Bottom: *Covenant Journey students at Ein Gedi Falls in southern Israel.*

Inside Masada, the Judean Desert fortress where Jewish rebels made their last stand against Roman armies.

lasting solution to the Israeli/Palestinian conflict. Intercede on behalf of Jewish believers in Jesus inside Israel, and for reconciliation and harmony with Palestinian Christians.

You can also bless Israel by voting for pro-Israel candidates for office—and by urging your elected officials to support pro-Israel policies at the local, state and federal level. Let your representatives know you support America's traditional alliance with Israel and want it strengthened and sustained. Oppose the Boycott, Disinvestment, and Sanctions (BDS) movement to delegitimize Israel and support anti-BDS legislation.

Covenant Journey and Christians in Defense of Israel are two more ways to support and bless Israel.

COVENANT JOURNEY

Covenant Journey provides a life-changing opportunity for Christian college-age students with demonstrated leadership potential. It offers an immersive educational and spiritual experience in Israel that strengthens their Christian faith and equips them to be goodwill ambassadors for Israel. Covenant Journey is having a profound and long-lasting impact on their lives and careers.

Top Right: *Covenant Journey group lined up to be baptized in the Jordan River.*

Bottom Right: *Mat Staver baptizes a Covenant Journey participant.*

Students selected for Covenant Journey are leaders and will be the future leaders in every industry and profession. In addition to visiting the traditional Biblical and historical sites in Israel, Covenant Journey provides expert speakers in government, national security, military, the Middle East, education, business and technology, and a rare experience to meet a Holocaust survivor. Covenant Journey also provides a variety of internship opportunities to student alumni in Israel and in the United States.

"I had always been very supportive of Israel as a state, but this trip honestly changed everything," said Brianna, who visited Israel on a Covenant Journey trip in 2016. "I absolutely fell hard in love with Israel. I came back to my campus with a strong conviction to minister to Jews, as well as advocate for Israel politically."

Jennifer Sullivan took a Covenant Journey visit to Israel in January 2016, joining 50 other college-age Christians on a 10-day trip of a lifetime. She visited ancient and biblical sites, and discovered firsthand why modern Israel is a place to be celebrated, not scorned.

When Jennifer returned home to Florida, she put what she learned about Israel to very good use. The youngest member of the Florida legislature at 24, she cosponsored Florida's anti-BDS legislation which became law three months after her Covenant Journey.

Left: *Mat Staver meeting Israeli Prime Minister Benjamin Netanyahu in 2011 in Jerusalem.*

The impact of Covenant Journey on the lives of Christian millennials is far beyond what we could have imagined. The Covenant Journey experience will strengthen the Christian faith of the student participants and awaken in them a passion for Israel while equipping them to become goodwill ambassadors for Israel and the Jewish people. Qualified students selected for the Covenant Journey experience pay only a $500 registration fee. All other expenses are covered by Covenant Journey.

For more information and to learn how you can help this important ministry, visit www.CovenantJourney.org.

Christians in Defense of Israel

Christians in Defense of Israel (CIDI) exists to help you stand with Israel and bless the Jewish people. CIDI's mission is to strengthen your Christian faith and inspire you to be a goodwill ambassador for Israel and the Jewish people. With the help of friends like you, we accomplish this mission through education and immersive experiences in Israel.

The impetus for CIDI stems from a meeting Anita and I had in 2011 with Prime Minister Benjamin Netanyahu. We arrived in Israel shortly after President Barack Obama stunned the Jewish state by calling for a return to its narrow and indefensible

***Right:** Liberty Ambassador Counsel tour group in Jerusalem.*

pre-1967 borders. Anita and I came to deliver a simple message: The American people strongly support Israel.

During the meeting, the Prime Minister asked us to help build relationships between Israel and American believers. We eagerly agreed.

Today, our Liberty Ambassador Counsel Tour takes American Christians to Israel, giving them memorable journeys to build their faith and equipping them to be well-informed advocates for Israel. There is no place on earth like Israel. "It is a land the LORD your God cares for; the eyes of the LORD your God are continually on it from the beginning of the year to its end" (Deuteronomy 11:12). That is why your life will never be the same after you visit the Holy Land.

Our internationally aired television series, *Why Israel Matters*, is bringing the inspiring truth about Israel to a global audience. CIDI also enjoys access to key leaders in Israeli government and society.

CIDI is here to give you the opportunity to learn about Israel, to discover the wonders of this land and the people, and to deepen your understanding of the Bible and God's plan for you. You can learn more and become a part of Christians in Defense of Israel when you visit www.CIDIsrael.org.

Kziv River in the upper Galilee flows from the western slopes of Mount Meron in northern Israel.

Seize the Opportunity to Stand with Israel

Finally, let me tell you a story.

A friend of mine was visiting the Holocaust Museum in Jerusalem years ago when an unfamiliar lady approached and asked if he was a Jew. He is a Jewish believer in Jesus, so he informed her of that fact.

Inexplicably. she began to weep. She told him that as a young woman during the Holocaust years, she had lived within sight of Nazi incinerators. Each morning, she could smell the stench of burning flesh. As she sobbed, she said in a broken voice, "I did nothing. I am so very sorry—I did nothing."

May it never be said of you ... may it never be said of me, that we did nothing on Israel's behalf when we had the opportunity. Now is the time to pray and act! Join me and others to bless Israel and stand in her defense.

Appendix A

Biblical and Historical Timeline of Israel

Israel's history stretches across more than 4,000 years, from God's call to Abraham up to the present moment. The preservation and prominence of the Jewish people throughout four millennia, despite exile, persecution, even genocide, is a sobering witness to God's enduring purpose for the people He chose.

The timeline on the following pages provides key markers of biblical and historical events in Israel's past that have shaped the Jewish people and shaped the world. In so doing, it reminds, once more, that Israel matters to the nations, the church, and you.

The lush HaMidron garden located on the scenic slope of Old Jaffa in Tel Aviv.

Biblical and Historical Timeline of Israel

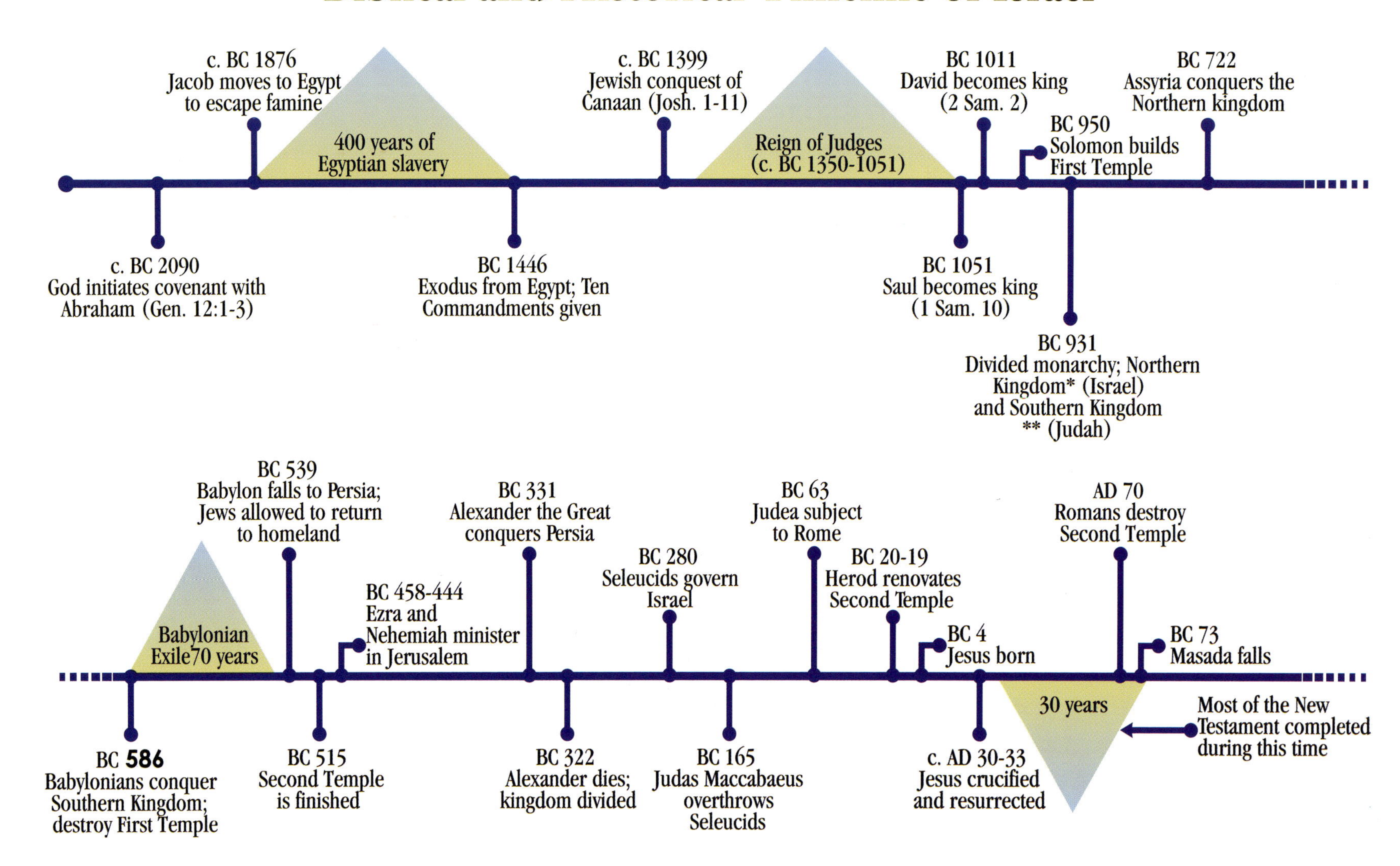

* Northern Kingdom tribes: Asher, Dan, Ephraim, Gad, Issachar, Manasseh, Naphtali, Reuben, Simeon, and Zebulun
** Southern Kingdom tribes: Judah and Benjamin

Biblical and Historical Timeline of Israel (continued)

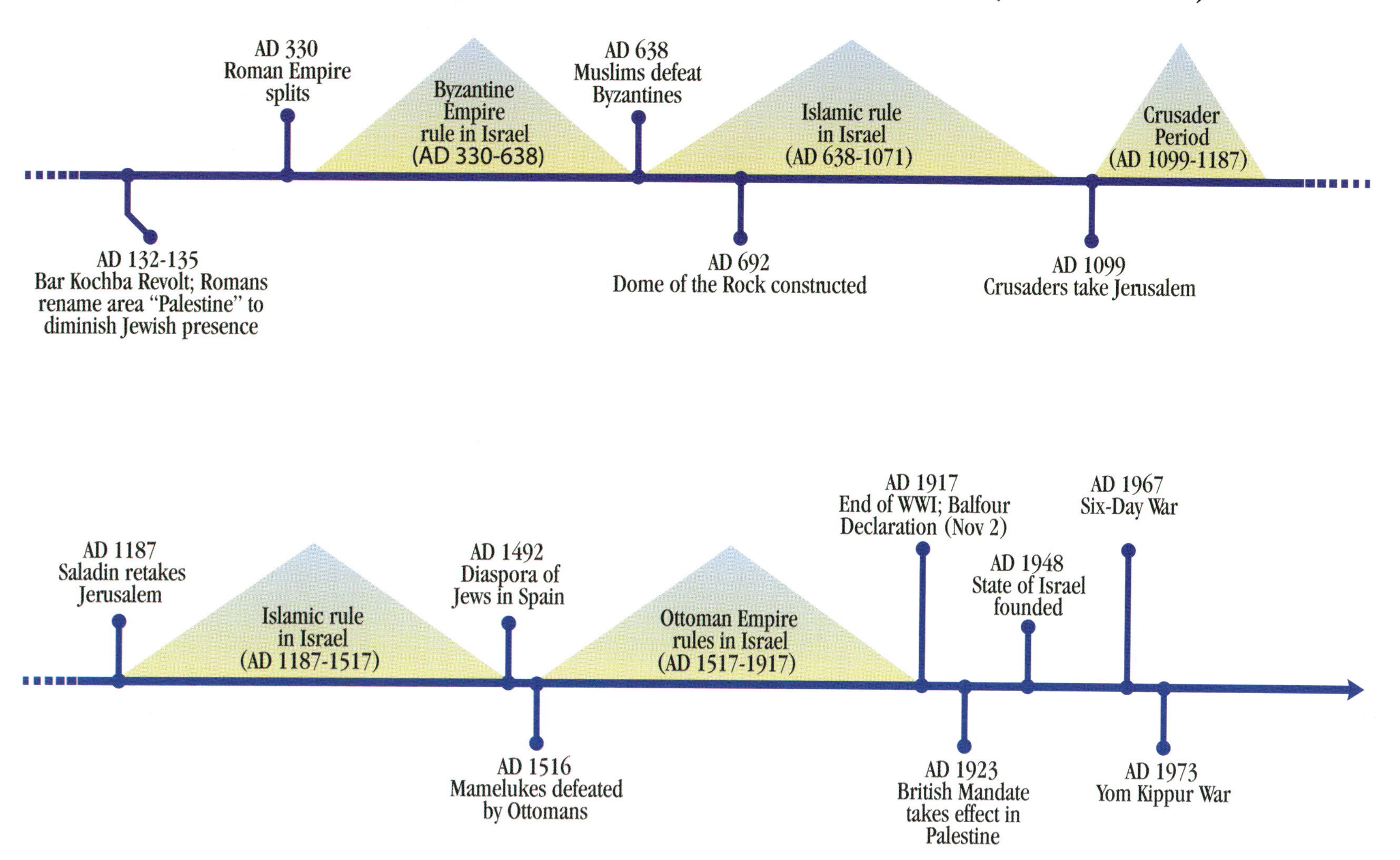

A luscious green spring valley in Israel.

APPENDIX B

*A BIBLICAL BASIS FOR ISRAEL'S RIGHT TO THE LAND**

Genesis 12:1-3: Now the LORD had said to Abram: "Get out of your country, from your family and from your father's house, **to a land that I will show you**. I will make you a great nation; I will bless you and make your name great; and you shall be a blessing. I will bless those who bless you and I will curse him who curses you; and in you all the families of the earth shall be blessed" (NKJV).

Genesis 12:7: Then the LORD appeared to Abram and said, "**To your descendants I will give this land**." And there he built an altar to the LORD, who had appeared to him (NKJV).

Genesis 15:18: On the same day the LORD made a covenant with Abram, saying: "**To your descendants I have given this land**, from the river of Egypt to the great river, the River Euphrates—the Kenites, the Kenezzites, the Kadmonites, the Hittites, the Perizzites, the Rephaim, the Amorites, the Canaanites, the Girgashites, and the Jebusites" (NKJV).

Genesis 17:7-8: (God said to Abraham) "**I will establish my covenant as an everlasting covenant between me and you and your descendants after you for the generations to come, to be your God and the God of your descendants after you. *The whole land of Canaan, where you***

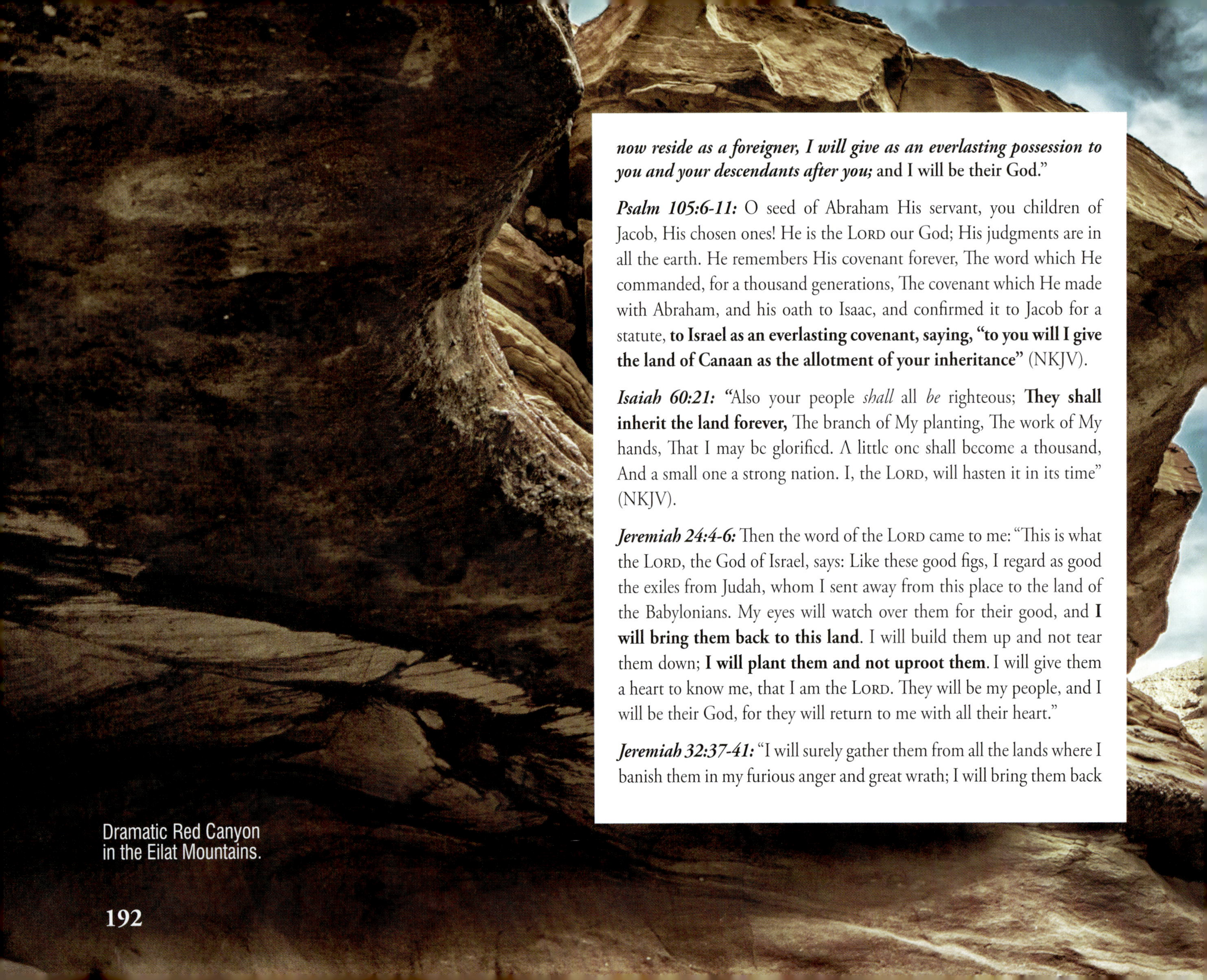

now reside as a foreigner, I will give as an everlasting possession to you and your descendants after you; **and I will be their God."**

Psalm 105:6-11: O seed of Abraham His servant, you children of Jacob, His chosen ones! He is the LORD our God; His judgments are in all the earth. He remembers His covenant forever, The word which He commanded, for a thousand generations, The covenant which He made with Abraham, and his oath to Isaac, and confirmed it to Jacob for a statute, **to Israel as an everlasting covenant, saying, "to you will I give the land of Canaan as the allotment of your inheritance"** (NKJV).

Isaiah 60:21: "Also your people *shall* all *be* righteous; **They shall inherit the land forever,** The branch of My planting, The work of My hands, That I may be glorified. A little one shall become a thousand, And a small one a strong nation. I, the LORD, will hasten it in its time" (NKJV).

Jeremiah 24:4-6: Then the word of the LORD came to me: "This is what the LORD, the God of Israel, says: Like these good figs, I regard as good the exiles from Judah, whom I sent away from this place to the land of the Babylonians. My eyes will watch over them for their good, and **I will bring them back to this land**. I will build them up and not tear them down; **I will plant them and not uproot them**. I will give them a heart to know me, that I am the LORD. They will be my people, and I will be their God, for they will return to me with all their heart."

Jeremiah 32:37-41: "I will surely gather them from all the lands where I banish them in my furious anger and great wrath; I will bring them back

Dramatic Red Canyon in the Eilat Mountains.

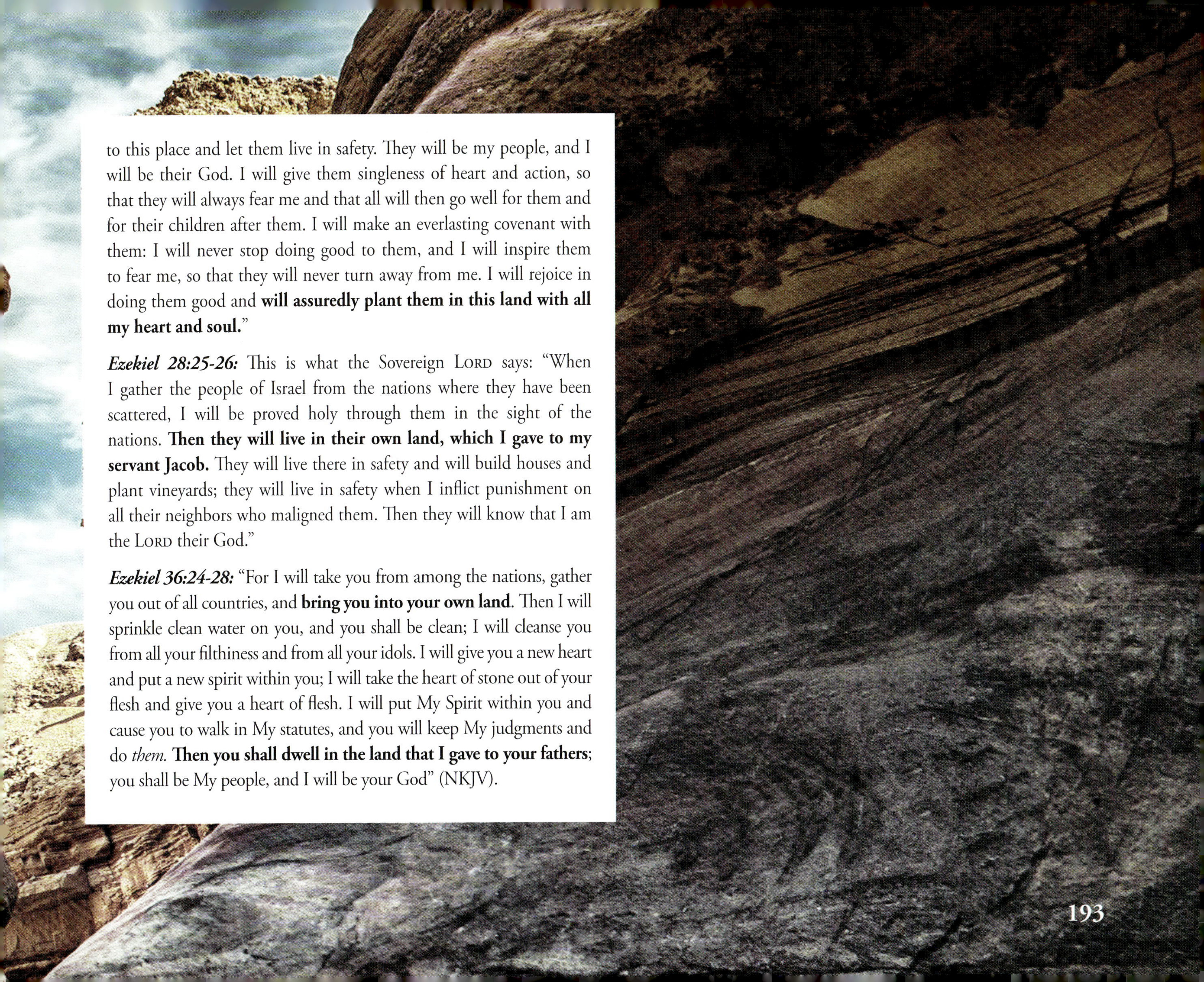

to this place and let them live in safety. They will be my people, and I will be their God. I will give them singleness of heart and action, so that they will always fear me and that all will then go well for them and for their children after them. I will make an everlasting covenant with them: I will never stop doing good to them, and I will inspire them to fear me, so that they will never turn away from me. I will rejoice in doing them good and **will assuredly plant them in this land with all my heart and soul.**"

Ezekiel 28:25-26: This is what the Sovereign LORD says: "When I gather the people of Israel from the nations where they have been scattered, I will be proved holy through them in the sight of the nations. **Then they will live in their own land, which I gave to my servant Jacob.** They will live there in safety and will build houses and plant vineyards; they will live in safety when I inflict punishment on all their neighbors who maligned them. Then they will know that I am the LORD their God."

Ezekiel 36:24-28: "For I will take you from among the nations, gather you out of all countries, and **bring you into your own land**. Then I will sprinkle clean water on you, and you shall be clean; I will cleanse you from all your filthiness and from all your idols. I will give you a new heart and put a new spirit within you; I will take the heart of stone out of your flesh and give you a heart of flesh. I will put My Spirit within you and cause you to walk in My statutes, and you will keep My judgments and do *them.* **Then you shall dwell in the land that I gave to your fathers**; you shall be My people, and I will be your God" (NKJV).

Ezekiel 37:14: "I will put My Spirit in you, and you shall live, and **I will place you in your own land**. Then you shall know that I, the LORD, have spoken *it* and performed *it,*" says the LORD (NKJV).

Ezekiel 37:21-24: Then say to them, "Thus says the Lord God: 'Surely I will take the children of Israel from among the nations, wherever they have gone, and **will gather them from every side and bring them into their own land**; and I will make them one nation in the land, on the mountains of Israel; and one king shall be king over them all; they shall no longer be two nations, nor shall they ever be divided into two kingdoms again" (NKJV).

Ezekiel 37:25-28: "**Then they shall dwell in the land that I have given to Jacob My servant, where your fathers dwelt; and they shall dwell there, they, their children, and their children's children, forever**; and My servant David *shall be* their prince forever. Moreover I will make a covenant of peace with them, and it shall be an everlasting covenant with them; I will establish them and multiply them, and I will set My sanctuary in their midst forevermore. My tabernacle also shall be with them; indeed I will be their God, and they shall be My people. The nations also will know that I, the Lord, sanctify Israel, when My sanctuary is in their midst forevermore" (NKJV).

Joel 2:17-18: Let the priests, who minister before the Lord, weep between the portico and the altar. Let them say, "Spare your people, Lord. Do not make your inheritance an object of scorn, a byword among the nations. Why should they say among the peoples, 'Where is their God?'" Then **the LORD was jealous for his land** and took pity on his people.

Joel 3:1-2: "In those days and at that time, when I restore the fortunes of Judah and Jerusalem, I will gather all nations and bring them down to the Valley of Jehoshaphat. There I will put them on trial for what they did to my inheritance, my people Israel, because they scattered my people among the nations and **divided up my land**."

Amos 9:14-15: "I will bring back the captives of my people Israel; They shall build the waste cities and inhabit *them*; They shall plant vineyards and drink wine from them; They shall also make gardens and eat fruit from them. **I will plant them in their land, And no longer shall they be pulled up from the land I have given them,"** says the LORD your God (NKJV).

Obadiah 20-21: This company of Israelite exiles who are in Canaan **will possess the land** as far as Zarephath; the exiles from Jerusalem who are in Sepharad will possess the towns of the Negev. Deliverers will go up on Mount Zion to govern the mountains of Esau. And the kingdom will be the LORD's.

Zechariah 8:7: This is what the LORD Almighty says: "I will save my people from the countries of the east and the west. **I will bring them back to live in Jerusalem**; they will be my people, and I will be faithful and righteous to them as their God."

Romans 9:3-4: For I could wish that I myself were cursed and cut off from Christ for the sake of my people, those of my own race, the people of Israel. Theirs is the adoption to sonship; theirs the divine glory, **the covenants**, the receiving of the law, the temple worship and **the promises**.

Red anemones blossom in spring on a green meadow.

Romans 11:1-2a: I ask then: Did God reject his people? By no means! I am an Israelite myself, a descendant of Abraham, from the tribe of Benjamin. **God did not reject his people whom he foreknew**.

Romans 11:11-12: Again I ask, did they (Israel) stumble so as to fall beyond recovery? Not at all! Rather, because of their transgression, salvation has come to the Gentiles to make Israel envious. But if their transgression means riches for the world, and their loss means riches for the Gentiles, **how much greater riches will their full inclusion bring**!

Romans 11:28-29: As far as the gospel is concerned, they (Israel) are enemies for your sake; but as far as election is concerned, they (Israel) are loved on account of the patriarchs, **for God's gift and his call are irrevocable**.

*Emphases added

The Jordan River, with 9,232 foot Mt. Hermon in the distance.

LIBERTY COUNSEL: A FAMILY OF MINISTRIES

Founded in 1989 by Mat and Anita Staver, Liberty Counsel's mission is restoring the culture by advancing religious freedom, the sanctity of human life, and the family. We advance this mission through education, litigation, and public policy.

Liberty Counsel also advances the mission through its family of affiliated ministries: Christians in Defense of Israel, Covenant Journey. Liberty Counsel Action, Liberty Relief International, and Liberty Prayer Network.

Liberty Counsel works every day to restore the culture by advancing religious freedom, the sanctity of human life, and the family. We advance the mission for a just and good society through litigation, education, and public policy.

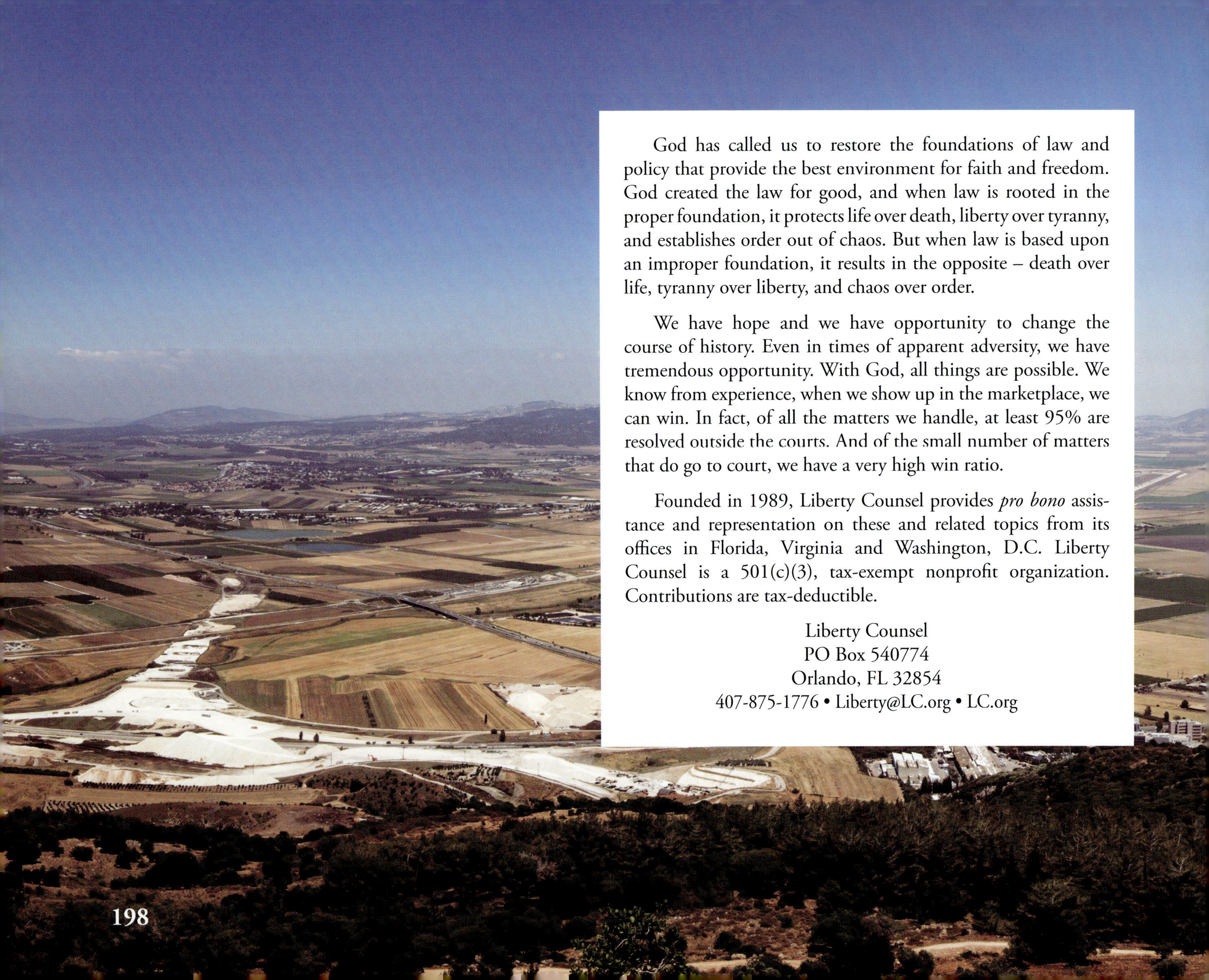

God has called us to restore the foundations of law and policy that provide the best environment for faith and freedom. God created the law for good, and when law is rooted in the proper foundation, it protects life over death, liberty over tyranny, and establishes order out of chaos. But when law is based upon an improper foundation, it results in the opposite – death over life, tyranny over liberty, and chaos over order.

We have hope and we have opportunity to change the course of history. Even in times of apparent adversity, we have tremendous opportunity. With God, all things are possible. We know from experience, when we show up in the marketplace, we can win. In fact, of all the matters we handle, at least 95% are resolved outside the courts. And of the small number of matters that do go to court, we have a very high win ratio.

Founded in 1989, Liberty Counsel provides *pro bono* assistance and representation on these and related topics from its offices in Florida, Virginia and Washington, D.C. Liberty Counsel is a 501(c)(3), tax-exempt nonprofit organization. Contributions are tax-deductible.

Liberty Counsel
PO Box 540774
Orlando, FL 32854
407-875-1776 • Liberty@LC.org • LC.org

Christians in Defense of Israel (CIDI) is an education and advocacy ministry to strengthen Christians in their faith and inspire goodwill ambassadors for Israel and the Jewish people. With offices in Florida and Washington, D.C., we urge believers throughout America to stand in solidarity with our Jewish brothers and sisters and the nation of Israel.

In additional to education and advocacy, CIDI provides unique tour opportunities in Israel where participants experience both ancient and modern Israel through an immersive experience that is life-changing. Everything centers around Israel – our faith, our history, and our heritage. This small nation is a world leader in business and technology. The CIDI tours are called "Liberty Ambassador Counsel VIP Tours."

The Bible makes it very clear that Israel occupies a unique place in God's revealed Word—and that God will bless those who bless Israel (Genesis 12:3). That is why support for Israel is

both urgently needed and crucially important. Now, more than ever, Israel needs America and America needs Israel.

Christians in Defense of Israel is a 501(c)(3), tax-exempt nonprofit ministry. Contributions are tax-deductible.

Christians in Defense of Israel
PO Box 540209
Orlando, FL 52854
407-875-1948 • Israel@CIDIsrael.org • CIDIsrael.org

Acacia tree grows in the shadow of sheer cliff in Negev.

Covenant Journey provides a life-changing educational and experiential journey to Israel for Christian college-age students who have leadership potential. Made possible by generous supporters, the 10-day tour introduces bright young Christian leaders to Biblical, historic, and modern Israel. The mission is to strengthen students' Christian faith and equip them to be goodwill ambassadors for Israel and the Jewish people.

Covenant Journey has offices in Florida and Washington, D.C.

"This trip will completely transform your life mentally and spiritually," exclaimed Covenant Journey alumnus Karley R. "You will be more in tune with God's heart and God's vision for the land of Israel, as well as the world."

Having worked with young people in a variety of circumstances, the ministry of Covenant Journey is the most impactful ministry for Christian college-age students. It is life-changing in so many ways.

Launched in 2014, Covenant Journey has already taken many young people to Israel from every conceivable profession

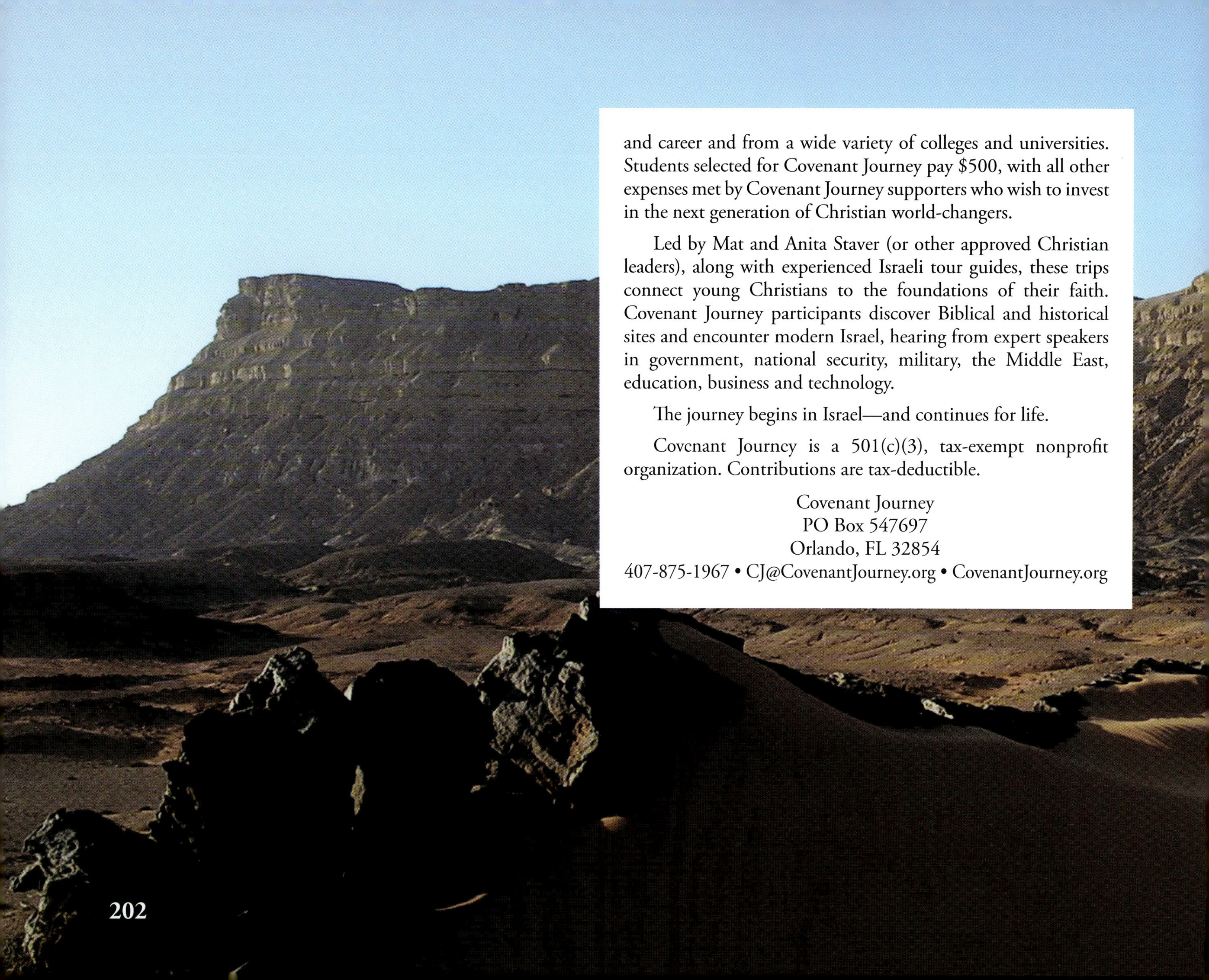

and career and from a wide variety of colleges and universities. Students selected for Covenant Journey pay $500, with all other expenses met by Covenant Journey supporters who wish to invest in the next generation of Christian world-changers.

Led by Mat and Anita Staver (or other approved Christian leaders), along with experienced Israeli tour guides, these trips connect young Christians to the foundations of their faith. Covenant Journey participants discover Biblical and historical sites and encounter modern Israel, hearing from expert speakers in government, national security, military, the Middle East, education, business and technology.

The journey begins in Israel—and continues for life.

Covenant Journey is a 501(c)(3), tax-exempt nonprofit organization. Contributions are tax-deductible.

Covenant Journey
PO Box 547697
Orlando, FL 32854
407-875-1967 • CJ@CovenantJourney.org • CovenantJourney.org

Liberty Counsel Action is a law and policy education and grassroots lobbying organization with a broad agenda for a better America. With offices in Florida and Washington, DC, Liberty Counsel Action advances religious liberty, the sanctity of human life, the family, responsible government, national security, and support for Israel at the federal, state, and local levels.

Liberty Counsel Action's rich heritage dates to 1979 when Dr. Jerry Falwell founded the Moral Majority. He later launched The Liberty Alliance in 1986 to expand Moral Majority's impact, renaming the group Liberty Alliance Action in 2004. In 2010, Liberty Alliance Action became Liberty Counsel Action under the leadership of Mat and Anita Staver.

Liberty Counsel is a 501(c)(4), tax-exempt nonprofit organization.

Liberty Counsel Action
PO Box 540629
Orlando, FL 32854
407-875-1789 • Liberty@LCAction.org •
LCAction.org • LibertyCounsel.com

Red sand dunes in Negev Desert.

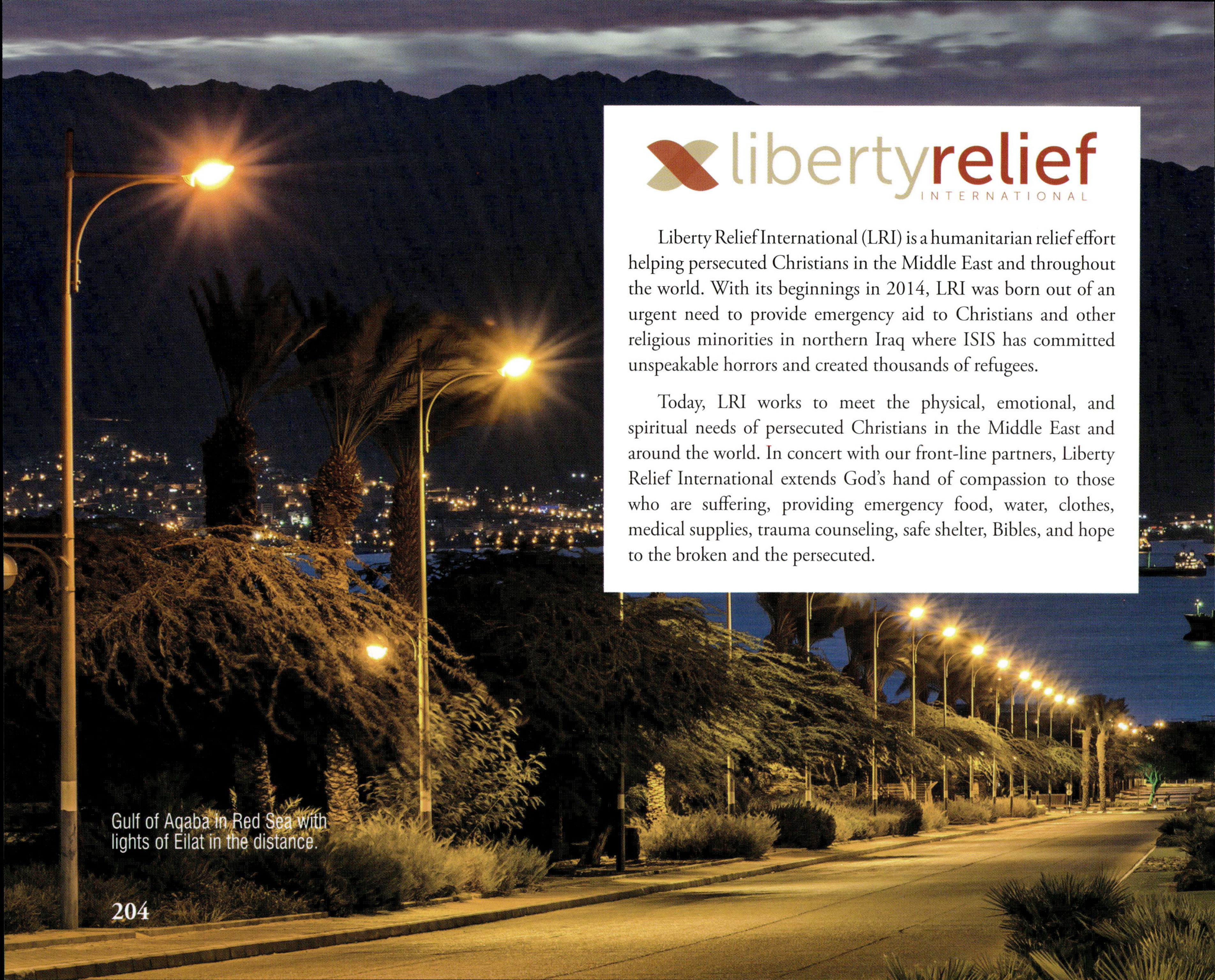

Liberty Relief International (LRI) is a humanitarian relief effort helping persecuted Christians in the Middle East and throughout the world. With its beginnings in 2014, LRI was born out of an urgent need to provide emergency aid to Christians and other religious minorities in northern Iraq where ISIS has committed unspeakable horrors and created thousands of refugees.

Today, LRI works to meet the physical, emotional, and spiritual needs of persecuted Christians in the Middle East and around the world. In concert with our front-line partners, Liberty Relief International extends God's hand of compassion to those who are suffering, providing emergency food, water, clothes, medical supplies, trauma counseling, safe shelter, Bibles, and hope to the broken and the persecuted.

Gulf of Aqaba in Red Sea with lights of Eilat in the distance.

Thanks to our generous donors, Liberty Relief International has provided millions of dollars to support persecuted Christians in Iraq, Syria, the Middle East, and elsewhere. In so doing, LRI has touched the lives of tens of thousands of brothers and sisters in Christ and other religious minorities.

When you give to LRI, you meet critical and urgent needs wherever Christians are under threat. You stand alongside fellow believers around the world with a "gift of hope" through your tax-deductible donation to Liberty Relief International.

Liberty Relief International is a 501(c)(3), tax-exempt nonprofit organization. Contributions are tax-deductible.

Liberty Relief International
PO Box 547309
Orlando, FL 32854
407-875-2015 • LRI@LibertyReliefInternational.org
• LibertyReliefInternational.org

LIBERTY PRAYER NETWORK

Liberty Prayer Network is the prayer ministry of Liberty Counsel. LPN enlists prayer intercessors to take a firm stand in their communities, lifting high the torch of liberty and calling others to worship God. The intercessors commit to spend time as they are able, alone or in groups, from wherever they live, to pray for His blessing over their states, the nations, and the world.

Maureen Bravo, who has been active in international onsite prayer intercession for many years, serves as International Director of LPN. She networks with other prayer ministries and leads intercession for those who champion the principles of life, liberty, and the family.

We partner with those in other nations who uphold the restoration of their cultures by advancing religious freedom, the sanctity of human life, and the family. You can also stay informed about our cases and other important work by reading our Liberty Alert emails so you can know how to pray.

Liberty Prayer Network
PO Box 540774
Orlando, FL 32854
407-875-1776
LC.org/project/prayer • Maureen@LibertyPrayerNet.org

About the Authors

Mat Staver is an attorney and the Founder and Chairman, Liberty Counsel, an international nonprofit litigation, education, and policy organization dedicated to advancing religious freedom, the sanctity of human life, and the family. He is also the Founder and President, Covenant Journey; President, Christians in Defense of Israel; Founder and President, Liberty Relief International; chairman, board of directors, National House of Hope; chairman, Liberty Counsel Action, Freedom Federation, and The Salt & Light Council; member, board of directors, Hispanic Israel Leadership Coalition; member, board of trustees, Supreme Court

Pumpkin plants in Samaria, with brown hills beyond.

Historical Society and Timothy Plan, a New York and Tel-Aviv Stock Exchange-traded family of mutual funds; member, board of reference, The Christian Film & Television Commission; director, Liberty Center for Law and Policy; vice president and Global Chief Counsel, National Hispanic Christian Leadership Conference/CONEL; member, board of advisors, Care for Pastors; former member, board of trustees, Liberty University; former vice president, Liberty University; former dean and tenured professor of law, Liberty University School of Law; founder and former president, Staver & Associates; founder and former president, The Staver Group; former vice president of law and policy, Liberty University.

Mat has over 230 legal opinions; author of eight scholarly law review publications, multiple books, and booklets, including *Faith & Freedom: A Complete Handbook for Defending Your Religious Rights*, *Same-Sex Marriage: Putting Every Household at Risk*, and *Eternal Vigilance: Knowing and Protecting Your Religious Freedom*. He produces and hosts *Faith and Freedom*, a 15-minute daily radio program, and *Freedom's Call*, a 60-second daily radio program. He is a frequent guest on international and many national network and cable television and radio programs, including print and electronic media.

Mat has filed numerous briefs and argued two landmark cases before the United States Supreme Court, *Madsen v. Women's Health Center* and *McCreary County v. ACLU of Kentucky*. He has the highest AV rating for attorneys and is Board Certified in Appellate Practice by the Florida Bar.

Barren landscape and brilliant sunrise in Negev Desert.

He received a B.A., Theology, *cum laude*, Southern Missionary College; M.A., Religion, *summa cum laude*, Andrews University; J.D., University of Kentucky; LL.D., *honoris causa*, Liberty University; D.D., *honoris causa*, South Florida Bible College.

Mat is married to Anita, who is also an attorney and is President of Liberty Counsel.

John Aman is the Director of Creative Services for Liberty Counsel and a communications professional with more than two decades of experience in policy communications, marketing, and corporate communications. He has served directly and indirectly for numerous Christian and conservative organizations and has written dozens of articles, papers, books

and resources on current issues. John is the author of *The Book on Obama* and *The Obamacare Death Panel.*

Along with his wife, Tewannah, he is active in pro-life ministry, serving as president of a local Right to Life organization.

John received a B.A. in English from the University of Washington in Seattle, and a M.A. in Journalism and Public Policy from Regent University.

ENDNOTES

1 Shelley Kleiman, "The State of Israel Declares Independence," Israel Ministry of Foreign Affairs, April 27, 1999. http://www.mfa.gov.il/MFA/MFA-Archive/1999/Pages/Shelley%20Kleiman%20-%20The%20State%20of%20Israel%20Declares%20Ind.aspx

2 "Declaration of Establishment of State of Israel," May 14, 1948, Israel Ministry of Foreign Affairs. http://www.mfa.gov.il/mfa/foreignpolicy/peace/guide/pages/declaration%20of%20establishment%20of%20state%20of%20israel.aspx

3 Benny Morris, *Righteous Victims: A History of the Zionist-Arab Conflict*, 1881-2001 (Vintage, 2001), 217.

4 "Understanding the Arab-Israeli Conflict," Compiled by Paul Bogdanor. http://www.paulbogdanor.com/israel/quotes.html

5 Danielle Ziri, "Israel warns UN: Hezbollah has 120,000 missiles aimed at us," JerusalemPost.com, July 12, 2016. http://www.jpost.com/Arab-Israeli-Conflict/Israel-warns-UN-Hezbollah-has-120000-missiles-aimed-at-Israel-460184

6 Ariel Ben Solomon, "Nasrallah: Israel is a cancer and the ultimate goal should be to remove it," JerusalemPost.com, August 15, 2014. http://www.jpost.com/Arab-Israeli-Conflict/Nasrallah-Israel-is-a-cancer-and-the-ultimate-goal-should-be-to-remove-it-371182

7 Denver Nicks, "ISIS Leader Reportedly Warns Israel 'We Are Getting Closer to You,'" Time.com, December 26, 2015. http://time.com/4161623/isis-leader-baghdadi-message-israel/

8 "The Iranian Leadership's Continuing Declarations of Intent to Destroy Israel, 2009-2012," Jerusalem Center for Public Affairs. http://jcpa.org/wp-content/uploads/2012/05/IransIntent2012b.pdf

9 Malcolm Hay, *The Roots of Christian Anti-Semitism* (New York: Liberty Press, 1981), p. 87. Quoted in Michael L. Brown. *Our Hands Are Stained with Blood* (Shippensburg, PA: Destiny Image Publishers, Inc., 1992), Kindle Locations 231-233.

10 Theodor Herzl, *The Jewish State*, Kindle Locations 171-174.

11 Ibid., 12.

12 Theodor Herzl, *Letters and Journals* (Jerusalem: Mizpa, 1928), p. 129. [Hebrew]. Cited in Natan Sharansky, "The Political Legacy of Theodor Herzl," AzureOnline, Summer 5765 / 2005, no. 21. http://azure.org.il/article.php?id=175&page=all

13 Elie Wiesel, *Night* (Farrar, Straus and Giroux. Kindle Edition), 8-9.

14 Herzl, *The Jewish State*, 53.

15 Ibid., 55.

16 David Baron, *Israel in the Plan of God* (Kindle edition), Kindle Locations 2792-2793.

17 Mark Twain, *Innocents Abroad*, 607-608. Located at "Mark Twain in His Times" website: http://twain.lib.virginia.edu/innocent/text/inn56.html

18 David Sugarman, "Melville in Jerusalem," Tabletmag.com, August 16, 2012. http://www.tabletmag.com/jewish-arts-and-culture/books/109333/melville-in-jerusalem

19 Ibid.

20 "Estimating the Population of Ancient Jerusalem," Magen Broshi, *Biblical Archaeology Review*, 4:02, June 1978.

21 Dore Gold, "Jerusalem in International Diplomacy: The 2000 Camp David Summit, the Clinton Plan, and Their Aftermath," Jerusalem Center for Public Affairs, February 1, 2001. http://jcpa.org/article/jerusalem-in-international-diplomacy-the-2000-camp-david-summit-the-clinton-plan-and-their-aftermath/

22 James Finn to the Earl of Clarendon, September 15, 1857. Cited in Alan Dershowitz, *The Case for Israel* (Turner Publishing Company, Kindle Edition), 26.

23 Samuel Bartlett, *From Egypt to Palestine* (New York: Harper, 1879), p. 409. Cited in Fred Gottheil, "The Population of Palestine, Circa 1875," Middle Eastern Studies, vol. 15, no. 3, October 1979. Cited in Dershowitz, 26-27.

24 Edward Wilson, *In Scripture Lands* (New York: C. Scribner's, 1890), 316. Cited in Gottheil. Cited in Dershowitz, 26-27.

25 W. Allen, *The Dead Sea: A New Route to India* (London: 1855), 113. Cited in Gottheil. Cited in Dershowitz, 26-27.

26 William Thomson, *The Land and the Book* (New York: Harper Bros., 1871), 466. Cited in Gottheil. Cited in Dershowitz, 26-27.

27 See fn 1 in Dore Gold, "Jerusalem in International Diplomacy: The 2000 Camp David Summit, The Clinton Plan, and Their Aftermath," Jerusalem Center for Public Affairs, February 1, 2001. http://www.jcpa.org/jl/vp447.htm

28 Karl Marx, "Declaration of War – On the History of the Eastern Question," *New-York Daily Tribune*, April 15, 1854. https://www.marxists.org/archive/marx/works/1854/03/28.htm

29 David S. Landes, "Palestine Before the Zionists," *Commentary*, February 1, 1976. https://www.commentarymagazine.com/articles/palestine-before-the-zionists/#18

30 Ibid.

31 Joan Peters, *From Time Immemorial: The Origins of the Arab-Jewish Conflict over Palestine* (JKAP Publications, 2001), 184.

32 Pierre Caquet, *The Orient, the Liberal Movement, and the Eastern Crisis of 1839-41* (Palgrave Macmillan, 2016), 167. Also see James Finn, *Stirring Times, or Records from Jerusalem Consular Chronicles*, Vol. I (London: C. Kegan Paul & Co., 1878), 106.

33 S. Zalman Abramov, *Perpetual Dilemma: Jewish Religion in the Jewish State* (Cranbury, New Jersey: Associated University Presses, Inc., 1976), 27.

34 See "Sir Moses Montefiore," *Harper's* Magazine, Volume 67, p. 890. Dovid Rossoff, "Moses Montefiore's Dream," *The Jewish Magazine*, August 1998. http://www.jewishmag.com/12mag/israel/israel.htm., and "Moses Montefiore," Montefiore Wines. https://www.montefiorewines.net/moses-montefiore/moses-montefiore/

35 Dovid Rossoff, "Moses Montefiore's Dream," *The Jewish Magazine*, August 1998. http://www.jewishmag.com/12mag/israel/israel.htm

36 "Ben-Yehuda, Eliezer (1858-1922)," The Jewish Agency for Israel. http://www.jewishagency.org/leaders/content/25936

37 "Immigration to Israel: The First Aliyah (1882 - 1903)" JewishVirtualLibrary.org. http://www.jewishvirtuallibrary.org/jsource/Immigration/First_Aliyah.html

38 George Gilder, *The Israel Test: Why the World's Most Besieged State is a Beacon of Freedom and Hope for the World Economy* (Perseus Books Group, 2010), 38-39.

39 "Our History," Jewish National Fund. http://www.jnf.org/about-jnf/history/?referrer=https://www.google.com/

40 Benny Morris, *Righteous Victims: A History of the Zionist-Arab Conflict, 1881-2001* (Vintage, 2001), 19.

41 David Baron, *Israel in the Plan of God* (Grand Rapids, Mich.: Kriegel Publications, 1983. Originally published: *The History of Israel.* London: Morgan & Scott, 1925), ix.

42 "Demographics of Israel: Jewish & Non-Jewish Population of Israel/Palestine (1517-present)," JewishVirtualLibrary.org. http://www.jewishvirtuallibrary.org/jsource/Society_&_Culture/israel_palestine_pop.html

43 Palestine Royal Commission, *Report Presented to the Secretary of State for the Colonies in Parliament by Command of his Majesty, July 1937* (London: HMSO; rep. 1946): 93 (vii). Found at http://www.meforum.org/3423/israel-arabs-deprived-radicalized#_edn5

44 Efraim Karsh, "1948, Israel, and the Palestinians: Annotated Text," *Commentary Magazine.* http://www.commentarymagazine.com/article/1948-israel-and-the-palestinians-annotated-text/

45 George Gilder, *The Israel Test*, 37.

46 Ibid., 41.

47 Ibid., 43.

48 See Samuel Kurinsky, "The Arabs and the Jews, Part I: The Pre-Islamic Period, Fact Paper 43-I," Hebrew History Federation. http://www.hebrewhistory.info/factpapers/fp043-1_preislam.htm

49 Robert Spencer, "The Qur'an: Israel Is Not for the Jews," *Middle East Quarterly*, Fall 2009, pp. 3-8. http://www.meforum.org/2462/the-quran-israel-not-for-jews

50 Sahih International translation. https://quran.com/2:65

51 Ibid., https://quran.com/7:166

52 Ibid., https://quran.com/5:60

53 Sahih al-Bukhari, Book 52, Hadith 177, www.muflihun.com. https://muflihun.com/bukhari/52/177

54 Surah 33:21 in the Koran states, "You have an excellent example in Allah's Messenger for those of you who put your hope in Allah and the Last Day and who praise Allah continually."

55 "The Myth: Muhammad Lived at Peace with the Jews, Part 3: The Banu Qurayza," TheReligionofPeace.com. https://www.thereligionofpeace.com/pages/muhammad/qurayza.aspx

56 "Benny Morris: 'The 1948 War Was an Islamic Holy War,'" *Middle East Quarterly*, Summer 2010, pp. 63-69. http://www.meforum.org/2769/benny-morris-1948-islamic-holy-war

57 Walter Laqueur, Barry Rubin, eds., *The Israel-Arab Reader: A Documentary History of the Middle East Conflict*, 7th Revised, Updated ed. (Penguin Books, 2008), 3-4.

58 Dershowitz, *The Case for Israel*, 20.

59 Ibid., 20-21.

60 Laqueur, Rubin, eds., *The Israel-Arab Reader*, 25.

61 Aref Pasha Dajani, Speech to the King-Crane Commission, June 18, 1919, Center for Online Judaic Studies. http://cojs.org/aref_pasha_dajani-_speech_to_the_king-crane_commission-_june_18-_1919/

62 Laqueur, Rubin, eds., *The Israel-Arab Reader*, 17.

63 Ibid., 19.

64 The Weizmann-Feisal Agreement, January 3, 1919, Israel Ministry of Foreign Affairs. http://www.mfa.gov.il/mfa/foreignpolicy/peace/mfadocuments/pages/the%20weizmann-feisal%20agreement%203-jan-1919.aspx

65 Laqueur, Rubin, eds., *The Israel-Arab Reader*, 17.

66 San Remo Resolution, April 25, 1920. Primary Sources, Council on Foreign Relations. http://www.cfr.org/israel/san-remo-resolution/p15248

67 Howard Grief, "Legal Rights and Title of Sovereignty of the Jewish People to the Land of Israel and Palestine under International Law," NATIV Online, Vol. 2, 2004. http://www.acpr.org.il/english-nativ/02-issue/grief-2.htm. Also see Howard Grief, *The Legal Foundation and Borders of Israel Under International Law: A Treatise on Jewish Sovereignty over the Land of Israel* (Mazo Publishers, 2013).

68 Martin Gilbert, *Churchill and the Jews: A Lifelong Friendship* (New York: Henry Holt & Company, 2007), 71.

69 Chaim Weizmann, *The Letters and Papers of Chaim Weizmann: August 1898-July 1931* (New Brunswick, NJ: Transaction Books, 1983), 290.

70 Grief, "Legal Rights and Title of Sovereignty of the Jewish People to the Land of Israel and Palestine under International Law."

71 "Allowed but Unwelcome: the Jews of Jordan," *Mosaic*, May 8, 2015. http://mosaicmagazine.com/picks/2015/05/allowed-but-unwelcome-the-jews-of-jordan/

72 "The Palestine Mandate," Article 6, The Avalon Project, Yale Law School. http://avalon.law.yale.edu/20th_century/palmanda.asp#art25

73 Churchill Papers, 17/20. Cited in Alan Baker, ed., *Israel's Rights as a Nation-State in International Diplomacy* (Jerusalem: Jerusalem Center for Public Affairs – World Jewish Congress, 2011), 28.

74 Ibid.

75 Grief, "Legal Rights and Title of Sovereignty of the Jewish People to the Land of Israel and Palestine under International Law."

76 Dershowitz, *The Case for Israel*, 41.

77 Palestine Royal Commission Report, July 1937, 141. https://palestinianmandate.files.wordpress.com/2014/04/cm-5479.pdf

78 Jacqueline Shields, "Pre-State Israel: Arab Riots of the 1920's," JewishVirtualLibrary.org. http://www.jewishvirtuallibrary.org/jsource/History/riots29.html

79 Howard Morley Sachar, *Aliyah: The People of Israel* (World Publishing Company, 1961), 231.

80 Theodor Herzl, *The Jewish State* (Kindle Edition), 18.

81 Dan Leon, "The Jewish National Fund: How the Land Was 'Redeemed,'" *Palestine-Israel Journal*, Vol 12, No. 4 & Vol 13 No. 1, 05/06 /. http://www.pij.org/details.php?id=410

82 Hope Simpson Report, Pg. 51. Cited in Mitchell Bard, *Myths & Facts: A Guide to the Arab-Israeli Conflict*. JewishVirtualLibrary.org. http://www.jewishvirtuallibrary.org/jsource/myths3/MFmandate.html#_edn21

83 Hillel Cohen, *Army of Shadows: Palestinian Collaboration with Zionism, 1917-1948* (University of California Press, 2008), 45.

84 Morris, *Righteous Victims*, 123.

85 Mitchell Bard, *Myths & Facts: A Guide to the Arab-Israeli Conflict*. JewishVirtualLibrary.org. http://www.jewishvirtuallibrary.org/jsource/myths3/MFmandate.html#5

86 Shabtai Teveth, *Ben-Gurion and the Palestinian Arabs: From Peace to War* (London: Oxford University Press, 1985), 32. Cited in Bard, *Myths & Facts*. http://www.jewishvirtuallibrary.org/jsource/myths3/MFmandate.html#5

87 Text of the Peel Commission Report (July 1937). JewishVirtualLibrary.org. http://www.jewishvirtuallibrary.org/jsource/History/peel1.html

88 Martin Gilbert, *The Routledge Atlas of the Arab-Israeli Conflict*, 10th ed. (Routledge, 2012), 3.

89 Jerold S. Auerbach, "Ben-Gurion Recognized Biblical Claim to Israel," Letter to the editor, *New York Times*, January 8, 1997. http://www.nytimes.com/1997/01/08/opinion/l-ben-gurion-recognized-biblical-claim-to-israel-078662.html

90 "David Ben-Gurion: Letter to French General Charles de Gaulle (December 6, 1967)," JewishVirtualLibrary.org http://www.jewishvirtuallibrary.org/jsource/History/BenGuriondeGaulle.html

91 Evidence of Haj Amin al-Husseini Before the Royal Commission, January 12, 1937, EretzYisroel.org. http://www.eretzyisroel.org/~jkatz/evidence.html. Also see Ernest Main, *Palestine at the Crossroads* (G. Allen & Unwin, 1937), 304.

92 "The Holocaust: The Mufti and the Führer," JewishVirtualLibrary.org. http://www.jewishvirtuallibrary.org/jsource/History/muftihit.html#1

93 Dershowitz, *The Case for Israel*, 7.

94 "British Palestine Mandate: Text of the Peel Commission Report (July 1937)," JewishVirtualLibrary.org. http://www.jewishvirtuallibrary.org/jsource/History/peel1.html

95 "The Partition Plan: Background & Overview," JewishVirtualLibrary.org. http://www.jewishvirtuallibrary.org/jsource/History/partition_plan.html

96 "British Policy in Palestine, 1937-8," H. G. L. and E. M. Bulletin of International News, Vol. 15, No. 23 (Nov. 19, 1938), pp. 3-7.

97 Efraim Karsh, *Palestine Betrayed* (Yale University Press, 2010), xiv.

98 Efraim Karsh, *Rethinking the Middle East* (Portland, OR: Frank Cass Publishers, 2003), 118.

99 David Barnett and Efraim Karsh, "Azzam's Genocidal Threat," *Middle East Quarterly*, Fall 2011, pp. 85-88. http://www.meforum.org/3082/azzam-genocide-threat#_ftnref10

100 J.C. Hurewitz, *The Struggle for Palestine* (NY: Shocken Books, 1976), 308. Cited in "Israeli War of Independence: Background & Overview (1947 - 1949)," JewishVirtualLibrary.org. http://www.jewishvirtuallibrary.org/jsource/History/1948_War.html

101 "Israeli War of Independence: Background & Overview (1947 - 1949)," JewishVirtualLibrary.org. http://www.jewishvirtuallibrary.org/jsource/History/1948_War.html

102 "The Declaration of the Establishment of the State of Israel, May 14, 1948," Israel Ministry of Foreign Affairs. http://www.mfa.gov.il/mfa/foreignpolicy/peace/guide/pages/declaration%20of%20establishment%20of%20state%20of%20israel.aspx

103 "Israel War of Independence: The Bernadotte Truce Plan (Summer 1948)," JewishVirtualLibrary.org. http://www.jewishvirtuallibrary.org/jsource/History/bernplan.html

104 *Middle Eastern Affairs*, (December 1956), p. 460. "Chapter 5: The 1956 Suez War," JewishVirtualLibrary.org. http://www.jewishvirtuallibrary.org/jsource/myths3/MF1956.html#_edn4

105 "Chapter 5: The 1956 Suez War," JewishVirtualLibrary.org. http://www.jewish-virtuallibrary.org/jsource/myths3/MF1956.html

106 Mark Tessler, *A History of the Israeli-Palestinian Conflict*, 2nd ed. (Bloomington, Ind.: Indiana University Press, 2009), 393.

107 Dershowitz, *The Case for Israel*, 96.

108 Howard Sachar, *A History of Israel: From the Rise of Zionism to Our Time*, 3rd Revised and Updated Edition (Alfred A. Knopf, 2007), 676.

109 "Peace or Terror? Israelis Killed in Palestinian Arab Terror Attacks," Information Regarding Israel's Security (IRIS). http://www.iris.org.il/terrcht2.htm

110 Kenneth R. Timmerman, *Preachers of Hate: Islam and the War on America* (Crown Forum, 2003), 197.

111 "The Palestinian National Covenant- July 1968," Israel Ministry of Foreign Affairs. http://www.mfa.gov.il/mfa/foreignpolicy/mfadocuments/yearbook1/pages/33%20the%20palestinian%20national%20covenant-%20july%201968.aspx

112 Benny Morris, "Arafat didn't negotiate - he just kept saying no," TheGuardian.com, May 22, 2002. https://www.theguardian.com/world/2002/may/23/israel3

113 Ibid.

114 Khaled Abu Toameh, "Mashaal vows Hamas will not concede land," *The Jerusalem Post*, December 8, 2012. http://www.jpost.com/Middle-East/Mashaal-vows-Hamas-will-not-concede-land

115 "Abbas: 'We will not agree to … a Jewish state'" Palestinian Media Watch. http://www.palwatch.org/main.aspx?fi=826

116 Michael B. Oren, *Ally: My Journey Across the American-Israeli Divide* (Random House, 2015), 139.

117 Coby Ben-Simhon, "Benny Morris on why he's written his last word on the Israel-Arab conflict," Haaretz.com, September 2, 2012. http://www.haaretz.com/weekend/magazine/benny-morris-on-why-he-s-written-his-last-word-on-the-israel-arab-conflict-1.465869

118 A.T. Robertson, *Word Pictures in the New Testament* (Lk 19:41) (Nashville, TN: Broadman Press).

119 Josephus, *The Wars of the Jews*, 6.406, translated by William Whiston. Lexundria.com. http://lexundria.com/j_bj/6.374-6.408/wst

120 David Baron, *The Shepherd of Israel and His Scattered Flock: A Solution of the Enigma of Jewish History* (Kindle edition. Previously published by Morgan and Scott, 1910), Kindle Locations 257-259.

121 See Isaiah 53: "he was led like a lamb to the slaughter" (v.7), and "... the Lord makes his life an offering for sin" (v. 10).

122 Michael L. Brown, *Our Hands Are Stained with Blood* (Shippensburg, Penn.: Destiny Image Publishing, 1992), Kindle Locations 1242-1244.

123 "GW's Reply to the Hebrew Congregation Newport, Rhode Island, 17 August 1790," The Papers of George Washington. http://gwpapers.virginia.edu/documents/hebrew/reply.html

124 Jonathan Edwards, Works, *Apocalyptic Writings*, vol. 5 (New Haven: Yale University Press, 1977), 133-34. Cited in Barry E. Horner, *Future Israel: Why Christian Anti-Judaism Must Be Challenged* (Nashville, TN: Broadman & Holman Academic), 336.

125 Baron, *The Shepherd of Israel*, Kindle Locations 279-280.

126 Brown, *Our Hands Are Stained with Blood*, Kindle Location 1052.

127 Meir Simcha Sokolovsky, *Prophecy and Providence* (Jerusalem/ New York: Feldheim, 1991), 79-80. Cited in Michael L. Brown, *Answering Jewish Objections to Jesus: Volume 1: General and Historical Objections* (Baker Publishing Group, 2000), Kindle Locations 2392-2397.

128 Theodor Herzl, *The Jewish State*, (Kindle edition), 48.

129 Ken Spiro, "Modern Zionism," SimpletoRemember.com. http://www.simpletoremember.com/articles/a/modern_zionism/

130 Shelley Kleiman, "The State of Israel Declares Independence," Israel Ministry of Foreign Affairs. http://mfa.gov.il/MFA/MFA-Archive/1999/Pages/Shelley%20Kleiman%20-%20The%20State%20of%20Israel%20Declares%20Ind.aspx

131 "David Ben-Gurion: Select Quotations," JewishVirtualLibrary.org. http://www.jewishvirtuallibrary.org/jsource/Quote/bg.html

132 "Israel's Religiously Divided Society," Pew Research Center, March 8, 2016, p. 7. http://www.pewforum.org/files/2016/03/Israel-Survey-Full-Report.pdf

133 Ibid., 97.

134 Ibid., 94.

135 "Yair Rosenberg, "On Israel's Liberal Abortion Policies," TabletMag.com, http://www.tabletmag.com/scroll/191538/on-israels-liberal-abortion-policies

136 Debra Kamin, "Israel's abortion law now among world's most liberal," *The Times of Israel*, January 6, 2014. http://www.timesofisrael.com/israels-abortion-law-now-among-worlds-most-liberal/

137 Rabbi Yitzchok Breitowitz, "Israel Health & Medicine: Legal Terms of Abortion," JewishVirtualLibrary.org. http://www.jewishvirtuallibrary.org/jsource/Health/abort1.html

138 Baron, *Israel in the Plan of God*, Kindle Locations 1511-1512.

139 Brown. *Our Hands Are Stained with Blood*, Kindle Locations 1339-1340.

140 David Baron, *Zechariah: A Commentary on His Visions & Prophecies* (Kindle Edition), Kindle Locations 5874-5876.

141 Dan Senor and Saul Singer, *Start-up Nation: The Story of Israel's Economic Miracle* (Grand Central Publishing, Kindle Edition), 16.

142 "Immigration to Israel: Introduction & Historical Overview," JewishVirtualLibrary.org. http://www.jewishvirtuallibrary.org/jsource/Immigration/immigration.html

143 "Among Israeli Jews, 20,000 embrace Christ," SRNNews.com, May 26, 2011. http://srnnews.townhall.com/news/faith/2011/05/26/among_israeli_jews,_20,000_embrace_christ

144 Sarah Posner, "Kosher Jesus: Messianic Jews in the Holy Land," TheAtlantic.com, November 29, 2012. http://www.theatlantic.com/international/archive/2012/11/kosher-jesus-messianic-jews-in-the-holy-land/265670/

145 Michael L. Brown, *The Real Kosher Jesus: Revealing the mysteries of the hidden Messiah* (Lake Mary, Fla.: Frontline, 2012), Kindle Locations 433-434.

146 Ibid., Kindle Locations 444-445.

147 Rowan Jacobsen, "Israel Proves the Desalination Era Is Here," *Scientific American*, July 29, 2016. http://www.scientificamerican.com/article/israel-proves-the-desalination-era-is-here/

148 Simona Weinglass, "How Israel became a water superpower," *Times of Israel*, December 1, 2015. http://www.timesofisrael.com/how-israel-became-a-water-superpower/

149 Jacobsen, "Israel Proves the Desalination Era Is Here," *Scientific American.*

150 Ariella Mendlowitz, "Netanyahu to Kenya's Christian Zionists: 'We Have No Better Friends in the World Than You,'" BreakingIsraelNews.com, July 6, 2016.

151 Ibid.

152 Mesfin M. Mekonnen and Arjen Y. Hoekstra, "Four billion people facing severe water scarcity," *Science Advances*, February 12, 2016. http://advances.sciencemag.org/content/2/2/e1500323.full

153 Simona Weinglass, "How Israel became a water superpower," *Times of Israel*, December 1, 2015. http://www.timesofisrael.com/how-israel-became-a-water-superpower/

154 Rowan Jacobsen, "Israel Proves the Desalination Era Is Here," *Scientific American*, July 29, 2016. http://www.scientificamerican.com/article/israel-proves-the-desalination-era-is-here/

155 Jonathan Leaf, "Israelis Have Made the Desert Bloom, But They Couldn't Make Socialism Work," Stream.org, July 30, 2016.

156 Ibid.

157 Douglas Feiden, "Bibi's Capital Idea Bye-Bye to Socialism in Israel, He Says," *New York Daily News*, July 12, 1996. http://www.nydailynews.com/archives/money/bibi-capital-idea-bye-bye-socialism-israel-article-1.740515

158 Gilder, *The Israel Test*, 99.

159 Ibid., 104-105.

160 "Gross domestic product 2015," World Bank. http://databank.worldbank.org/data/download/GDP.pdf

161 "Table 1: Human Development Index and its components," United Nations Development Programme Human Development Index. http://hdr.undp.org/en/composite/HDI

162 Organisation for Economic Co-operation and Development (OECD) Data, Israel. https://data.oecd.org/israel.htm

163 "Consumer Prices Index," Israel Central Bureau of Statistics, July 2016. http://www.cbs.gov.il/price_new/a3_2_e.pdf

164 "Labour Data Based On Labour Force Surveys," Israel Central Bureau of Statistics. http://www.cbs.gov.il/ts/databank/series_one_e.html?codets=41097

165 Richard Behar, "Inside Israel's Secret Startup Machine," Forbes.com, May 11, 2016. http://www.forbes.com/sites/richardbehar/2016/05/11/inside-israels-secret-startup-machine/#6c727be157d3

166 "Patent Counts by Country, State, and Year - All Patent Types," U.S. Patent and Trademark Office. http://www.uspto.gov/web/offices/ac/ido/oeip/taf/cst_all.htm

167 "Invest in Israel," Ministry of Economy and Industry, State of Israel. http://investinisrael.gov.il/resources/invest_in_israel_-_brochure.pdf

168 "One in Six US Drugs Will Soon Be Made in Israel," Forward.com, August 5, 2016. http://forward.com/news/world/346969/one-in-six-us-drugs-will-soon-be-made-in-israel/

169 "Israel sold $5.7 billion in military hardware in 2015," *The Times of Israel*, April 6, 2016. http://www.timesofisrael.com/israel-sold-5-7-billion-in-military-hardware-in-2015/

170 "Top List TIV (Trend Indicator Values) Tables," Stockholm International Peace Research Institute. http://armstrade.sipri.org/armstrade/page/toplist.php

171 "Israel's Diamonds May Not Be For Ever After All," JewishBusinessNews.com, January 17, 2016. http://jewishbusinessnews.com/2016/01/17/israels-diamonds-may-not-be-for-ever-after-all/

172 "Essential Tremor Study: John Watterson," Focused Ultrasound Foundation, see at 3:50 and following. https://www.youtube.com/watch?v=NwZ0FTUOQuw

173 See video interview with Dr. Kobi Vortman in "Beyond The Cutting Edge – Operating Room of the Future," Technion External Relations & Resource Development. http://pard.technion.ac.il/beyond-the-cutting-edge-2/

174 Gilder, *The Israel Test*, 4

175 Brodie Hart, "Adam Gorlitsky reflects on historic Cooper River Bridge Run," ABCNews4.com, April 4, 2016. http://abcnews4.com/news/local/adam-gorlitsky-reflects-on-historic-cooper-river-bridge-run

176 Gilder, *The Israel Test*, 61.

177 Senor and Singer, *Start-up Nation*, 63.

178 "7 Facts About Drip," Netafim. https://www.youtube.com/watch?v=1R_1rjgVezE&feature=iv&src_vid=NflV5LS42KY&annotation_id=video%3A7bf072ce-d2a5-439a-aee6-52cb939620f9

179 "Full text of Netanyahu 2015 address to the UN General Assembly," TimesofIsrael.com, October 1, 2015. http://www.timesofisrael.com/full-text-of-netanyahu-2015-address-to-the-un-general-assembly/

180 Hagai Amit, "Israel's Hazera: From Tomato Seeds to International Growth," Haaretz.com, February 1, 2015. http://www.haaretz.com/israel-news/business/.premium-1.639907

181 Mark Michelson, "More Details on Landa's Nanographic Digital Press Rollout for U.S. Market," *Printing Impressions*, June 16, 2016. http://www.piworld.com/article/more-details-on-landas-drupa-presence-and-product-rollout-for-the-u-s-market/

182 Abigail Klein Leichman, "Step aside, Gutenberg, Israel is about to revolutionize printing – again," Israel21c.org, May 7, 2012. http://www.israel21c.org/step-aside-gutenberg-israel-is-about-to-revolutionize-printing-again/

183 Charles Levinson and Adam Entous, "Israel's Iron Dome Defense Battled to Get Off Ground," *Wall Street Journal*, November 26, 2012. http://www.wsj.com/articles/SB10001424127887324712504578136931078468210. Also see Viva Sarah Press, "15 things you didn't know about the Iron Dome," Israel21c.org, July 14, 2014. http://www.israel21c.org/15-things-you-didnt-know-about-the-iron-dome/

184 Dara Kerr, "Google reveals it spent $966 million in Waze acquisition," Cnet.com, July 25, 2013. http://www.cnet.com/news/google-reveals-it-spent-966-million-in-waze-acquisition/

185 Abigail Klein Leichman, "Why Israel has become a mighty mobile app machine," Israel21c.com, June 9, 2016. http://www.israel21c.org/why-israel-has-become-a-mighty-mobile-app-machine/

186 David Shamah, "Massive Israeli presence at world's biggest mobile event," *Times of Israel*, February 24, 2014. http://www.timesofisrael.com/massive-israeli-presence-at-worlds-biggest-mobile-event/

187 Nicky Blackburn, "Made in Israel – The top 64 innovations developed in Israel," Israel21C.org, April 22, 2012. http://www.israel21c.org/made-in-israel-the-top-64-innovations-developed-in-israel/

188 Brad Stone, Adam Satariano, and Gwen Ackerman, "The Most Important Apple Executive You've Never Heard Of," Bloomberg Business Week, February 18, 2016. http://www.bloomberg.com/features/2016-johny-srouji-apple-chief-chipmaker/

189 "Apple Used an Israeli Technology to Build the Revolutionary Camera of The iPhone 7," Happyintlv.net, September 8, 2016. https://happyintlv.net/item/apple-iphone-7-linx-revolution-camera/

190 "The Israeli Innovation Enhancing Your iPhone…," Knowledge@Wharton, January 26, 2012. http://knowledge.wharton.upenn.edu/article/the-israeli-innovation-enhancing-your-iphone/

191 Sam Shead, "Apple is quietly developing 'iPhone 8' hardware in Israel," BusinessInsider.com, September 28, 2016. http://www.businessinsider.com/apple-developing-iphone-8-in-israel-2016-9?r=UK&IR=T

192 Viva Sarah Press, "Intel Skylake made in Haifa," Israel21c.org, September 2, 2015. http://www.israel21c.org/intel-skylake-made-in-haifa-2/

193 Senor and Singer, *Start-up Nation*, 38.

194 Ibid., 17.

195 David Shamah, "Microsoft CEO to visit in November," *The Times of Israel*, August 30, 2012. http://www.timesofisrael.com/microsoft-ceo-steve-ballmer-set-to-visit-israel-in-november/

196 "Google chief: Israeli tech second only to Silicon Valley," YNETnews.com, June 18, 2016. http://www.ynetnews.com/articles/0,7340,L-4817334,00.html

197 Allison Kaplan Sommer, "Israelis launch aid efforts for Katrina victims," Israel21c.com, September 4, 2005. http://www.israel21c.org/israelis-launch-aid-efforts-for-katrina-victims/

198 "Humanitarian Aid on the Volatile Syrian Border," IDF Blog, February 22, 2015. https://www.idfblog.com/blog/2015/02/22/humanitarian-aid-volatile-syrian-border/

199 "Israeli doctors rally to save 5-year-old Syrian girl," *Times of Israel*, April 7, 2016. http://www.timesofisrael.com/israeli-doctors-spies-rally-to-save-5-year-old-syrian-girl/

200 "Israeli Doctors Save Syrian Girl After Security Services Smuggle Out Family Bone Marrow Donor," News4Security, August 23, 2016. http://news4security.com/posts/2016/08/israeli-doctors-save-syrian-girl-after-security-services-smuggle-out-family-bone-marrow-donor/

201 Viva Sarah Press, "Syrian refugee creates website to thank Israelis," Israel21c.com, February 21, 2016. http://www.israel21c.org/syrian-refugee-creates-website-to-thank-israelis/

202 Daniel Meron, "Israeli humanitarian aid saves lives," Israel Ministry of Foreign Affairs, August 18, 2016. http://mfa.gov.il/MFA/ForeignPolicy/Pages/Israeli-humanitarian-aid-saves-lives-18-August-20160818-6941.aspx

203 Yehuda Avner, "A jilted love affair in Africa," *The Jerusalem Post*, February 8, 2006. http://www.jpost.com/Features/A-jilted-love-affair-in-Africa

204 Dr. Arye Oded, "Fifty years of MASHAV activity," Jerusalem Center for Public Affairs, October 26, 2009. http://jcpa.org/article/fifty-years-of-mashav-activity/

205 "Israel Humanitarian Operations: 2015 Earthquake in Nepal," JewishVirtualLibrary.org, May 2015. http://www.jewishvirtuallibrary.org/jsource/Society_&_Culture/nepalquake.html

206 "Live Updates: #IDFinPhilippines Rescue Mission," Israel Defense Forces, November 14, 2013. https://www.idfblog.com/blog/2013/11/14/31296/

207 Judah Ari Gross, "UN ranks IDF emergency medical team as 'No. 1 in the world,'" *The Times of Israel*, November 13, 2016. http://www.timesofisrael.com/un-ranks-idf-emergency-medical-team-as-no-1-in-the-world/

208 "About Us," DreamDoctors.org. http://www.dreamdoctors.org.il/en/Category/2/About_us

209 Abigail Klein Leichman, "Israeli medical clowns bring smiles to Nepalese earthquake victims," Israel21c.org, May 7, 2015. http://www.israel21c.org/israeli-medical-clowns-bring-smiles-to-nepal/

210 "Israeli Doctors Restore Sight to 90 Kyrgyzstanis in 'Eye From Zion' Initiative," Algemeiner.com, August 26, 2015. http://www.algemeiner.com/2015/08/26/israeli-doctors-restore-sight-to-90-kyrgyzstanis-in-eye-from-zion-initiative/

211 Joshua Muravchik, *Liberal Oasis: The Truth About Israel* (Encounter Books, 2014, Kindle Edition), Kindle Locations 899-901.

212 Fares Akram, "Gaza Strip patients find help in Israeli hospital," *The Times of Israel*, May 19, 2015. http://www.timesofisrael.com/israeli-hospitals-treat-gaza-residents-children/

213 Marissa Newman and AP, "Hamas leader's daughter receives medical care in Israel," *The Times of Israel*, October 19, 2014. http://www.timesofisrael.com/hamas-leaders-daughter-said-to-receive-medical-care-in-israel/

214 "8 years, 8 Quotes by Hamas Leader Ismail Haniyeh," Hamas Terrorism 101, IDF Blog, February 19, 2014. https://www.idfblog.com/hamas/2014/02/19/8-years-8-quotes-hamas-leader-ismail-haniyeh/

215 Tovah Lazaroff, "Netanyahu phones Abbas, offers condolences on brother's death," *The Jerusalem Post*, July 22, 2016. http://www.jpost.com/Arab-Israeli-Conflict/Netanyahu-phones-Abbas-offers-condolences-on-brothers-death-462127

216 William E. Blackstone, *Jesus is Coming* (Fleming H. Revell Company, 1908), 172.

217 Paul W. Rood, "William E. Blackstone (1841-1935): 'Zionism's Greatest Ally Outside of Its Own Ranks,'" *Western States Jewish History*, Winter 2015, Vol. 48, Issue 2, pp.52-53. See note 12.

218 Yaakov Ariel, "A Neglected Chapter in the History of Christian Zionism in America: William E. Blackstone and the Petition of 1916," in Jonathan Frankel, ed., *Studies in Contemporary Jewry: Volume VII: Jews and Messianism in the Modern Era* (Oxford University Press, 1991), 70.

219 Paul C. Merkley, *The Politics of Christian Zionism 1891-1948* (Routledge, 1998), 60.

220 Anita Lebeson, "Zionism Comes to Chicago," in *Early History of Zionism in America*, ed. Isidore S. Meyer, 155–90; (New York: American Jewish Historical Society and Theodore Herzl Foundation, 1958), 166. Cited in Jonathan Moorhead, "The Father of Zionism: William E. Blackstone?" *The Journal of the Evangelical Theological Society*, 53/4 (December 2010), 789.

221 See Rood, "William E. Blackstone (1841-1935): "Zionism's Greatest Ally Outside of Its Own Ranks," 56. Also see Moorhead, "The Father of Zionism: William E. Blackstone?", 792.

222 Blackstone to Benjamin Harrison and James G. Blaine; n.d. Billy Graham Archive Center (BGAC) Box 7, Folder 3, Page 6. Cited in Moorhead, "The Father of Zionism: William E. Blackstone?", 792-793.

223 *Public Papers and Addresses of Benjamin Harrison, Twenty-third President of the United States* (Washington: Government Printing Office, 1893), 100. Cited in Rood, "William E. Blackstone (1841-1935), 60.

224 "Hyman L. Meites, Publisher of Chicago Jewish Chronicle, Dies at 67," Jewish Telegraphic Agency, May 5, 1944. http://www.jta.org/1944/05/05/archive/hyman-l-meites-publisher-of-chicago-jewish-chronicle-dies-at-67

225 In a 1916 letter, Nathan Straus wrote Blackstone: "Mr. Brandeis is perfectly infatuated with the work that you have done along the lines of Zionism. It would have done your heart good to have heard him assert what a valuable contribution to the cause your document is. In fact he agrees with me that you are the Father of Zionism, as your work antedates Herzl." Nathan Straus to Blackstone; May 8, 1916, Billy Graham Archive Center, Box 7, Folder 6, Page 3. Cited in Jonathan Moorhead, "The Father of Zionism: William E. Blackstone?" *The Journal of the Evangelical Theological Society*, 53/4 (December 2010), 796.

226 Rood, "William E. Blackstone (1841-1935)," 65.

227 "America and Zionism," Jewish Telegraphic Agency, February 1, 1935. http://www.jta.org/1935/02/01/archive/america-and-zionism

228 Rood, "William E. Blackstone (1841-1935)," 53.

229 Shalom Goldman, "Professor George Bush: American Hebraist and Proto-Zionist," American Jewish Personalities, American Jewish Archives. http://americanjewisharchives.org/publications/journal/PDF/1991_43_01_00_goldman.pdf

230 George Bush, *The Valley of Vision; Or The Dry Bones of Israel Revived* (New York: Saxton & Miles, 1844), 17.

231 Ibid., 21.

232 "Professor George Bush," Friends of Zion Museum. http://www.fozmuseum.com/bush

233 Alexis de Tocqueville, *Democracy in America*, Vol. 1 (London: Longman, Green, Longman and Roberts, 1862), 361.

234 James Carroll, *Jerusalem, Jerusalem: How the Ancient City Ignited Our Modern World* (New York: Houghton Mifflin Harcourt, 2011), 211.

235 Ibid.

236 Peter Grose, *Israel in the Mind of America* (New York: Knopf, 1983), 25–26; Cited in Michael B. Oren, *Power, Faith, and Fantasy: America in the Middle East: 1776 to the Present* (W. W. Norton & Company. Kindle Edition), Kindle Locations 11792-11793.

237 Allen C. Guelzo, *Abraham Lincoln: Redeemer President* (Grand Rapids, Mich.: Eerdmans, 1999), 434.

238 Michael B. Oren, "Jimmy Carter's Book: An Israeli View," *Wall Street Journal*, December 26, 2006. http://www.wsj.com/articles/SB116709330748759250

239 Michael B. Oren, *Power, Faith, and Fantasy: America in the Middle East, 1776 to the Present* (New York: W.W. Norton & Company, 2007), 89.

240 Robert O. Smith, *More Desired Than Our Owne Salvation: The Roots of Christian Zionism* (Oxford University Press, 2013), 125.

241 Jonathan Edwards, *Apocalyptic Writings*, Ed., Stephen J. Stein (Jonathan Edwards Center at Yale University, WJE Online Vol. 5), 134-135.

242 Mark Musser, "The Puritans and Israel," The 1024 Project. http://1024project.com/2014/01/14/the-puritans-and-israel/

243 Carl F. Ehle, Jr., "Prolegomena to Christian Zionism in America: The Views of Increase Mather and William E. Blackstone Concerning the Doctrine of the Restoration of Israel," Ph.D. Dissertation at New York University, [1977], Abstract. Cited in Thomas Ice, "Lovers of Zion: A History of Christian Zionism," Pre-Trib Research Center. http://www.pre-trib.org/articles/view/lovers-of-zion-history-christian-zionism#_edn72

244 Ezra Stiles, "The United States Elevated to Glory and Honor (1783)," Reiner Smolinski, Ed., DigitalCommons@University of Nebraska – Lincoln. http://digitalcommons.unl.edu/cgi/viewcontent.cgi?article=1041&context=etas

245 "From John Adams to Mordecai M. Noah, 15 March 1819," Founders Early Access, The University of Virginia Press. http://rotunda.upress.virginia.edu/founders/default.xqy?keys=FOEA-print-03-02-02-7097

246 Elias Boudinot, *A Star in the West: Or, A Humble Attempt to Discover the Long Lost Ten Tribes of Israel* (Trenton, NJ: D. Fenton, S. Hutchinson, and J. Dunham, 1816), 43.

247 Ibid., 297-298.

248 Yaacov Ariel, "A Neglected Chapter in the History of Christian Zionism in America: William E. Blackstone and the Petition of 1916," in Jonathan Frankel, ed., *Studies in Contemporary Jewry: Volume VII: Jews and Messianism in the Modern Era* (Oxford University Press, 1991), 80-81.

249 Jonathan Moorhead, "The Father of Zionism: William E. Blackstone?" *The Journal of the Evangelical Theological Society*, 53/4 (December 2010), 798.

250 Wilson, quoted by Rabbi Stephen Wise, in Bartley Cavanaugh Crum, *Behind the Silken Curtain* (Kennikat Press, 1969), 16.

251 Paul C. Merkley, *The Politics of Christian Zionism*, 91-92.

252 Thomas Ice, "HAPPY BIRTHDAY ISRAEL," Tom's Perspectives. http://www.pre-trib.org/data/pdf/Ice-HappyBirthdayIsrael.pdf

253 David Brog, *Standing With Israel* (Lake Mary, Fla.: Charisma House, 2006), Kindle Location 1462-1464.

254 Paul C. Merkley, *The Politics of Christian Zionism*, 191.

255 "Middle East: Mortal Friends," *Time* magazine, Monday, Aug. 16, 1982. http://content.time.com/time/magazine/article/0,9171,950718,00.html

256 "Holocaust Rescue: Operation Texas," JewishVirtualLibrary.org. http://www.jewishvirtuallibrary.org/jsource/Holocaust/optexas.html

257 Public Papers of the Presidents of the United States: Lyndon B. Johnson, 1968-69 (U.S. Government Printing Office), 474. Cited in "U.S. Presidents & Israel: Quotes About Jewish Homeland & Israel," JewishVirtualLibrary.org. http://www.jewishvirtuallibrary.org/jsource/US-Israel/presquote.html#johnson

258 All quotations taken from "U.S. Presidents & Israel: Quotes About Jewish Homeland & Israel," JewishVirtualLibrary.org. http://www.jewishvirtuallibrary.org/jsource/US-Israel/presquote.html

259 Caroline B. Glick, "Column One: God, Jerusalem and American foreign policy," *Jerusalem Post*, September 6, 2012. http://www.jpost.com/printarticle.aspx?id=284167

260. "United Nations Security Council Resolution 2334," http://www.un.org/ga/search/view_doc.asp?symbol=S/RES/2334(2016), and "FULL TRANSCRIPT: Kerry Blasts Israeli Government, Presents Six Points of Future Peace Deal," Haaretz.com, December 28, 2016. http://www.haaretz.com/israel-news/1.761881

261 "Freedom in the World 2016," Freedom House, pp. 20-24. https://freedomhouse.org/sites/default/files/FH_FITW_Report_2016.pdf

262 "The Global Gender Gap Report," World Economic Forum, pp. 8-9. http://www3.weforum.org/docs/GGGR2015/cover.pdf. Also see Tova Dvorin, "Israel Ranked as Best Country for Women in Middle East," IsraelNationalNews.com, March 14, 2014. http://www.israelnationalnews.com/News/News.aspx/178504

263 Tamar Hermann, "The Israeli Democracy Index 2015," Israel Democracy Institute, p. 29. http://en.idi.org.il/media/4256544/democracy_index_2015_eng.pdf

264 Muravchik, *Liberal Oasis*, Kindle Locations 261-264.

265 Khaled Abu Toameh, "Islam Today," Hudson Institute, May 18, 2009, p. 5. http://www.hudson-ny.org/ 511/ islam-today-1. Quoted in Muravchik, *Liberal Oasis,* Kindle Locations 753-754.

266 Michael Oren, "The Ultimate Ally," ForeignPolicy.com, April 25, 2011. http://foreignpolicy.com/2011/04/25/the-ultimate-ally-2/

267 Ibid.

268 Jason Gewirtz, "Big US military aid package to Israel has strings attached," CNBC.com, September 15, 2015. http://www.cnbc.com/2016/09/15/big-us-military-aid-package-to-israel-has-strings-attached.html

269 "U.S.-Israel Strategic Cooperation: Israeli Military Equipment Used by the U.S.," JewishVirtualLibrary.org. http://www.jewishvirtuallibrary.org/jsource/US-Israel/israelisystems.html

270 Oren, "The Ultimate Ally," ForeignPolicy.com.

271 "U.S.-Israel Strategic Cooperation: F-35 Joint Strike Fighter Plane," JewishVirtualLibrary.org. http://www.jewishvirtuallibrary.org/jsource/US-Israel/jetfighter.html

272 "FACT SHEET: Memorandum of Understanding Reached with Israel," The White House, September 14, 2016. https://www.whitehouse.gov/the-press-office/2016/09/14/fact-sheet-memorandum-understanding-reached-israel

273 "U.S.-Israel Strategic Cooperation: Intelligence Collaboration," JewishVirtualLibrary.org. http://www.jewishvirtuallibrary.org/jsource/US-Israel/intell_coop.html

274 Jeremy Havardi, *Refuting the Anti-Israel Narrative: A Case for the Historical, Legal and Moral Legitimacy of the Jewish State* (Jefferson, NC: McFarland & Company, Inc., 2016), 192.

275 Yair Seroussi, "The US: Israel's most important trading partner," Globes.co.il., March 5, 2015. http://www.globes.co.il/en/article-the-us-israels-most-important-trading-partner-1001032635

276 "Top U.S. Trade Partners," 2015, International Trade Administration. http://www.trade.gov/mas/ian/build/groups/public/@tg_ian/documents/webcontent/tg_ian_003364.pdf

277 "Foreign Direct Investment (FDI) Israel," SelectUSA.commerce.gov. http://selectusa.commerce.gov/country-fact-sheets/2015-09-10%20Israel%20Fact%20Sheet.pdf

278 Senor and Singer, *Start-up Nation*, 17.

279 Einat Paz-Frankel, "Why The World's Largest Tech Companies All Want A Piece Of The Israeli Pie," NoCamels.com, September 30, 2015. http://nocamels.com/2015/09/multinational-high-tech-companies-presence-israel/

280 Rev. Isaac Boyle, *A Historical View of the Council of Nice with a Translation of Documents* (Boston: James B. Dow, Bookseller, 1836), 55-56. Emphases added.

281 Michael J. Vlach, "The Church as a Replacement of Israel: An Analysis of Supersessionism," (PhD dissertation at Southeaster Baptist Theological Seminary, Wake Forest, NC, 2004), p. xv. Quoted in Dr. Thomas Ice, "What is Replacement Theology?" Pre-Trib Research Center. http://www.pre-trib.org/articles/view/what-is-replacement-theology#_edn1

282 H. Wayne House, "The Church's Appropriation of Israel's Blessings" in H. Wayne House, editor, *Israel: The Land and the People* (Grand Rapids: Kriegel, 1998), p. 77. Quote in Ice, "What is Replacement Theology?"

283 Brog, *Standing With Israel*, Kindle Location 260-261.

284 Ibid., Kindle Location 299-302.

285 Quoted in Brown, *Our Hands Are Stained with Blood*, Kindle Locations 199-203.

286 Malcolm Hay, *The Roots of Christian Anti-Semitism* (New York: Liberty Press, 1981), p. 32. Cited in Brown, *Our Hands Are Stained with Blood*, Kindle Locations 1537-1538.

287 Brown, *Our Hands Are Stained with Blood*, Kindle Locations 207-213.

288 David Rausch, *Legacy of Hatred: Why Christians Must Not Forget the Holocaust* (Chicago: Moody, 1984), 27.

289 Brog, *Standing With Israel*, Kindle Location 327.

290 David Baron, *The Shepherd of Israel and His Scattered Flock: A Solution of the Enigma of Jewish History* (Kindle Edition), Kindle Locations 341-342.

291 Baron, *The Shepherd of Israel and His Scattered Flock*, Kindle Locations 344-345.

292 Fourth Lateran Council, 1215, Canons on Jews, Canon 68. http://history.hanover.edu/courses/excerpts/344latj.html.

293 Baron, *The Shepherd of Israel and His Scattered Flock*, Kindle Locations 350-352.

294 "THOMAS AQUINAS, 'Letter on the Treatment of Jews' (1271)," Council of Centers on Jewish-Christian Relations. http://www.ccjr.us/dialogika-resources/primary-texts-from-the-history-of-the-relationship/268-aquinas

295 Brown, *Our Hands Are Stained with Blood*, Kindle Locations 236-237.

296 Brog, *Standing With Israel*, Kindle Location 345.

297 Brown, *The Real Kosher Jesus*, Kindle Locations 299-302.

298 Ibid., Kindle Locations 177-182.

299 A. James Rudin, "Vatican II: The beginning of the end of Catholic anti-Semitism," WashingtonPost.com, October 25, 2012. https://www.washingtonpost.com/national/on-faith/vatican-ii-the-beginning-of-the-end-of-catholic-anti-semitism/2012/10/25/f2a2356e-1ee2-11e2-8817-41b9a7aaabc7_story.html

300 "Pope John Paul II: Relations with Jews and Israel," JewishVirtualLibrary.org. http://www.jewishvirtuallibrary.org/jsource/anti-semitism/johnpaul.html

301 "World Council of Churches (WCC)," NGO Monitor, September 19, 2016. http://www.ngo-monitor.org/ngos/world_council_of_churches/

302 "Outgoing World Council of Churches Leader Slams Israel's 'Sin Against God,'" Institute on Religion and Democracy press release, August 31, 2009.

http://www.christiannewswire.com/news/3684411393.html

303 "World Council of Churches and National Council of Churches Statement on Israel Further Exposes 'Historic Anti-Israel Bias,'" Anti-Defamation League, September 15, 2016. http://www.adl.org/press-center/press-releases/israel-middle-east/world-council-of-churches-and-national-council-of-churches-statement.html?referrer=http://www.adl.org

304 Sarah Pulliam Bailey, "How some evangelicals are challenging a decades-long stance of blanket support for Israel's government," WashingtonPost.com, December 14, 2015. https://www.washingtonpost.com/news/acts-of-faith/wp/2015/12/14/how-some-influential-evangelicals-are-challenging-a-decades-long-stance-of-blanket-support-for-israels-government/

305 Steve Haas, "'All of Me,' Engaging a world of poverty and injustice," Lausanne Global Analysis, January 2015, Volume 4 / Issue 1. https://www.lausanne.org/content/lga/2015-01/all-of-me#_ednref1

306 See "Alex Awad: Palestinian Christians in the Shadow of Christian Zionism," Christ at the Checkpoint 2010 conference. https://www.youtube.com/watch?v=LMwEu_CQP2U. Rev Awad is introduced by man who states: "It was over a year ago that Rev. Alex Awad shared with the faculty of Bethlehem Bible College, shared with us his dream about this conference. And in fact this conference has been in our minds, we always talked about it, but it was really Rev. Alex's assistance last year and he pushed us to do it…. So he's really to thank for when it comes to this conference."

307 Robert W. Nicholson, "Evangelicals and Israel: What American Jews Don't Want to Know (but Need to)," *Mosaic* magazine, October 6, 2013. http://mosaicmagazine.com/essay/2013/10/evangelicals-and-israel/

308 "CHRIST AT THE CHECKPOINT: How the U.S., U.K. and Dutch Governments Enable Religious Strife and Foment Mideast Conflict," NGO Monitor, March 2014, p. 7.

309 "World Vision – Willow Creek Association: Leadership Tour of the Holy Land," StephenSizer.com. http://www.stephensizer.com/2010/07/world-vision-willow-creek-association-leadership-tour-of-the-holy-land/

310 "CHRIST AT THE CHECKPOINT," NGO Monitor, p. 4.

311 Ron Cantor, "Sizer Reaffirms: Messianic Jews in Israel an Abomination," CharismaNews.com, March 13, 2014. http://www.charismanews.com/opinion/43110-sizer-reaffirms-messianic-jews-in-israel-an-abomination

312 See Andrew C. McCarthy, "The Father of Modern Terrorism; The True Legacy of Yasser Arafat," NationalReview.com, November 12, 2004. http://www.defenddemocracy.org/media-hit/the-father-of-modern-terrorism-the-true-legacy-of-yasser-arafat/. See also Mario Loyola, "Arafat's True Legacy," *The Weekly Standard*, November 22, 2004. http://www.weeklystandard.com/article/6127

313 Alexander H. Joffe, Ph.D., "Bad Investment: The Philanthropy of George Soros and the Arab-Israeli Conflict," NGO Monitor, May 2103, pp. 49-50. http://www.ngo-monitor.org/soros.pdf

314 "Response to recent criticism of World Vision's position on and work in the Middle East," World Vision statement. http://www.worldvision.org/press-release/response-recent-criticism-world-visions-position-and-work-middle-east

315 Tricia Miller, "Where are Empowered21 and Oral Roberts University Headed in Relation to Israel?" Camera.com, August 10, 2015. http://www.camera.org/index.asp?x_context=7&x_issue=51&x_article=3077

316 Dexter Van Zile, "CAMERA Asks Mart Green to Unwind Damage to Israel's Reputation by Movie," Committee for Accuracy in Middle East Reporting in America, June 14, 2016. http://www.camera.org/index.asp?x_print=1&x_context=7&x_issue=20&x_article=3369

317 "Israel's Wars & Operations: First Intifada (1987 - 1993)," JewishVirtualLibrary.org. http://www.jewishvirtuallibrary.org/jsource/History/intifada.html

318 Ryan Rodrick Beiler, "I was 'part of a terror organization,' says Israeli pilot turned activist," *The Electronic Intifada*, February 10, 2015. https://electronicintifada.net/content/i-was-part-terror-organization-says-israeli-pilot-turned-activist/14253

319 "Breaking the Silence (Shovrim Shtika)," NGO Monitor, June 28, 2016. http://www.ngo-monitor.org/ngos/breaking_the_silence_shovirm_shtika_/

320 Tricia Miller, "Where are Empowered21 and Oral Roberts University Headed in Relation to Israel?" Camera.com, August 10, 2015. http://www.camera.org/index.asp?x_context=7&x_issue=51&x_article=3077

321 Ibid.

322 Dexter Van Zile, "CAMERA Asks Mart Green to Unwind Damage to Israel's Reputation by Movie," CAMERA.org, June 14, 2016. http://www.camera.org/index.asp?x_context=7&x_issue=20&x_article=3369

323 Bailey, "How some evangelicals are challenging a decades-long stance of blanket support for Israel's government," WashingtonPost.com.

324 Jan Markell, "When Social Justice Equals No Justice," WND.com, October 19, 2012. http://www.wnd.com/2012/10/when-social-justice-equals-no-justice/

325 "Press Release: Whose Land? Whose Promise? Marred by Errors, Hostile Theology," Committee for Accuracy in Middle East Reporting in America, September 17, 2007. http://www.camera.org/index.asp?x_context=2&x_outlet=118&x_article=1372

326 "Anti-Semitism at post-war high," *Jewish News*, August 18, 2016. https://www.jewishnews.net.au/anti-semitism-post-war-high/55451

327 "Latest Trends in Religious Restrictions and Hostilities," Pew Research Center, Religion and Public Life, February 26, 2015. http://www.pewforum.org/2015/02/26/religious-hostilities/

328 "Antisemitism and radical Islam could drive Jews from Europe, rabbi warns," *The Jerusalem Post*, October 2, 2016. http://www.jpost.com/Diaspora/Antisemitism-and-radical-Islam-could-drive-Jews-from-Europe-rabbi-warns-469290

329 "Natan Sharansky: No future for Jews in France," Jewish Telegraphic Agency, June 28, 2016. http://www.jta.org/2016/06/28/news-opinion/world/sharansky-arab-far-right-anti-semitism-mean-no-future-for-jews-in-france

330 Jennifer Rubin, "Anti-Semitism spikes on U.S. campuses," WashingtonPost.com, July 26, 2016. https://www.washingtonpost.com/blogs/right-turn/wp/2016/07/26/anti-semitism-spikes-on-u-s-campuses/?utm_term=.77b2468de102

331 Alan M. Dershowitz, "Israel-Hatred on Campus," Frontpagemag.com, March 9, 2004. http://archive.frontpagemag.com/Printable.aspx?ArtId=13858

332 "BBC poll: Germany most popular country in the world," BBC.com, May 23, 2013. http://www.bbc.com/news/world-europe-22624104

333 Barak Ravid, "World Sees Israel as a Pariah State, Senior Gov't Official Says," Haaretz.com, August 7, 2016. http://www.haaretz.com/israel-news/1.735598

334 "Netanyahu slams Palestinians over Israel boycott campaign," CBSNews.com, May 31, 2015. http://www.cbsnews.com/news/netanyahu-slams-palestine-over-israel-boycott-campaign/

335 "What is BDS?" BDSmovement.net. https://bdsmovement.net/what-is-bds

336 Itamar Marcus and Nan Jacques Zilberdik, "PA TV to kids: Israeli cities Haifa, Jaffa, Lod, Ramle, Acre are all 'occupied cities,'" Palestinian Media Watch, August 29, 2010. http://palwatch.org/main.aspx?fi=157&doc_id=2962

337 Dan Diker and Harold Rhode, "The world from here: BDS: A weapon of Islamic warfare," JerusalemPost.com, January 5, 2016. http://www.jpost.com/Opinion/The-world-from-here-BDS-A-weapon-of-Islamic-warfare-439491

338 Roberta P. Seid, PhD, "Omar Barghouti at UCLA: A speaker who brings hate," JewishJournal.com, January 16, 2014. http://www.jewishjournal.com/opinion/article/omar_barghouti_at_ucla_echoes_of_1930s_europe

339 Michael Lipka, "Strong support for Israel in U.S. cuts across religious lines," Pew Research Center, February 27, 2014. http://www.pewresearch.org/fact-tank/2014/02/27/strong-support-for-israel-in-u-s-cuts-across-religious-lines/

340 "Billy Graham Voices Staunch Support for Israel, Concern for State's Security," Jewish Telegraphic Agency, December 26, 1967. http://www.jta.org/1967/12/26/archive/billy-graham-voices-staunch-support-for-israel-concern-for-states-security

341 David Brog. *Standing With Israel* (Lake Mary, Fla.: Charisma House, 2006), Kindle Location 1548.

342 Merrill Simon, *Jerry Falwell and the Jews* (Middle Village, NY: Jonathan David Publishers, 1999), 64. Quoted in Brog, *Standing With Israel,* Kindle Locations 806-808.

343 Brog, *Standing With Israel*, Kindle Locations 798-799.

344 "Understanding the Arab-Israeli Conflict," Compiled by Paul Bogdanor. http://www.paulbogdanor.com/israel/quotes.html

345 Quoted in Erwin W. Lutzer, *Hitler's Cross: How the Cross Was Used to Promote the Nazi Agenda* (Moody Publishers, Kindle Edition, 2016), 192.

346 Basilea Schlink, *Israel, My Chosen People: A German Confession before God and the Jews* (Old Tappan, N.J.: Chosen, 1987), 42-43. Quoted in Michael L. Brown, *Answering Jewish Objections to Jesus: Volume 1: General and Historical Objections* (Baker Publishing Group. Kindle Edition) Kindle Location 4172-4179.

347 "Elie Wiesel - Acceptance Speech," The Nobel Peace Prize 1986. https://www.nobelprize.org/nobel_prizes/peace/laureates/1986/wiesel-acceptance_en.html

348 D. A. Carson, R. T. France, J. A. Motyer, & G. J. Wenham (Eds.), *New Bible Commentary*: 21st century edition (Leicester, England; Downers Grove, IL: Inter-Varsity Press, 4th ed.), 812.

349 J. F. Walvoord & R. B. Zuck (Eds.), *The Bible Knowledge Commentary: An Exposition of the Scriptures*, Vol. 1 (Wheaton, IL: Victor Books), 1457.

350 Schlink, *Israel: My Chosen People*, 85–86. Quoted in Teplinsky, *Why Still Care about Israel?*, 253-254.

351 Walvoord & Zuck (Eds.), *The Bible Knowledge Commentary*, 81.

352 Teplinsky, *Why Still Care about Israel?*, 252-253.

353 Ibid., 20-21.

354 "The Promise Theater," Friends of Zion Heritage Center. http://www.fozmuseum.com/print?c0=31382

355 Teplinsky, *Why Still Care about Israel?*, 128.